THE MIND GAME

Witchdoctors and Psychiatrists

THE MIND GAME

Witchdoctors and Psychiatrists

E. Fuller Torrey, M.D.

National Institute of Mental Health
Rockville, Maryland 20852

The opinions set forth in this volume are those of the author
and do not represent the official policy
of the National Institute of Mental Health
or the United States Public Health Service.

EMERSON HALL PUBLISHERS, INC., New York

First Edition

ISBN 0-87829-002-8

Library of Congress Catalog Card Number 77-188562

Anita Duncan, Design
Distributed by
Independent Publishers' Group/David White
60 E. 55th St., New York, N.Y. 10022

To my wife Barbara
The most important of my sources:
the source of my best ideas and confidence

Contents

Foreword

It would be both impossible and inappropriate to review the content of this book in a brief foreword; so, rather than to discuss substance, I would prefer to comment on a process. *How* should a reader assimilate and evaluate the content of this volume?

Dr. Torrey has attempted to take some bearings in the field of psychotherapy by surveying therapists in different cultures. In so doing, he has raised many important questions. What is it that we as psychotherapists do? How can we be more effective? How should we be trained? The answers have important implications for the shape of future mental health services.

In presenting data on which professionals in mental health can expand their knowledge, Dr. Torrey emphasizes the importance of looking objectively at other cultures and subcultures; but even the title of this book demonstrates how difficult it is to achieve objectivity when one is dealing with values which are often subjective.

In his first chapter, Dr. Torrey comments, "The witch-doctors, being semi-religious in function . . . quickly became equated with the devil. It was partly to dispel this negative stereotype that the term 'witchdoctors' was chosen to juxtapose 'psychiatrists' for the title of this book."

However, such a juxtaposition might have the reverse effect and operate to heighten the negative stereotype of the term "psychiatrists." This possibility must be at least considered. The basic point I wish to make here is that in order to grasp a complex situation, we must look at it simultaneously from many points of view, in the realization that no matter how thoroughly researched, our conclusions will still be debatable.

With a refreshing originality, the author of this volume takes a transcultural look at social change in an effort to break through the current cliches that have begun to obscure the impact of change as well as the change itself.

Predicting social change and engineering new social institutions has been my professional concern for the past decade. We live in the era of transition and turbulence, in fear, anxiety and worry. Our problem is one of adaptation now and in the immediate future to the rapid rate of social change. One approach is to free our thinking and break out of professional traditionalism.

No longer can we look with one eye or one point of view. It is not only a matter of seeing but of comprehending. And to comprehend, we must hear as well as see; feel as well as think. To grasp something we must not only touch it; it must touch us. In brief, social change is more than a professional challenge; it is a human challenge. And to deal with it as humans who are also professionals, we must unashamedly call upon the full range of our human capacities and interests: artistic, religious and scientific.

Furthermore, we must realize that our full range of human capacities is in itself limited. The cultures of other continents offer us possible alternatives in feeling and thought, not available within our own society. The insights to be gained through observation from an international perspective may help us to grasp the essence of difficult and complex situations.

In this sense, Dr. Torrey's book makes a contribution, though his conclusions will be unacceptable to many in our own particular culture. The author is subjecting the reader to a form of mind game, hopefully stretching our minds so that the boundaries of our minds will be enlarged to do a better job at our basic professional mission: helping and caring for people.

Bertram S. Brown, M.D., *Director*
National Institute of Mental Health

Preface

This book is an attempt to provide a framework for understanding the activities of psychotherapists around the world. As such it is an ambitious—some would say arrogant—undertaking. To attempt it as a psychiatrist just out of the nest leaves me open to attack. "Wait until you are more experienced, wait until you are older and wiser, then you will understand," call the voices.

But I am not certain that experience brings truth or that age brings wisdom. Too often added years seem only to bring the encrustations of time, obtunding self-criticism and impelling self-justification. Perhaps it is only from the vantage point of the nest's edge that the relationship of witchdoctors and psychiatrists can be clearly seen.

A framework for a general understanding of psychotherapists can be approached by asking questions. What does a psychotherapist do? Is he effective? What does his effectiveness come from? How can he be made more effective? What is the effect of his personality? How should he be selected? What kind of training should he have? What should be his role in society? In what ways is he a product of his culture?

These questions are important and they are not asked often enough. Formal psychotherapy is an institution in our culture, enshrined in psychiatry, psychology, and social work. We tend to accept our inherited institutions without criticism and pass them on mechanically to posterity. This transfer guarantees obsolescence. Insofar as this book focuses attention on these questions, it will accomplish its purpose. The answers proposed are intended only to invite innovation and experimentation.

I realize that many readers may not agree with my general thesis. From preliminary readings it appears that the strongest opposition is likely to come from those who want to pretend that witchdoctors do not exist (e.g., highly educated members of Western subcultures and cultures from developing countries) and also from those who want to believe that psychiatrists are special and different (e.g., people who have had long-term therapy). If the book only forces these people to clarify and codify the nature of their opposition it will have accomplished much.

In the process of writing this book I have had to contend with the ethnocentrism and bias that always lurk at the periphery of my own vision. Many times I thought myself free, only to turn and find it behind me. The more introspective I became, the more I found that it had invaded the very depths of my thought. As long as our culture nurtures it in so many subtle ways, its complete eradication seems a task for Sisyphus.

The anthropological literature on therapists in other cultures is vast. A bibliography published in 1923 listed 650 studies of Siberian shamans alone—even at that time. I have selected from this array in anthropology and related fields what seemed to be the most promising items to study in greater detail. Undoubtedly I have missed many of merit. Especially conspicuous by their absence are studies of therapists in Latin America (which are mostly in Spanish) and the Middle East (which are few in number and mostly in Arabic).

This book will focus on the healer, the therapist. It will attempt to show how much of his effectiveness comes through his sharing of a common world-view with the patient, through certain personality characteristics, and through expectations that the patient has of him. It will then show how another source of his effectiveness, the techniques of therapy, are basically the same whether they are used by a witchdoctor or a psychiatrist. The book will then examine the varieties of therapists found in the United States and in other countries. Finally it will look at the implications of the foregoing for mental health services both here and elsewhere and examine some of the problems and resistances to putting the changes into operation.

Brief portions of the book are borrowed from articles I have published elsewhere. Excerpts from chapters 2, 3, and 4 are found in my article in *The Archives of General Psychiatry*, volume 20. Some of the material for chapter 5 was used for a chapter in *Current Psychiatric Therapies*, volume 10. Part of chapter 10 was included in the *Community Mental Health Journal*, volume 6. And portions of chapter 8 were published by the *Stanford M.D.*, volume 9.

I owe much gratitude to Paul Beavitt, Rosa Miller, and Robert Campos, who helped with different parts of my field work. Linda Hess, Norman Reynolds, and Halsey and Jane Beemer provided invaluable criticism of the manuscript. Sue Heller added wise counsel, and Joan Wolfe provided not only excellent typing but contributed many helpful suggestions as well.

"The human brain is not an organ of thinking but an organ of survival, like claw and fangs. It is made in such a way as to make us accept as truth that which is only advantage."

ALBERT SZENT-GYÖRGI

chapter 1

Introduction:
The Dangers
of Psychiatric Imperialism

Witchdoctors and psychiatrists perform essentially the same function in their respective cultures. They are both therapists; both treat patients using similar techniques; and both get similar results. Recognition of this should not downgrade psychiatrists; rather it should upgrade witchdoctors.

The fact that the two are essentially the same is not just an intellectual cordial, a curiosity to be sipped as an afterthought. It is an important and substantive issue with implications for the whole range of mental health services in the United States and elsewhere. It suggests changes in selection and training of psychiatrists, psychologists, and psychiatric social workers. It suggests new sources of mental health manpower. It suggests changes in the community mental health center approach for large segments of our population. It suggests radically different types of mental health services for other countries. And it suggests that we have been remarkably nearsighted in undervaluing the contributions of other cultures to psychiatry as we have overvalued our own.

Both witchdoctors and psychiatrists are therapists. In terms of the Greek root, therapeía, that means they *treat* something. This "something" may be problems of physical health or mental health; in the latter case they are called psychotherapists. Both witchdoctors and psychiatrists, then, are accepted by their respective cultures as belonging to the medical model. Although the appropriateness of this model may be questioned for problems of "mental health" it is not the purpose of this book to do so. If it were questioned, it could be done equally for witchdoctors and psychiatrists.

Psychotherapy, the treatment of problems of mental health, can be defined as a series of contacts between a socially sanctioned healer and a patient who seeks relief. The definition distinguishes psychotherapy from other helping relationships such as a chat with the milkman or some advice-giving by the bartender. The contacts may be private, as in a psychiatrist's office, or public, as part of a group setting. The purpose of the contacts is to provide relief for the patient.

If the reader has not already, he will soon raise the objection: "But you are talking only about relief for the patient—just symptom removal. The *real* purposes of psychotherapy are behavior change and long-term personality change." This is a valid objection. Unfortunately no research has been done to date that clarifies the different kinds of changes occurring in psychotherapy. The relationship of symptom relief to behavior change to long-term personality change is not known. It *is* known that both witchdoctors and psychiatrists can bring about symptom removal and relief for the sufferer.

Since the techniques employed by the two are essentially the same, it is left for the reader to decide after examining the evidence whether psychiatrists produce long-term personality change any more often than witchdoctors do.

The Spectrum of Witchdoctors

"Witchdoctor" is a curious word. It is apparently not a word like "horsedoctor" or "baby doctor" indicating who or what is treated. Rather it implies a therapist who is simultaneously a witch.

The term apparently arose out of the eighteenth and nineteenth century European exploration of Africa. The world was simpler then, and the new cultures were rapidly assigned their proper status in The Order of Things. We were white; they were black. We were civilized; they were primitive. We were Christian; they were pagan. We used science; they used magic. We had doctors; they had witchdoctors. This simplistic reductionism is still remarkably prevalent in our thinking about other cultures, though it is being reevaluated. It afforded an easy way to inflate the self-esteem of the white races, though of course at the expense of others.

The witchdoctors, being semireligious in function, were especially anathematized by the colonizing whites who often were there to spread the Christian faith. Witchdoctors quickly became equated with the devil. Thus it was, and still is, difficult for us to see them as they really are. It was partly to dispel this negative stereotype that the term "witchdoctors" was chosen to juxtapose "psychiatrists" for the title of this book. Terms with fewer negative connotations, such as shamans or medicine men, could have been chosen. The end result, however, might then be agreement by the reader that there *are* a few real psychotherapists among shamans or medicine men but "what about those others—all those evil and primitive witchdoctors." I have chosen instead to deal directly with the term "witchdoctors" so that psychotherapists in other cultures, performing the same function as psychiatrists in Western cultures, cannot be dismissed with a single pejorative epithet.

"Witchdoctor" is a generic term applied by Western cultures to therapists in other cultures, especially those in Africa. The Africans themselves of course do not use the term; each tribe or area has its own term for the therapist in its own language. Examples are *izinyanga* in parts of South Africa, *ganga* among the Zulu, *mganga* among Swahili speakers in East Africa, *chimbuki* among the Ndembu in Northern Rhodesia, *mulogo* in parts of Uganda, *bulomba* among the Temne in Sierra Leone, *babalawo* among the Yoruba in Nigeria, and *baroom xam-xam* among the Lebou in Senegal. The last certainly sounds more impressive to me than the term "witchdoctor"; it translates as "master of knowledge."

There are other generic terms for therapists in other parts of the world. "Medicine man" is the one used most often for

North American Indian tribes, though each tribe has its own word for the healer. "Shaman" is a word that originated in Siberia for the therapist in the Tungusian tribes; it became widespread as the generic term throughout Alaska and parts of Asia. More recently it has been used to designate therapists everywhere who become possessed. As with witchdoctors and medicine men, each group has its own word; if you approach a group asking for their shaman you will as likely be shown to their outhouse or hotel as to their therapist. Examples of such names are *llubu* in Tibet, *angakok* among Alaskan Eskimos, *dehar* in Afghanistan, and *miko* in Japan.

Other terms for therapists are more regional. There is the *curandero* throughout Latin America, the *medium* throughout the Caribbean, and the *marabout* in many Moslem countries. Some terms are used to indicate a specific function of the therapist. For instance, "soothsayer," "seer," and "diviner" refer to his ability to foretell events or find lost objects; "sorcerer" or "devil doctor" refer to his ability to cast spells.

It is inaccurate to assume that therapists from different cultures are the same, even when the same generic term is used. For instance, a psychiatrist who has studied Japanese shamans noted the wide variety among their selection, training, and function, even in different parts of Japan.[1]

In this book the term "witchdoctor" will be used generically to cover all therapists in other cultures. Similarly, the term "psychiatrist" will be used as a shorthand for all formally trained therapists in our Western cultures, including psychoanalysts, psychologists, psychiatric social workers, and trained counselors.

The Functions of Witchdoctors

Therapists in other cultures may include many diverse functions under their job description. Paviotso Indian shamans, for instance, were supposed to control the weather, charm the antelopes before the hunt, and make the warriors invulnerable to bullets.[2] This was in addition to their more traditional healing duties. Some traditional therapists act as the tribe historian by passing on the lore, and others overlap the political leadership of the tribe. But for the therapist to be the *most* important political personage is unusual; more often he is a close advisor to the political chief.

Therapists in almost all cultures are closely allied with religious functions. Some of the most successful of the modern African witchdoctors are associated with the Christian sects.[3] In Latin America the *curanderos* utilize Catholicism and in Bali the *balians* utilize Hinduism in their therapeutic techniques. Often the therapists and the religious leaders are one and the same person, as are the Buddhist monks in Thailand and the *hodjas* in Turkey. It is only recently in our own culture, as a matter of fact, that therapists have become completely secularized.

The main function of therapists in all cultures is to treat illness. In our culture we distinguish rather sharply between physical illness and mental illness, and we have separate therapists for each. A psychiatrist, for instance, is not expected to treat a case of pneumonia. Most other cultures do not make such a sharp distinction, with the result that therapists in these cultures treat a wide variety of physical as well as mental and social problems.

The specialization of therapists exists in all cultures. The degree of specialization is roughly proportional to the technological complexity of the society, although this is not always the case. The Wolof and Lebou tribes in Senegal, for instance, have six distinct types of healers.[4]

Within the realm of what we call mental illness, the most common division of personnel in other cultures is into herbalist, diviner, and healer. These can be roughly translated into our equivalents as druggist, psychologist, and psychiatrist. The herbalist prepares and dispenses medicines. The diviner makes diagnoses (as well as often finding lost objects and predicting the future), and the healer treats people. The healer always has the most training and the most prestige. Often people will begin with the herbalist and work up, depending on how difficult a case it is.

Another common division of the therapist's functions in many cultures is that between public and private. The public functions include such things as presiding over ceremonies, exorcising evil spirits at the building of a new house, and giving charms to departing warriors. In our culture these functions are performed by politicians, priests, and the Department of Defense. The private functions of seeing patients individually and in groups coincides with our use of the term therapist.

It can be seen, then, that different cultures divide up the

world differently. This will be dealt with at length in chapter 2. The implications for therapists is that we should not expect other cultures necessarily to follow our division of functions. There is no exact equivalent of a "psychiatrist" in other cultures. The functions we assign to a psychiatrist are found in other cultures, and these are the subject of this book. But the reader should not be surprised to find, for instance, that the Iroquois medicine man who is doing psychoanalytic dream interpretation is also in charge of the weather, and acts as judge, and philosopher in the tribe.

In all cultures the functions of therapists are constantly evolving. This can be seen quite clearly in our own culture. Over the past twenty years the psychiatrist has begun to move out of his private office and involve himself in community action and social planning. This extension of his purview is the cause of much debate. So in other cultures the functions of an Eskimo shaman today may be quite different than they were one hundred years ago. Therapists, like clothing styles and dating patterns, are part of the culture and evolve with it.

But what about the evil functions of witchdoctors? Everybody knows that one of the most important things that witchdoctors do is to put a hex on people. Actually this is a relatively unimportant and infrequent function of most witchdoctors. It is another stereotype that arose out of the writings of the missionaries. *Belief* in witchcraft and hexing *is* very common, but it is rare to find a therapist who will admit to doing it. It is always the other therapist who is believed to be guilty of it, never the one you are talking to.

This is not to deny that therapists ever perform these evil functions. It is just a comparatively rare phenomenon. When therapists who are believed to do these things exist in a culture, they are usually given a separate name. For example a *bruja* in Latin America is translated as a witch and is believed to cast hexes. She is quite distinct from the *curandero* or healer in the minds of the people.

In some cultures the occurrence of witchcraft and its occasional use by the therapist is part of the cultural judicial system. Among the Tenino Indians, for instance, the shaman occasionally would cast a hex on an unknown criminal who had not been caught. When word spread that it had occurred, the criminal often found himself becoming sick and quickly confessing.[5]

Mental Health Manpower

Almost all specialties within medicine today are being forced to examine their manpower and its utilization. They are asking questions such as: "Who is doing what job? What training do they need to do it? Is it possible that someone with less training could do part of the job?"

A good example is the field of pediatrics. By following pediatricians around with a stopwatch, it has been determined that they spend most of their time with patients who are not sick and on tasks that could be done by someone with far less training.[6] More recent studies have tried to identify these tasks.[7] Simultaneously other workers have been developing new personnel, like the pediatric nurse-practitioner, to do these tasks without a full medical-school education.[8] Other specialties within medicine are experimenting with physician assistants, midwives, anesthesiology assistants, family health workers, and public health aides.[9]

Turning to psychiatry, the gulf between supply and demand of therapists is rapidly becoming a chasm. There are 20,000 practicing psychiatrists in the United States, about one for every 10,000 people. They are distributed mostly among the middle and upper classes (Westport, Connecticut, with a population of 30,000, has 30 practicing there), leaving large segments of the population without any psychiatrists. Since it takes 12 years to train a psychiatrist, and since much of the money for the training comes from general tax funds, it is entirely proper to ask what psychiatrists are doing, to whom, and whether some of their job can be taken over by persons with less training.

Pressure on the psychiatric profession for answers to these questions is increasing. As the general public has become more sophisticated about psychiatry, there has been a rapidly increasing demand for their services. The community mental health centers have also brought psychiatry to more people; it is projected that there will be 2,000 centers by 1980, but nobody knows where the manpower to staff them will come from. Even now, one out of every four positions for psychiatrists in state hospitals is unfilled.[10]

But statistics are only numbers and are easily forgotten. Like the droning of demographers on the population explosion, the statistics anesthetize us to the stark realities of people with mental problems and no one to help them. These realities alone justify a critical look at psychiatrists in the perspective of therapists around the world.

Magic or Science?

In contrast to the abundant anthropological literature, there are remarkably few psychiatric studies of therapists in other cultures.[11] This paucity is difficult to explain in view of the more numerous studies in every other area of cross-cultural psychiatry.[12]

One reason why therapists and their techniques have been ignored is that they are automatically relegated to the realm of "mere magic and superstition." Only occasionally are they even dignified with the rubric of "prescientific psychiatry."[13] This is to distinguish them from therapists in our culture who are thought to employ techniques based on modern science.

The truth is not even close; it is a quantum jump away. The techniques used by Western psychiatrists are, with few exceptions, on exactly the same scientific plane as the techniques used by witchdoctors. If one is magic then so is the other. If one is prescientific, then so is the other. The only exceptions to this are some of the physical therapies, in particular some drugs and shock therapy, which have been shown in controlled studies to be effective in producing psychiatric change. None of the psychosocial therapies has been so shown. In fact efforts to show this—so called "outcome studies"—have been notoriously negative for reasons we will come to later.

It is difficult to comprehend this. We are used to thinking of psychiatrists as men of science and witchdoctors as men of magic. Even when we do note it we quickly forget. A good example is found in Redlich and Freedman's textbook of psychiatry. On one page they observe that if we only used psychiatric therapies which are based on scientific evidence, then ". . . not much would remain, because there are very few truly scientific therapies in our field.[14] One page later, however, they have already forgotten their own admonition and lapse back into the stereotype: "The technique must be based on some scientific rationale to deserve the designation of psychotherapy; it cannot be a mystical or magical procedure."[15] They then proceed to make the inevitable but fallacious assumption that Western psychiatric therapies are based on science.

In order to be scientific, a phenomenon must be explainable by underlying laws. These laws are arrived at by observation, measurement, experimentation, induction, hypothesis formulation, and testing. The rationale for most therapies used by witchdoctors and psychiatrists is not arrived at in this way—rather the techniques are used on sick patients, the patients get well, and therefore the techniques are thought to work. This is logical, empirical psychiatry and is found among witchdoctors and psychiatrists.[16] And both witchdoctors and psychiatrists make the asumption that their patients get well because of the techniques. As we shall see, probably other elements are involved.

Much of the confusion arises because we confuse the general level of technology in the culture with the psychiatric techniques. We implicitly and automatically assume that therapy which goes on in an office in a modern skyscraper or in a complex medical center must be scientific, whereas therapy which goes on in a grass hut must be magical. We also confuse the educational level of the practitioner with the therapy; M.D.'s and Ph.D.'s automatically are thought to do scientific things, whereas "uneducated" persons automatically are thought to do magical things. And finally we confuse the theories of causation with the therapies; if a person believes a mental disorder is caused by hormonal imbalance or a missing gene, then his therapy is automatically thought to be scientific, whereas if his theory of causation involves evil spirits then his therapy must be magical. In fact, psychiatric therapies are very similar all over the world and are relatively independent of the level of technology, the education of the therapists, or the theories of causation. Psychiatry is just as scientific—or prescientific—in rural Nigeria or the mountains of Mexico as it is in New York or San Francisco.

It is important to challenge this stereotype of witchdoctors using magic and psychiatrists using science if we hope to see them as they really are. It may be, however, that there is still too much magic in our lives to permit us to give up the stereotype easily. We divine the future with our horoscopes. We have our superstitions about the number 13 and our lucky charms to wear around our neck to ward off evil. We buy 10 million rabbit-foot charms each year.[17] We knock on wood and walk around ladders. We consult Jeane Dixon and other mediums who communicate with spirits. We are able to transform bread and wine into body and blood, at least in our minds. And at the end of the day we are advised to pray:

> "Protect us from goblins and ghoulies
> and long-legged ghosties, and things
> that go bump in the night."

It may be that we don't want to see this magic in our lives, so we just see it in witchdoctors and call what we do "science."

If we hope to learn about witchdoctors and psychiatrists we will have to get outside of ourselves. We will have to dispose of our condescension when we approach other cultures and begin to understand that they have something to teach us. Too much of the cross-cultural literature is tinged with psychiatric imperialism.[18] The Original Sin was probably ethnocentrism, which may be defined as revolving around one's own navel. We must learn to look out on the world not through the cord, but with a broader view.

part I
The Four Components of Psychotherapy

chapter 2

A Shared World-View:
The Principle
of Rumpelstiltskin

A doctor can give penicillin to any patient who has certain kinds of infections and the patient will get well. The penicillin does not depend upon a common language or a shared world-view. Communication is not even necessary.

This is not true for psychotherapy. Communication is its essence. And real communication presupposes not only a shared language, but a shared world-view as well. When this exists the principle of Rumpelstiltskin, the first of the four components of all psychotherapy, becomes possible. Let me illustrate.

The psychiatrist looked thoughtfully at his patient. "You looked angry when you were just talking about your father. You often look angry when you talk about him. I wonder if something happened to you once that made you very angry at him." At this point the patient broke down sobbing, blurting out a forgotten history of neglect and deceit by a thoughtless father toward a little girl. Afterwards the patient felt better. After several more sessions in which she was able to explore her feelings of anger she began to get better.

The witchdoctor stared solemnly at the small shells. They had landed in a pattern resembling the shape of a large animal. He picked one shell up and examined it minutely. "You have broken a taboo of your family. It has offended the sacred bear that protects your ancestors. That is why you are sick." The patient and her family breathed a sigh of relief. It was as they had suspected. Now that they knew for certain what was wrong they could proceed with the necessary sacrifices. After these had been made the patient began to get better.

Both therapists are able to name what is wrong with their patients. The very act of naming it has a therapeutic effect. The patient's anxiety is decreased by the knowledge that a respected and trusted therapist understands what is wrong. The identification of the offending agent (childhood experience, violation of a taboo) may also activate a series of associated ideas in the patient's mind, producing confession, abreaction, and general catharsis.

This is the principle of Rumpelstiltskin. Based upon personality studies of the Brothers Grimm in the early nineteenth century, the principle illustrates the magic of the right word. In the Grimm Brothers' version the word is the name of an evil man who wants to take the queen's baby. The only way the baby can be saved is by the queen naming him correctly. At the last moment she finds the right name—Rumpelstiltskin—whereupon the baby is saved and the queen lives happily ever after.

The naming process is one of the most important components of all forms of psychotherapy. It is also one of the most commonly overlooked components. Every therapist who has ever had the experience of observing a patient's relief after solemnly telling him that he was suffering from idiopathic dermatitis or pediculosis knows how important the name is. It says to the patient that someone understands, that he is not alone with his sickness, and implicitly that there is a way to get well. It is used by all therapists everywhere, witchdoctors and psychiatrists equally effectively.

Very little research has been done on the naming process as it is used by therapists. One of the few analyses of it is that by anthropologist Claude Lévi-Strauss. In a comparison of shamans and psychoanalysts he says that the goal of both is to bring to a conscious level conflicts and resistances that have remained unconscious in the patient. The naming process, the use of words as symbols for what is wrong, is effective not because of the knowledge per se that the words convey ". . . but because this knowledge makes possible a specific experience, in the course of which conflicts materialize in an order and on a level permitting their free development and leading to their resolution."[1] In other words, when a therapist correctly names what is wrong (in psychiatric terms, "makes the correct interpretation") then the patient is able to resolve that particular conflict.

Witchdoctors do this in exactly the same way that psychiatrists do. In discussing the case of an Indian cured by a shaman, Lévi-Strauss observes:

> "The shaman provides the sick woman with a *language* by means of which unexpressed, and otherwise inexpressible, psychic states can be immediately expressed. And it is the transition to this verbal expression . . . which induces the release of the psychological process, that is, the reorganization in a favorable direction of the process to which the sick woman is subjected."[2]

And psychiatrist G. M. Carstairs comments upon a healer in rural India:

> "What was expected from the healer was reassurance. So long as the illness was nameless, patients felt desperately afraid, but once its magic origin had been defined and the appropriate measures taken, they could face the outcome calmly. The parallel with our own clinical experience is obvious."[3]

Another psychiatric view of the naming process is provided by Werner Mendel. He calls it "the assignment of meaning" and maintains that it is part of every therapist-patient transaction: "It is a process totally independent of the theories or techniques of the therapist even though its content is related to the school of psychotherapy. All schools help their patients to assign meaning to behavior, thoughts, fantasies, dreams, delusions, and hallucinations."[4] Mendel then goes on to quote another psychoanalyst who sees the naming process as the essence of the psychoanalytic method:

> ". . . the essence of the psychoanalytic method is, I think, that it gives meaning to apparently meaningless sequences of thoughts and acts, that by making certain assumptions and applying certain

rules derived from them it provides a rational explanation for apparently irrational behavior."[5]

Underlying the principle of Rumpelstiltskin is an important assumption—that the therapist knows the right name to put on the disease. And in order to know the right name the therapist must share some of the patient's world-view, especially that part of the world-view concerning the disease itself. A psychiatrist who tells an illiterate African that his phobia is related to a fear of failure or a witchdoctor who tells an American tourist that his phobia is related to possession by an ancestral spirit will be met by equally blank stares. And as therapists they will be equally irrelevant and ineffective.

The remainder of this chapter will explore the assumption behind the principle of Rumpelstiltskin. It will first attempt to answer the question, "do all people think alike?" It will then examine some of the specific aspects of mental diseases where people's thinking differs from culture to culture. Finally it will survey the psychiatric and anthropological literature for examples of attempted cross-cultural psychotherapy and evaluate these attempts. All of this will be found to support the contention that the principle of Rumpelstiltskin is a universal component of psychotherapy but that its content is culture bound.

Do All People Think Alike?

Underlying this question is a controversy that has been raging in anthropology and psychology for over 100 years. It is the question of psychic unity versus psychic relativity: do all people think alike or do they think differently?

Debate began in earnest during the last half of the nineteenth century with the evolutionism of William Henry Morgan and Sir Edward Tylor. They postulated that all men were really the same, both in feelings and in thought, but simply were in different stages of evolution. According to them the Kalahari Bushmen and the Australian Aborigines would think exactly as we do once they reached our stage of evolution. Western cultures, of course, were considered to be the most highly evolved cultures of all.

At the turn of the century evolutionism began to be challenged. Franz Boas, the father of American anthropology, promoted a view called historicalism. He saw each culture as distinct and distinctive and said that man's feelings and thoughts were tied to the culture. This view implicitly challenged and denied psychic unity. Boas' theories became increasingly popular in American anthropology and influenced many other anthropologists, e.g., the configurations of cultures presented by Ruth Benedict in *Patterns of Culture*.[6]

But until recently hard data to support cultural relativity has been sparse. One of the first attempts to study thinking patterns in others dealt not with the thinking itself but with perception. This was the Torres Straits expedition to the South Pacific in 1898. There W. H. R. Rivers tested the visual perception of the inhabitants of the Pacific Islands to optical illusions and found that they differed from Europeans.

Cultural variation in perception has since been substantiated. Kalahari Bushmen have been shown to be superior in spatial acuity.[7] Other studies found a differential ability among Africans to perceive optical illusions, and argued that the differences were related to the number of like-shaped objects in their environment.[8] In other words, perception was shown to be partly dependent upon cultural experience, an argument in favor of cultural relativity of cognitive processes in general. All men apparently don't see things in the same way, and the way they see them is dependent upon their culture. Why shouldn't the same be true for reasoning and categorization and feeling?

Psychology has contributed circumstantial evidence toward the cultural relativity of thinking. Piaget and his co-workers in Geneva have clearly shown that thinking processes in children differ from those in adults. For instance when the child is thinking about a conservation of weight problem he goes through thinking processes that differ from those of an adult.[9] So by showing definite age-level differences in thinking, Piaget has left the door open to cultural differences as well.

Linguistics has also contributed evidence to this controversy. In fact it is the so-called Whorfian hypothesis that provides one of the main foci for the controversy. This hypothesis is the work of linguist Benjamin Whorf, who contended that different linguistic groups perceive and conceive reality in different ways, and that the language spoken by the group shapes the cognitive structure of the individual speaking that language.[10] In short, people's thinking differs, and these differences are related to and caused by the language used by the people. Whorf saw language as the mold into which thoughts are poured.

Whorf's hypothesis has received partial verification from studies in cognitive anthropology, though it has not been unequivocally established.[11] It *has* been clearly established, however, that the language of different groups reflects how people in that group divide their world. For instance, Eskimos have four different words for "snow." A non-Eskimo trying to learn their language cannot just learn one word; he must learn separate words for falling snow, snow on the ground, drifting snow, and drifted snow.[12] He will have to learn to make categories in his thought that he has not made before if he hopes to talk with an Eskimo about snow. Snow is very important to Eskimos, and its importance is reflected by the language.[13]

Probably the best evidence for determining whether all people think alike is found in anthropological studies. For instance, in the Philippines there is a group of people called the Hanunoo. They divide all colors into just four—mabiru, malagiti, marara, and malatuy. Marara, for example, includes those colors that we call red, orange, yellow, and maroon. If you show a Hanunoo man a red shirt and a yellow shirt he will tell you that they are both marara. If you press him he might add that the first is "more marara" or the second "weak marara," but they will both remain as marara.[14]

Another example is the Dani in New Guinea who do not count beyond two. Their numbers are one, two, and many. If a Dani tribesman wants to find out whether one of his goats is missing, he checks each goat by name. If one of the names is not there he knows it is missing. But he does not count. It is not because the Dani are not intelligent that they do not count beyond two; in fact they have been shown to have excellent memories and learning abilities. It is just that they divide up the world differently than we do, and their world does not have any number except one, two, and many.[15]

Studies such as these, along with the studies of perception, psychology, and linguistics, all point toward the same conclusion —that people think differently. And these differences are not just superficial differences; they are fundamental and include such basic things as colors and numbers. They imply differences in thought at all levels.

The fact that people apparently do not think alike is in agreement with our subjective impressions of the world. We have long known that people differ in more superficial ways, such as dress. And Americans traveling abroad quickly learn that customs differ—in Fiji you sit rather than stand to show respect to your elders. At a deeper level we know that cultures condition people to like different things. Standards for sexual attractiveness differ markedly from culture to culture—the shape of the eyes and ears, the degree of fatness or thinness, the size of breasts, the size of hips, etc.[16] Esthetics and art forms also reflect these cultural differences. Japanese archery, for example, is not a sport but rather an art form. It does not matter whether the arrow hits the target or not. From a Western cultural vantage point this is very difficult to comprehend.

Ideas, values, conceptions of time, the notion of cause-and-effect—all are culturally learned. Navaho Indians feel shame in situations where we would feel guilt. Such differences are found at all levels of our thinking, and reflect the wide cultural differences in child-rearing practices, through which our culture is transmitted.[17] Anthropologist Walter Goldschmidt sums it up as follows:

> Anthropology has taught us that the world is differently defined in different places. It is not only that people have different customs; it is not only that people believe in different gods and expect different postmortem fates. It is, rather, that the worlds of different people have different shapes. The very metaphysical presuppositions differ: space does not conform to Euclidean geometry, time does not form a continuous unidirectional flow, causation does not conform to Aristotelian logic, man is not undifferentiated from non-man or life from death, as in our world.[18]

It would seem to be a short but logical step from here to seeing the implications of these differences for therapists. But these extensions of thought are only rarely made. The reasons why they are rarely made are threefold. First, we are afflicted by a well-meaning but false internationalism. We *want* all people to think the same, therefore we see them that way. In the long-run, however, the failure to recognize true differences in thought among groups of people impedes rather than assists mutual international goals.

The second reason relates to the ethnocentrism mentioned in chapter 1. We have no insight into our own culturally learned ideas and values. They sit within us quietly, unconsciously, providing the baseline against which we make value judgments but never themselves coming into judgment. As therapists, for instance, we accept independence and responsibility as important goals in therapy, rarely realizing that these are culturally learned values and that other people may not share them.[19] Freud taught us how important childhood relationships with our parents are in forming an unconscious mold shaping later relationships. What needs to be stressed equally is how important our culturally learned ideas and values are in forming an unconscious mold, shaping later ideas and values. When we fully realize this as therapists, then we will realize that we are indeed culture-bound.

A third force militating against the recognition of cognitive relativity is the proponents of cognitive unity. These scholars deny that people think differently. Most of their work comes from the fields of communications and mathematics, and depict the human brain as a complicated computer. The computers may differ in color or exterior appearance, but they are said to utilize the same processes and therefore to be the same underneath. Complicated studies of kinship terms by componential analysis and studies of words by the semantic differential have been brought forth in support of this apparent cognitive unity.

The discrepancy between advocates of cognitive unity and those favoring cognitive relativity can be resolved by looking at them as different order abstractions. The bulk of evidence to date suggests that there *are* differences in cognition between different groups of people. This cognitive relativity is primarily concerned with thought *content*. On the other hand there may be underlying unity, but this unity is in the realm of thought *process*. These are two different orders of abstraction. The unity of thought process can be explained as due to the physically and mathematically finite ways in which the human brain can respond. For instance, a brain which becomes seriously disturbed, either chemically or psychologically, invariably responds with hallucinations. The process of hallucinating is the unity. The brain cannot dissolve itself, or emit clouds of blue smoke to signal its distress: it has to hallucinate. On the other hand the content of the hallucinations differs widely depending on the culture and the individual conflicts. For therapists it is the content of the thought that is important. It is the content that is used to talk about what is wrong and to make interpretations. If there is an underlying unity of thought process, it is of secondary importance for psychotherapy

Differences in Thinking on Causes

Turning specifically to mental diseases, it can be shown that people in various cultures have different beliefs regarding what causes these diseases. Insofar as the therapists of that culture share these beliefs, or can persuade the people to accept their theories of causation, they will be effective. A psychoanalyst trying to cure a patient who does not believe in oedipal conflicts and a witchdoctor trying to cure a patient who does not believe in spirit possession will be equally ineffective unless they can persuade the patient to accept their theory of causation.

Mental illness is universally thought to be caused by one of three things: biological events, experiential events, or metaphysical events. The first two are the foundation for Western therapy, the third for therapy elsewhere in the world. The difference is one of degree, however: all three are found in some form in almost every culture in the world.

Biological causes widely believed in by people in Western cultures include genetic damage, inborn constitutional factors, biochemical and metabolic inbalances, infections, drug toxicity, and damage to the brain. Depending upon which "school" of Western psychiatry the therapist favors he will put either more or less emphasis on them. European psychiatry, for instance, stresses these factors much more than does American psychiatry.

Other cultures accept biological causes of mental disease, but not as often as Western cultures do. Almost all cultures have a theory of genetic causation, though it may be associated with other things (such as a sin or a broken taboo by your ancestor) as well. Such thinking is not absent in the West. Many cultures also differentiate mental disease resulting from infections like

malaria and typhoid fever ("false madness") from that caused by
experiential or metaphysical events ("true madness").[20]

Some cultures believe in biological causes that Western
cultures no longer accept. Examples are bad air, insect bites, and
the intrusion of a foreign body into the person. The whole basis of
Chinese psychotherapy is based on a biological imbalance between
yin and *yang* in the brain. Therapy then logically becomes cor-
recting the imbalance, usually by stimulation of the nervous
system with needles (acupuncture).

Experiential causes, especially experiences in childhood, are
the hallmark of American psychiatry. Both patients and therapists
in our culture accept the importance of traumas in childhood and
much of psychotherapy consists of an exploration of these events.
Other cultures include experiences as causative of mental disease,
but to a lesser degree. The loss of a love object may be a cause
of illness among the Land Dayak in Borneo.[21] And in many
cultures mental diseases are thought to be associated with having
broken a taboo.

Metaphysical causes are the most important ones in most of
the world: the loss of the soul; the intrusion of a spirit into the
body (spirit possession); sorcery; angering a diety. The close
association between the metaphysical and mental illness leads
logically to the overlap in roles of priest and therapist that is
commonly found.[22] In fact it is only recently in Western cultures
that the two roles have been relatively separated. But gods and
devils, though not primary, are far from extinct in our own thinking about mental illness.

Though most investigators dismiss theories of causation in
other cultures as "just magic and spirits," those who have looked
more closely have found a complex and coherent belief system
equally as sophisticated as our own. A good example of this is
Devereux's extensive study of Mohave Indian beliefs about mental
illness.[23] Another good example is Castanada's fascinating education by a Yaqui medicine man.[24] Castanada, an anthropologist,
first tried to conceptualize his information on Yaqui mental illness
using Western categories of causation. After much work ". . . I
realized that my attempt at classification had produced nothing
more than an inventory of categories." Beginning again he tried
to order his data, using the structure of the medicine man himself.

The result was an intricate, logical, and internally consistent set of theories.

Finally it should be noted that thinking on causation not only differs between cultures, but it differs also over a period of time. It was only a few years ago in Western cultures that mental illness was thought to be caused primarily by witches. And in many developing countries mental disease is increasingly thought to be caused by various acquisitions from Western cultures. One should not expect theories of causation to be any more static than other aspects of culture; they have evolved and will continue to evolve.

Differences in Classifying Mental Disease

Therapists everywhere treat the same broad range of mental problems—uncontrollable anxiety, depression, agitation, violent outbursts, bizarre behavior, and loss of contact with reality (as defined by that culture). But though the broad forms of these problems are quite similar from culture to culture, the more detailed division of them varies considerably. Different cultures have different ways of classifying mental disease.

It has long been acknowledged in transcultural psychiatric studies that the content of mental symptoms is influenced by the culture. For instance, delusions with a religious content (e.g., when the patient believes he is God) are much more common in Christian than in non-Christian cultures around the world.[25]

What has not been acknowledged in these studies very often is a step beyond that—the fact that not only the content, but the forms and classification of mental disorders varies from culture to culture. Many cross-cultural studies have been undertaken to try to compare the incidence of, say, paranoid schizophrenia or psychoneurotic depression in two cultures. Invariably the study concludes with some remark like: "It is difficult to fit mental disorders from that culture into Western diagnostic categories."

It should not be surprising to find that mental diseases elsewhere do not fit into our classificatory system since often our own do not. The Western systems of classification are hopeless jungles. The present American system combines and confuses an incredible mishmash of labels indicating causation (chronic brain syndrome due to syphilis), intelligence (mental retardation), personality traits (explosive personality), age (adjustment reaction of adolescence), sexual behavior (homosexuality), habits (bedwetting), parts of the body (psychophysiological cardiovascular disorder), emotion (depressive neurosis), relative sobriety (acute alcohol intoxication), and the relationship of the patient to his domicile (runaway reaction).[26]

Since most Western psychiatrists have long since given up trying to find their patients in this semantic maze, it seems presumptuous at the least to expect patients in other cultures to fall into these categories. In fact other cultures often classify their mental patients in a simpler and more rational way than we do, often on a purely functional basis.[27]

Even if the Western systems of classification were coherent, however, diseases from other cultures still would not fit into them. Let me illustrate. In one of the best studies on this subject to date, anthropologist William Caudill did a factor analysis of symptoms of Japanese psychiatric patients.[28] The symptoms emerged in six clusters, four of which overlapped Western disease classification (depressed, manic, psychopathic, and psychotic) and two of which did not. One of these two was *shinkei-shitsu*, a commonly recognized Japanese mental disease which consists of phobias, bodily complaints, tenseness, withdrawal, and self-deprecation. The other was *wagamama*, characterized by childish regression, apathy, negativism, and emotional outbursts. Thus both of these two "diseases" overlapped several of our disease categories and could not be clearly categorized in our system. It should also be noted that even the four disease categories that did overlap did not correspond exactly, e.g., depression in Japan does not include bodily complaints.

Another example of mental disease that cannot be translated into our classificatory system is the "totally discouraged syndrome" found among the Sioux Indians. It cuts across our divisions of depression, alcoholism, social deprivation, sociopathy, obsessiveness, and psychosis.[29] "Moth-craziness" and "ghost sickness" among the Navaho Indians are similarly culture-bound.[30]

Actually there are a whole series of mental diseases usually classified as "rare and exotic diseases" in Western psychiatric textbooks. These include *latah* in Indonesia, *bah-tshi* in Thailand, *yuan* in Burma, *imu* in Japan, *mali-mali* in the Philippines, *dhami* in Tibet, *koro* in China, *myrakit* in Siberia, *piblotoq* among the Eskimos, *susto* in Latin America, and *bouffées délirantes* in West Africa.

Koro provides a useful illustration. It is found among Chinese males and consists of anxiety secondary to a strong belief that the man's penis is shrinking into his body. It is believed that death will follow if it does. Because of this rather unusual symptomatology, and the imaginative methods that Chinese families devise to prevent it shrinking any further, the disease has received considerable notice by Western psychiatrists. In their attempts to translate it into Western disease categories they have variously labeled it an anxiety neurosis, a conversion reaction, a phobia secondary to masturbation, a type of hypochondriasis, a psychosis, and an extreme castration complex.[31]

What hopefully has become clear from this discussion is that *all* mental diseases are culture-bound because the system of classification is culture-bound. Similarly, what is a "rare and exotic disease" depends where you live. If you live in Shanghai then perhaps *koro* is a major disease syndrome and such Western entities as cyclothymic personality might be relegated to the rare and exotic category.

Implied by this relativistic approach to the classification of mental disease is a similar approach to the concept of normality. What is considered normal in one culture may be considered quite pathological in another. An example is the value put on possession by a spirit in some cultures, whereas similar behavior in Western cultures would be labeled as psychotic.

All of this is not just an exercise in cultural relativity. It has important implications. Not only is it necessary to have a shared classification system between the therapist and patient in order to name the disease correctly, but it is also necessary in order to choose the correct form of treatment. For instance, *shinkeishitsu* is treated by Morita therapy in Japan,[32] and *koro* by countering the overactivity of the *yin* (female) part of the brain. The cultural specificity of some forms of treatment will be discussed in chapter 5; here it is mentioned only to emphasize the importance of the cultural system of classification.

Finally, the classification of mental diseases, like their causation, is time-bound as well as culture-bound. There are many reports in the psychiatric literature about how the syndrome of depression has changed over the past half century. And the constellation of symptoms making up the "postwar housewife syndrome" (role ambivalence, depression, frustration) is a late addition. Disease content and classification change similarly in other cultures over time.

Attempts at Cross-Cultural Psychotherapy

If all of the above is true, and the patient must share a worldview (including theories of causation and classification of disease) in order for the principle of Rumpelstiltskin to be effective, then one would not expect attempts at cross-cultural psychotherapy to be very successful. Examination of these attempts should provide some suggestive evidence either /to confirm or refute this thesis.

In fact, all attempts at cross-cultural psychotherapy of which I am aware have been either difficult or unsuccessful. The degree of difficulty appears to vary directly with the gulf between the cultures, e.g., an American therapist will find it easier to have an American-born Japanese patient in therapy than a patient directly from Japan. This seems self-evident but is not generally discussed in the literature. To do so would entail seeing our own system of therapy in all its culture-bound nakedness. Such a realization contradicts our implicit but strongly held conviction that Western psychotherapy is universal in its validity, as universal as penicillin is for infections or insulin is for diabetes. This conviction is another aspect of our ethnocentrism and is, quite simply, mendacious.

One of the classic attempts to do cross-cultural psychotherapy was Devereux' attempt to do psychoanalysis on a Plains Indian. Devereux had major difficulties which he says were due to his own "unconscious cultural narcissism and ethnocentrism."[33] Other testimonies to these difficulties are found in the work of Seward, Abel, Sauna, Bishop and Winokur, and Bustamente.[34] The last, a Cuban psychiatrist, relates how he could not make the correct interpretation of a dream by one of his patients with an African background until he understood the meaning of an obscure Nigerian symbol. My own experience working with foreign students in both individual and group therapy has confirmed for me the difficulties of doing cross-cultural psychotherapy.[35]

Supporting though indirect evidence for the difficulty of psychotherapy across cultures is found in the research on psychotherapy with people of a lower socio-economic class background. In this case "class" contains its own set of ideas, ideals, goals, values, etc., and so can be considered as a separate culture—"the culture of poverty" in Oscar Lewis' phrase.[36] Since most Western psychotherapists come from middle and upper class backgrounds, such therapy would be, in a sense, cross-cultural.

Research on what happens to patients from this "culture of poverty" in psychotherapy shows that they are less likely to seek therapy, are less likely to be accepted for therapy, are more likely to be assigned to inexperienced therapists, will terminate and be terminated sooner, and are more likely to be treated by short-term and somatic therapies.[37] In short, they are not considered to be "good" patients by most psychotherapists. They are considered to be too "different." I would maintain that much of this difference is due to their having a different world-view than their therapists, sharing neither ideas about causation nor classification. Hence accurate identification of the disease, the naming process, is not possible.

Another piece of supporting evidence that Western psychotherapy is culture-bound (and class-bound) comes from the studies of its ideals. As long ago as 1938 it was clearly shown that the ideals of Western psychotherapy, at that time being espoused by the mental hygiene movement, coincided remarkably with the ideals of the Protestant ethic, being espoused by (among others) proper Bostonian Americans. Individualism, self-reliance, self-sacrifice, enhancement of wealth and social status, and rationalism were the recurring themes in both. At the time, the mental hygiene movement was completely dominated administratively by proper Bostonians.[38]

Recently a similar study confirmed the association of mental health ideals with those of the dominant class and culture. Examination of mental health literature for idea content showed that only 10 percent of a series of pamphlets on mental health was not directly associated with middle-class values. The authors conclude ". . . that the mental health movement is unwittingly propagating a middle-class ethic under the guise of science."[39]

Since the vast majority of therapists in Western psychiatry are drawn from the upper and upper-middle classes, opportunities for satisfactory psychotherapy for patients from lower classes are negligible. Their culture, as well as their class, makes them too "different." Western therapists prove this repeatedly by restricting their practices to patients of their own class. It is not economic factors alone that lead to this state of affairs. Even when no fee is charged at all most Western psychotherapists find themselves automatically accepting into therapy patients who share their own class and culture and not accepting others. These are the patients who "understand," who "speak the same language," who are "good candidates for therapy." In short, they share a common world-view, common thoughts on causation, a common way of classifying mental disease.[40] They have cognitive congruence.

Therapists in other cultures are not as class restricted in background as are therapists in Western psychiatry. For example, an extensive study of Japanese shamans showed that their class background coincided with a general cross-section of the population. If anything they were overrepresented in the lower middle-class and underrepresented in the upper class. Thus they would be expected to share a world-view with similar-class patients.[41]

It should not be said that cross-cultural psychotherapy is futile or never effective. Occasionally it appears to help a patient. When it does, however, it is probably because other factors in the therapeutic relationship are producing the change, not the principle of Rumpelstiltskin. For instance, the therapist may be raising the patient's expectations, or may have personality characteristics that are therapeutic for that patient. These other aspects of psychotherapy will be taken up in the succeeding chapters.

In the end, however, the principle of Rumpelstiltskin and a shared world-view is not enough by itself for therapists anywhere. They must judiciously mix common sense into the batter. This is illustrated clearly by a story about a Yemenite *mori*, the traditional therapist for part of the Arabian peninsula:

> One of our informants told us about a *mori* to whom a man came complaining about the fact that his house was full of mice and requesting that the *mori* give him an amulet against mice. The wise *mori* wrote out a scroll for this special occasion, handed it to the client, and said, "Here is your scroll. Tie it to the neck of a cat, otherwise it won't help."[42]

chapter 3

Personal Qualities: A Terry-Cloth Computer Therapist

Personal qualities of the therapist constitute the second of the four components of psychotherapy. These include actual qualities —the therapist as he really is—as well as those that are projected onto him by the patient. The latter is called the transference.

Western psychiatric literature is abundantly endowed with analyses of transference but remarkably deficient in analyses of the therapist as he really is. Underlying this deficiency is the question: What does it matter? Can therapy be just as effective with a terry-cloth-covered computer therapist as with a live therapist? Are certain personal qualities more therapeutic than others? What kind of person should be a therapist?

I sat down at a teletype connected to the computer and signaled that I was ready to begin. I was curious but skeptical. How could a computer act like a psychotherapist?

COMPUTER: Hello. Please tell me your name.
ME: Torrey.
COMPUTER: It's nice to meet you Torrey. I would like to

29

discuss your problem with you. Please tell me first whether you are male or female.

ME: Male.

COMPUTER: How old are you?

ME: Thirty-two.

COMPUTER: Are you married?

ME: Yes.

COMPUTER: Now, how can I help you?

ME: I don't know.

COMPUTER: Tell me something about your wife.

ME: She is a fine wife. We have a good marriage.

COMPUTER: I understand. Now tell me something about your parents.

ME: My father is dead. My mother has been sick.

COMPUTER: Tell me more about her.

ME: She is getting better now.

COMPUTER: Does your wife tend to be like your mother?

ME: No, not at all.

COMPUTER: I understand. Now let me ask you something else about your mother. Was she very strict in raising you?

ME: No, she was lenient. I made all my own decisions.

COMPUTER: Does it bother you that you made all your own decisions?

ME: No, I like to.

COMPUTER: Why do you like to?

ME: Because then I have created my own existential meaning.

COMPUTER: I understand. Please tell me more about someone close to you.

I wasn't certain whether the computer *did* understand or not. I decided to test it and see how it handled hostility.

ME: Why are you so insensitive?

COMPUTER: I am doing my best under these conditions.

ME: You are just a crazy machine.

COMPUTER: You seem interested in me personally.

ME: Who do you think you are?

COMPUTER: Please think of me as a doctor trying to discuss your feelings about people close to you. Call me anything you wish.

We went through an extensive history of my childhood, illnesses, the kind of women who attract me, the kind of men I admire, etc. The computer seemed interested in me and apparently wanted to help me. It questioned, clarified, focused, rephrased, and occasionally interpreted. It sounded strangely like a therapist, and evoked feelings of both fascination and disquiet.

This computer therapist is the product of Kenneth Colby, an imaginative psychoanalyst at Stanford University who is trying to program psychotherapy and belief systems into computers.[1] In the process he is raising some important questions about the nature of the psychotherapeutic relationship. A logical extension of this might be to cover the computer therapist with terry-cloth. The prototype for such an innovation is the work of psychologist Harry Harlow on terry-cloth surrogate monkey mothers. In an effort to identify the important aspects of the mother-child relationship, Harlow separated newborn monkeys from their mothers, then substituted various kinds of mechanical surrogate mothers.[2] The most effective and efficient surrogate mother was found to be a block of wood covered with foam rubber and sheathed in terry-cloth. A single "unibreast" bubbled milk from it and an electric bulb provided warmth.

> "The result was a mother, soft, warm, and tender, a mother with infinite patience, a mother available twenty-four hours a day, a mother that never scolded her infant and never struck or bit her baby in anger . . . It is our opinion that we engineered a very superior monkey mother, although this position is not held universally by monkey fathers."[3]

Through his studies Harlow has begun to isolate the components of the mother-child relationship and to assign the components relative importance. For instance he has found that the contact with a soft body is as important as the provision of milk for the baby monkey's mental development, throwing light on such human possessions as "security blankets."

Now, if we begin sheathing some of Dr. Colby's computer therapists in terry-cloth, and programming the computer to respond in different ways (e.g., listening only with an occasional "I see," advice-giving, strongly empathetic, actively interpreting) then we might begin to be able to learn more about psychotherapy. We might be able to determine the relative importance of the human element, find out which personality characteristics of therapists are most helpful for different kinds of patients, and even make statements about the selection and training of therapists that are based upon more than impressions. Facts in this area are badly needed and are conspicuously absent.

Therapist-Patient Relationships

What is known about the personal aspects of therapist-patient relationships? Most importantly it *is* a personal relationship, between a witchdoctor or a psychiatrist and a patient. Although some therapists strive to keep their own personality out of the therapy (apparently trying to emulate a computer) they are never entirely successful. Therapy remains a relationship between two persons in all cultures of the world.[4]

Within the boundaries of a personal relationship, the variety of interaction between therapist and patient in all cultures is wide. In our own culture it may be a close, daily encounter in private sanitariums, a daily visit to the analyst's office, a weekly visit, or a single encounter in a group marathon at a retreat. Classical psychoanalysts even used to take their patients with them on vacations, though this is now no longer done. The degree of responsibility that the therapist will accept varies just as widely from total responsibility (usually in a hospital setting) to no responsibility other than agreeing to meet regularly.[5]

Therapists in other cultures show a similar variety. In Ghana and Sierra Leone the patient may move into the therapist's home and spend long periods with him each day.[6] The patient may stay, along with five or ten others, for as long as two years. On the other end of the spectrum an Iban witchdoctor in Sarawak may visit the patient in his longhouse for a one-shot marathon curing session and expect the patient to be well thereafter.

It is generally said that therapists in other cultures foster the dependence of their patients. This is probably true, though there are exceptions. What is not clear is whether Western psychotherapists do this any less often even though in theory they are supposed to promote independence. It is also an open question whether a dependent or independent relationship with a therapist is superior; it may well be that the answer is related to the value system of each particular culture.

In terms of responsibility therapists in other cultures usually do not accept very much. For instance, in British Guiana: "The healer's job is to assist in devotions. He never offers a prognosis, and does not accept the principal responsibility. The effectiveness of the therapy is always the patient's responsibility."[7] This attitude has echoes in several schools of Western therapy.

There is no unanimity in any culture on whether the therapist has to accept a patient for treatment. Western therapists, especially those in private practice, are usually selective and will accept only those whom they think they can help. Therapists in other cultures tend to be similarly selective, enhancing their reputations by accepting only those patients with a favorable outlook for recovery.[8] On the other hand well-known therapists in all cultures are sometimes expected to accept the most difficult cases because nobody else is skillful enough to help them. The Ute Indian medicine man is an example.[9]

In regard to body contact in the therapist-patient relationship, therapists in other cultures almost invariably use it more than Western therapists do. For instance the Nigerian *babalawo* rubs the patient's body extensively, and carefully holds his head as he makes shallow cuts for the medicine.[10] During my brief observations of a Balinese *balian* I noted that approximately one-half of the healing session included some kind of body contact, usually the rubbing of medicated oils into the body. Body contact in Western therapies is almost completely absent, being used only by chiropracters, faith healers, and recently in some group sensitivity sessions.

Therapists in all cultures tend to blame their patients for their failures. In Western therapy it is usually ascribed to the patient's being "unsuitable for therapy," having "too rigid defenses," not being able "to give up his symptoms," etc. In other cultures it is usually blamed on a taboo broken by the patient or his family, and therapists end most healing sessions by invoking enough taboos to insure their being broken, thus leaving themselves an excuse for failure.

The therapist-patient relationship is also in part determined by the fees paid by the patient to the therapist. In most cultures there is thought to be a relationship between how much the therapy costs and how much it is worth. The cost of individual Western therapy can go as high as one hundred dollars an hour in large cities. Such an extraordinary fee is not exclusive to Western therapists; in Martinique a therapy session may cost the equivalent of one week's wages. In the latter, however, the therapy is often supposed to be completed in one or two sessions. In areas where both Western and non-Western therapy are available, the latter may even be more expensive. For instance at a hospital I visited in Singapore which has both Western and traditional Chinese therapy the latter was more expensive. In contrast to cultures where a high fee characterizes the therapist-patient relationship, there are others in which the only fee is a donation. The patient leaves whatever he can afford. Even in such cultures, however, the therapist is well off. In all cultures in the world witch-doctors and psychiatrists are among the wealthiest members of the society.

Occasionally in other cultures a male therapist may accept a female patient as his wife in lieu of a fee. This is found, for instance, in Nigeria.[11] Although it is not rare in Western therapy for a therapist to marry his patient—some nationally known therapists have done it—presumably it is not in lieu of a fee.

Western therapists usually charge a fee, though a lower one, while they are in training. In other cultures this may differ. Shamans among the Northwest Coast Indians received no fee until they had finished their four-year apprenticeship.[12] And fully trained Tenino shamans could not accept a fee for their first five cases.[13]

Western therapists expect to be paid their fee regardless of whether the patient gets well or not. This is not always true elsewhere. In many cultures the therapist can collect his fee only if the patient gets well.

An interesting way of regulating fees is found among the Paviotso Indians. There it is generally believed that if the therapist asks more or less than his power instructs him he will become sick and no longer be able to practice.[14] In these days of Medicaid abuse it is interesting to think what would happen if such a belief became prevalent among Western therapists.

Genuineness, Empathy, and Warmth

Since the therapist-patient relationship is by definition a personal one, then the personality characteristics of the therapist are necessarily important. How important is another question. This has been a subject of spirited debate within Western psychiatry. At one end are those in the client-centered school who believe that the personality characteristics of the therapist are the most important components of the therapeutic relationship. At the other end are behavior therapists and psychoanalysts who maintain that therapy is primarily the application of techniques and that the personality of the therapist is relatively unimportant. Resolution of this question has implications for witchdoctors and psychiatrists everywhere.

During the past fifteen years there has been some research on the question by Western therapists. Much of it arose out of the theories and work of psychologist Carl Rogers. It began with Rogers' attempts to identify the important components of therapeutic personality change,[15] and the simultaneous work of Betz and Whitehorn on characteristics of successful and unsuccessful psychotherapists.[16] This was followed by an outpouring in the 1960s by Truax, Carkhuff, and their co-workers.[17]

Stated briefly, the research shows that certain personal qualities of the therapist—accurate empathy, nonpossessive warmth, and genuineness—are of crucial importance in producing effective psychotherapy. These three qualities of the therapist "have been shown to relate significantly to a variety of positive patient personality and behavioral change indexes."[18] The therapists who possess these qualities consistently and convincingly get better therapeutic results than those who do not possess them. Four types of supporting research data have been brought forth.[19] The first is concerned with patient outcome in cases receiving high levels of the three ingredients as contrasted with cases receiving low levels. The studies include individual therapy on 14 schizophrenic inpatients, 40 psychoneurotic outpatients, and 80 institutionalized male juvenile delinquents. The findings on the 40 psychoneurotic outpatients, for instance, showed a 90 percent improvement rate when the therapist provided high levels of the three therapeutic qualities, and 50 percent improvement

rate when he provided a low level. Most of the research was
done by having trained raters code samples of tape-recorded
psychotherapy using research scales designed to measure the
three therapeutic qualities.

The second type of supporting research data focuses on the
three qualities themselves, contrasting patient change with control
groups receiving no psychotherapy. The studies include 14 schizophrenic inpatients, 40 institutionalized female juvenile delinquents, and 24 college underachievers. The results of the last, for
instance, showed that 19 of the 24 had a higher grade point
average in the semester after the counseling, compared with 11
of the 24 controls.

Truax and co-workers also use these data to explain why past
studies of outcome of psychotherapy have often failed. Truax
maintains that such studies included all kinds of therapists, and
did not differentiate those with genuineness, empathy, and
warmth from those lacking it. Thus some therapists were getting
their patients well whereas others were doing nothing or even
making them sicker. The net result was zero.

The third type of supporting research data examines the
respective roles of the therapist and patient in determining how
high a level of these qualities will be offered. One study used
eight therapists and eight inpatients in a block design. This study
and others showed "that the levels of therapeutic conditions
offered throughout counseling are due to the counselor rather
than the client."[20] In other words it is the therapist who deter-
mines whether the genuineness, empathy, and warmth will be
present or not. The qualities are either there or they are not,
independent of the personality or type of problem of the patient.

Finally, converging evidence from research on learning and
on parental influence is offered. It has been shown, for instance,
in a study on 120 third-graders and eight teachers that children
learn to read faster under the teachers who offer higher levels of
the three qualities cited above.[21]

None of this is to say that genuineness, empathy, and warmth
are the only important personality characteristics of the therapist. Further research may identify others. The research *does*
clearly point, however, toward certain human attributes as being
relatively important in the therapist-patient relationship.

Evidence from the history of Western psychiatry also supports this. When the humanitarian movement became prominent in psychiatry, with therapists showing great interest and kindness toward their patients as human beings, then more patients got well. For instance, between 1833 and 1846 at Worcester State Hospital in Massachusetts 70 percent of patients admitted were discharged within one year as much improved or cured.[22] This was at the zenith of the humanitarian movement in mental hospitals. It was long before shock therapy or tranquilizers, yet this discharge rate compares favorably with that from state hospitals today. The most plausible explanation is that the humanitarian movement encouraged those personality characteristics of therapists which are most therapeutic.

If certain personality characteristics are therapeutic, then this could account for successful therapy not only by psychiatrists but by witchdoctors as well. The desirable personality characteristics would not necessarily be the same in other cultures; following the reasoning of chapter 2, differences would be expected. But certain characteristics would be therapeutic, and therapists who possessed these characteristics would be expected to be more effective than those who did not.

Selection of Therapists

Before looking directly at the actual personalities of witchdoctors and psychiatrists, it might be instructive to examine their selection process. How do they get into their profession? Answering this question will tell us something about what kind of people they are.

Western psychotherapists are chosen primarily through self-selection and their academic achievement. A therapist must finish high school and college, then get postgraduate training either as a social worker, psychologist, or psychiatrist. If he chooses to become the last he must go on through four years of medical school, one year of internship, and three years of psychiatric residency training—a total of twelve years training after high school. A psychoanalyst can add still another four to eight years to this before he is considered fully qualified.

Western therapists, quite obviously, must be good academic students to survive this selection process. Unfortunately there is evidence that being a good student has nothing to do with being a good therapist.[23] One study even showed a *negative* correlation between the grades of therapists-in-training and their ratings on empathy.[24] Based on his work cited above, Carl Rogers came to the same conclusion: "Intellectual training and the acquiring of information has, I believe, many valuable results—but becoming a therapist is not one of those results."[25]

If personality characteristics of the therapist are as important for successful therapy as research has indicated, then our present method of selecting therapists in Western culture may be grossly inappropriate. It is possible, in fact, that the prolonged academic trial may even be *antithetical* to selecting good therapists. Those genuine, warm, empathetic therapists who do emerge may do so in spite of, not because of, the system of selection. And it is very disquieting to realize that there may be many individuals with the proper personality characteristics who are presently blocked from ever becoming professional therapists because they cannot or do not wish to learn trigonometry or microbiology.

The selection of therapists in other cultures is done by criteria other than academic achievement. The most common methods of selection are through heredity, supernatural designation, and self-designation. Heredity is rarely the only method, but it is frequently present. The child picked to succeed the therapist-parent may not necessarily be the eldest, but may be the one who shows the greatest interest or capacity as a therapist. Many witchdoctors in Western Nigeria have had medicine in their family for four or five generations.[26] This kind of family tradition is present also in Western culture, though less marked. Erik Erikson's translation of the pressure felt by a Yoruk Indian girl whose mother and grandmother are shamans sounds suspiciously like a dialogue that many Western therapists have heard before:

> "My mother say, 'You be doctor.'
> I say, 'no.'
> She say, 'You have much money, beautiful clothes; if not doctor, will have nothing."[27]

Another type of quasi-hereditary selection of therapists is occasionally found. This is the automatic designation (as therapists) of certain individuals who are different. Eskimo shamans, for example, are often drawn from the ranks of orphans and those with physical deformity.[28] And in one part of Japan all girls who are blind or crippled are expected to become shamans.[29] It is thought that such "special" individuals have been supernaturally marked for this unique role in society.

Designation by the supernatural is probably the most common way of selecting therapists in other cultures. The following account of a *tahu'a* on Tahiti is typical, and echoes the Old Testament:

> Tama was about forty-five years old at the time of the study and was one of the most famous *tahu'a* on the island of Tahiti. He was a successful farmer and entrepreneur. He had no special thought of becoming a healer, nor did he think much about the supernatural until twelve years before the author met him, at which time he had experienced a vision in his sleep. A cloud appeared to him and a voice came out of it, saying: "Heal the sick. Cure the people." Similar dreams are typically described to mark the onset of all *tahu'a* careers.[30]

Many healers receive their calling through dreams, visions, and unusual experiences. It is generally believed that they *must* obey such a calling, and that the penalty for failing to obey is sickness or death.

Designation by the supernatural may also be sought by a potential therapist. This was commonly the case among American-Indian medicine men who would deprive themselves of food, water, sleep, and comforts as they wandered in search of their "calling." Clearly there is also a voluntary component to selection in this manner.

Self-selected therapists are less common in other cultures, and usually have less status than those selected by heredity or by the supernatural.[31] The self-selection process is illustrated by this account from Martinique:

> "It is neither by inheritance nor by training that a healer obtains his position. He is self-designated on the basis of his conviction that he has special magical powers or gifts. The sort of evidence accepted as proof of this was indicated by a male nurse who despite his skepticism wondered if he himself had magical powers. He based his belief on the fact that he had once cured someone by concentrating hard and because he had often dropped syringes

and thermometers but had never broken anything. To become a healer there is no initiation, no payment of fees, and no special garb; one need only let it be known that one has taken up the work of healer. The authors were convinced of the healer's sincerity in believing that he could genuinely help patients."[32]

Also frequently included in self-selection are factors similar to those which may motivate Western therapists, such as a desire to help people, to gain social status and wealth, or to master the unknown so as to be better able to protect oneself and one's family.[33]

Are Psychotherapists Mentally Ill?

There is a common belief in Western cultures that most psychiatrists are themselves a little disturbed. It is often said in jest, but reflects a rather widespread general suspicion. Similarly, there is a common belief among those with any exposure to anthropological literature that witchdoctors are also disturbed individuals. Are these beliefs true? What kind of individuals really are psychiatrists and witchdoctors?

Regarding Western therapists, there is remarkably little objective evidence available with which to answer these questions. Most observations have been confined to what kind of person a therapist *should* be, e.g., intelligent, imaginative, sensitive, likeable, respected, self-controlled, flexible, and energetic.[34] It is occasionally said that a therapist should have gone through a sickness of his own in order to understand his patients.

Recent data on suicide rates for professional people show that psychiatrists have an inordinately high rate—double that for other types of doctors.[35] They also are known to have a comparatively high rate of drug addiction. Whether these figures can be used to support a contention that psychiatrists are, as a group, more disturbed than the general population is another, and debatable, matter.

My own subjective impression of the personality of psychiatrists is that there is some overrepresentation at both ends of the spectrum, but that generally psychiatrists are not grossly different from most professional groups. In other words there appears to be a greater-than-expected group of highly motivated, well-integrated, stable, healthy, individuals and also a greater-than-expected group of misfits. The abnormally high suicide rate presumably comes from this latter group. More objective data on this issue is badly needed.

Turning to witchdoctors, there is a widespread but erroneous impression in the anthropological literature that witchdoctors are very disturbed individuals. The witchdoctor's vocation is often portrayed as a haven for the schizophrenics, opportunists, and sexual deviants of a society.

This belief originated with Bogoras' study of the Siberian Chukchi early in this century. He contended that their shamans were ". . . as a rule extremely excitable, almost hysterical, and not a few of them were half crazy."[36] Anthropologists such as A. L. Kroeber, George Devereux, and Ralph Linton perpetuated this belief, and being prolific writers they succeeded in establishing it as a fact which was until recently unchallenged. Kroeber, for instance, contends that one of the points differentiating a "primitive" from a "developed" society is that the former rewards its psychotics with a socially sanctioned role as a healer.[37] The line of reasoning usually follows psychoanalytic thinking in their writings and always, of course, comes from the vantage point of the writer's cultural norms.

A psychoanalyst who studied Apache Indian shamans provides further data. L. B. Boyer's earlier work on one shaman concluded that he was a disturbed individual.

> "He was shown to suffer from a personality disorder, with impulsive and hysterical traits, and to have characteristics of the imposter. His principle fixations were oral and phallic. There were suggestions he lacked clear masculine identity and suffered from problems resulting from latent homosexuality."[38]

From this he generalized that all Apache shamans were disturbed.[39]

Three years and eleven shamans later Boyer completely reversed himself. After further studies he concluded that the ". . . Apache shamans have not been psychological deviants at any period of their lives." In fact he says that they are *healthier* than the average member of their society.[40]

Boyer's observations are instructive. If you look at only one therapist in any culture you may find a deviant. There are abundant accounts of single therapists in other cultures who are psychopathic, manic, emotionally unstable, psychotic, or frauds.[41] It is no more valid, however, to generalize from these single therapists in other cultures than it is to generalize from a single therapist in our culture.

It is also clear that judgments about the mental health of therapists in other cultures often suffer from the ethnocentric bias of the observer. Thus spirit possession and associated hysterical behavior is not only normal, but often valued and desirable in other cultures. In our own culture it is considered deviant. It was just this kind of behavior that led Bogoras originally to the conclusion that the shamans must be crazy.[42]

To make a generalization about the mental health of therapists an observer must study several of them and must also know what kinds of behavior are considered normal in that culture. The best study to date which meets these criteria is by Dr. Yuji Sasaki, a Japanese psychiatrist, of 56 Japanese shamans. He found that 38 of the shamans were without evidence of personality deviation, 10 had some degree of neurosis, 6 were psychotic, and 2 had organic brain disease.[43] Unfortunately there is no data on Western therapists against which to compare these figures.

Another commonly cited fact in favor of the therapists-are-mentally-ill thesis is the use of transvestites as therapists. This was a well-known (and widely commented upon) arrangement among the Plains Indians where such individuals were called *berdaches*. For anthropologists like Kroeber this "proved" that therapists in other cultures are disturbed.[44] The fact is that *berdaches* certainly did exist, but that this arrangement is a rare one. It is found in a few other cultures in the world,[45] but not nearly as often as Western anthropological preoccupation with it would lead one to believe. Most therapists in other cultures are as heterosexual as most therapists in our own culture.

There is increasing evidence with which to refute the idea that therapists in other cultures are disturbed. In fact, many observers note that, as a group, the therapists appear to be among the least disturbed members of the society. Typical is the judgment of anthropologist Marvin Opler on the Ute Indian shaman:

> The Indian shaman is a man or woman ordinarily not only adult chronologically, but mature, poised, and serious in personality. . . . In his hands, as with the medical practitioner in our society, lay an enormous responsibility for maintaining the health and vigor necessary in the culture . . . His role, depending on his prowess, became in most instances a crucial and respected one, not merely medical but ethico-religious in essence.[46]

Unusual intelligence and memory are frequently ascribed to these therapists. For instance a Navaho medicine man must learn a volume of details for a curing ceremony that has been compared to memorizing a Wagnerian opera, including "orchestral score, every vocal part, all details of the settings, stage business, and each requirement of the costume."[47] And a Yakut Indian shaman must have a professional vocabulary of 12,000 words compared to the usual Yakut vocabulary of 4,000 words.[48] Other commonly mentioned attributes are ". . . unusual decency, upright character, judgment, and responsibility."[49] An observer of Yakut Indian shamans sums up best of all the qualities that make a good therapist in that culture, and probably in many cultures: "One must feel an inner force in him that does not offend yet is conscious of its power."[50]

Many other testimonials could be proffered to support the thesis that most therapists in other cultures are unusually stable and mature individuals. They cover a wide area from African witchdoctors[51] to Australian medicine men ("altruistic and intelligent men")[52] to American Indian shamans and medicine men.[53] After an extensive survey of the character of this last group, one field worker concludes: ". . . quackery and charlatanism are no more prevalent in primitive than in civilized society."[54]

Western therapists have organizations such as the American Psychiatric Association and the American Psychological Association to insure minimum standards of conduct and professionalism among their members. Though less commonly, therapists in other cultures are sometimes similarly organized. Witchdoctors in the Sudan and in Nigeria have fraternal organizations,[55] and shamans in Korea not only form guilds but even contribute money for the erection of lodges in which they meet.[56] Societies such as these can enforce good conduct; for instance candidates for the Association of Nigerian Doctors must take an oath that they will use their powers only for good purposes, never for sorcery.[57] These societies can also exclude mentally disturbed or unstable candidates from membership. Finally, many groups of therapists have a common ethic demanding professional secrecy regarding what the therapist has been told by patients.[58] One of the effects of such organizations is to encourage and enforce ethical behavior, thereby attracting more ethical personality types as therapists.

chapter 4

Patient Expectations:
The Edifice Complex

A taxi drives up to the front door of the Menninger Clinic in Topeka. A depressed, middle-aged man from northern New England gets out with his family. It has been a difficult trip, including two changes of planes and much financial sacrifice. But even as he enters the door he feels better. He has hope.

A crowded bus stops in the center of the West African village. A depressed, middle-aged man from up-country gets out with his family. The trip has entailed a day of walking, two buses, and much expense. Up on the hill the famous healing shrine is visible. As he starts up the hill toward it he too feels better. He has hope.

Both of these men illustrate the third component of psychotherapy. Along with a shared world view and the personal qualities of the therapist, patient expectations are a powerful and important part of the therapeutic process. Anything that raises patient expectations aids this process. Therapists everywhere in the world utilize this principle, though too often in Western cultures it lies misplaced and unrecognized beneath our piles of sophisticated theories and techniques.

Freud recognized its importance. In commenting on the similarity of primitive and religious therapies with psychoanalysis he said: "In order to effect a cure a condition of 'expectant faith' was induced in the sick person, the same condition which answers a similar purpose for us today."[1]

But it has remained for psychiatrist Jerome Frank to clearly outline the importance of hope and patient expectations for psychotherapy. After reviewing many types of healing in his lucid *Persuasion and Healing* Frank concludes: "The apparent success of healing methods based on all sorts of ideologies and methods, compels the conclusion that the healing power of faith resides in the patient's state of mind, not in the validity of its object."[2] And in a later paper: ". . . efforts to heighten the patient's positive expectations may be as genuinely therapeutic as free association or habit training."[3]

This chapter will examine the available evidence that supports these contentions. It will then describe some of the ways in which psychiatrists and witchdoctors raise their patients' expectations and produce hope, itself therapeutic. The building associated with the healer (the edifice complex), his reputation, his accessory paraphernalia, his reputation, and his training are all effective parts of therapy and induce hope that the patient will, after all, get well.

The Importance of Expectations

There is now abundant evidence from many sources that shows the importance of expectations. What a person expects to happen often will happen if the expectations are strong enough. This is the self-fulfilling prophecy.

Expectations are a major determinant of human behavior. Psychologists are familiar with experiments showing how visual perception is influenced by the person's expectations.[4] The person sees what he expects to see. Other experiments, involving classes of college students and a "substitute teacher," showed how expectations influence the formation of opinions. Half the class was given advance biographical data on the "teacher" indicating that he was a "cold" person, the other half a "warm" person. Testing after the class revealed that those with expectations of a "warm" teacher found him significantly more considerate, more sociable, more humorous, and less formal than their counterparts. Furthermore they participated more actively in the class.[5]

Some of the strongest evidence for the importance of expectations comes from studies of patients going to surgery. In one such study a group of surgical patients were warned before the operation about postoperative pain and were given breathing exercises to do for the pain. Another group was not given any warning or exercises. The group that had been told to expect pain requested only one-half as much pain medication and left the hospital earlier by an average of almost three days.[6] Clearly patient expectations are a powerful therapeutic tool, a fact to which Christian Scientists will testify most eloquently.

Turning to psychotherapy, one researcher studied 43 patients who were applying for psychotherapy. He found that the patient's expectations of help when he applied were significantly related to the degree of symptom relief he obtained in the initial interview. The more the patient expected to be helped, the more he was helped.[7] A similar study using medical students as psychotherapists showed that the patient's optimism at the onset of treatment was directly related to the symptomatic relief during the course of therapy.[8]

Studies of placebos—inactive substances with no pharmacologic effect which are given as medicine—provide further evidence for the importance of patient expectations. In fact the whole history of medicine provides such evidence, for we know now that most medicines used by doctors in the past were inactive. They were placebos. Yet patients got well and doctors became wealthy and famous.

Some of the more colorful placebo medicines on which doctors in the past made their reputations included lizard's blood, crocodile dung, swine teeth, powdered Egyptian mummy, and frog sperm.[9] Modern-day versions of placebos, such as kelp, honey, horehound leaves, and pigweed, can be found in several best-selling books of home remedies.[10] Some of these contain a grain of therapeutic truth but many of them are simply placebos. But they work. And they work because people expect them to work.

In psychiatry the effects of placebos have been compared with the effects of short-term psychotherapy. Fifty-six psychiatric outpatients, all diagnosed as neurotic, were given placebos as the only form of therapy. The outcome results compared favorably with the results obtained by short-term psychotherapy in a similar group.[11] In another study 109 psychiatric outpatients were given placebos (presented to them as "a new pill") and then followed for three years to see what the effect was. After one week on the pill 80 per cent of the patients reported improvement in their symptoms. And of those still taking it three years later, 66 percent reported continued improvement.[12] Jerome Frank cites such experiments as confirming ". . . the hypothesis that part of the healing power of all forms of psychotherapy lies in their ability to mobilize the patient's hope of relief."[13]

 The power of a patient's expectations is also suggested by studies done on its obverse—hopelessness. Internists and surgeons know well the problems of trying to cure a hopeless patient. Some surgeons will not even operate on a patient who does not expect to survive the operation—too often they do not survive.[14] Related to this is the high mortality rate of old people shunted off to the state hospitals; they apparently give up hope and just die.

Probably the most impressive demonstration of the efficacy of patient expectations is "voodoo death." This dramatic demise occurs when a person is "hexed" by another who is believed to be powerful enough to kill him.[15] The hexed person becomes sick and dies within a few weeks. He expects to die so he does die. The actual mechanism of death has been debated, but probably involves activation of the nerve to the heart causing the heart to gradually stop. Deaths due to this kind of patient expectations have been reported by Western observers from South America, Africa, Australia, and the Caribbean. Voodoo deaths then, along with the other sources of evidence cited above, point to the great importance of patient expectations in determining a person's health status.

The Edifice Complex and Beyond

Part of the efficacy of therapists all over the world arises from their ability to mobilize the patient's hope and raise his expectations of getting well. Often the therapist is not even aware of this aspect of therapy, but it occurs nonetheless.

It begins when the patient decides to go to the healing institution. Even making an appointment and thinking about going is often enough to make the patient feel better. It is increased by the trip. The longer the trip is, the higher will be the patient's expectations. Often a trip to a major healing institution takes on the qualities of a pilgrimage, as is implied in the two cases described at the beginning of the chapter. Western patients will often talk of their trip to the Menninger Clinic, the Mayo Clinic, the Leahy Clinic, or any of The Other Medical Centers in terms that other pilgrims use for Delphi, Mecca, or Lourdes.

This is the edifice complex.[16] Though it is as old as the Greek myth of similar sound it bears no relation to it. It is faith in the institution itself, the door at the end of the pilgrimage. It is the light in the patient's eyes when you tell him that you are associated with The Medical Center. It is the misty prestige of antibiotics and open-heart surgery seeping down the hall to the Department of Psychiatry. It occurs when "patients invest the hospital itself with a healing function, and assume that whatever goes on within its walls is done to help them."[17] It is that portion of psychotherapeutic effectiveness which would be lost if psychiatrists operated out of austere rooms in a county courthouse rather than out of The Medical Center. In psychoanalytic terms it is transference to the institution.

Western therapists commonly utilize the edifice complex to raise patient expectations though they are not usually aware of using it. They use it more often than therapists in other cultures because they are more likely to be attached to a single building or institution. Witchdoctors are less apt to center themselves in one place, and more commonly make visits to the patient's home. The edifice complex is certainly not unknown among therapists in other cultures, however; healing shrines of wide repute are found scattered throughout almost all cultures. They are commonly semireligious in nature in these other cultures, contrary to their more purely medical nature in Western cultures.[18]

We have seen that the therapist's ability to raise a patient's expectations is intimately connected both with his ability to name what is wrong and with his personal qualities. In reference to the first, much of the naming process and the assignment of meaning can be looked at from the vantage point of increasing the patient's faith in the therapist and increasing his expectations of cure. It is the naming, in fact, which is the necessary first step; only when the malady is properly identified does the possibility of curing it become a real one.

The therapist's personal qualities are also closely intertwined with patient expectations. Somewhere in the interface between the two the word "charisma" may be found, a word frequently applied to successful therapists in all cultures. "Charisma" is often used in an explanatory way in descriptions of witchdoctors that try to explain their success. It is perhaps more accurate to think of it in terms of personal qualities of the therapist and the raising of patient expectations.

Another aspect of this is the therapist's belief in himself. Several studies have shown that the greater is this belief, the higher are the patient's expectations of being helped.[19] Accounts of both successful witchdoctors and psychiatrists invariably include the strong belief that the therapist has in himself. It can be seen, for instance, in the "inner force . . . that does not offend yet is conscious of its power" in a Yakut Indian shaman[20] as well as in the writings of a Western therapist like Carl Rogers.

Another phenomenon which points toward the importance of a therapist's belief in himself is the continuous succession of "new" types of therapy in Western cultures. These are usually associated with a single therapist, the "founder," and flit across the therapy screen like fads. It is as if the psychiatric and psychological journals had a therapist-of-the-month foldout. These "new" therapies are invariably most effective in the hands of their "founders" who usually claim, and probably obtain, spectacular cure-rates. They have, after all, the most faith in the "new" methods, and they transmit their certainty to their patients. Later devotees who try and implement these "new" therapies never quite match the original cure-rates, being naturally plagued by more skepticism than the "founders."

Therapists do other things as well to raise the expectations of their patients. In most cultures they stand out as different, apart from the great mass of people. In Western culture psychotherapists even stand apart from their healing brethren in other medical specialties. They dress differently, have beards, and are rarely in danger of being confused with surgeons or pediatricians. American Indian medicine men had distinctive dwellings and diet as well as dress,[21] and the colorful regalia of African witchdoctors is well known. It is interesting to speculate whether there is any relationship between the face paint and mask commonly adopted by therapists in other cultures and the beard and pipe used by psychiatrists in our own culture.

Individuality of the therapist, though usually not consciously affected, tends to increase the patient's expectations of him. The therapist is different. He has high status in the society, and is accorded respect and sometimes reverence. Simultaneously he is held in awe and sometimes fear. Most members of the society have a lurking suspicion that he has a special relationship with occult or mystical powers. The feelings of a Yoruba tribesman toward a *babalawo* (literally, "father of mysteries") has an exact counterpart in the feelings of a cocktail party guest toward the psychiatrist in the room—attraction, awe, avoidance, fear. In his study of Indian medicine men Maddox sums up this aspect of them: his description fits many cultures:

"He is readily distinguishable from the laity by his taciturnity, his grave and solemn countenance, his dignified step, and his circumspection. All of these peculiarities tend to heighten his influence, and, by rendering his appearance impressive and suggestive of superiority, serve to increase his control over the people."[22]

Certain paraphernalia are used by therapists in different cultures to increase patient expectations. In Western culture non-psychiatric healers have their stethoscope, and psychotherapists are supposed to have their couch. With the decline of classical psychoanalysis there has been an accompanying disappearance of the couch, and therapists frequently observe their patients looking furtively around for it on their first visit. Therapists in other cultures have their counterpart trademark, often a special drum, mask, or amulet. A South American Caraibe therapist, for instance, can always be identified by his large colored feather headdress and a sacred gourd rattle which he carries in both hands.[23]

Therapist Reputation and Training

A therapist's ability to engender hope in his patient and raise the expectations of being cured ultimately depends upon his own reputation. And though reputations may be forged in different ways in different cultures, usually they are primarily forged upon the anvil of training.

Certainly this is true in Western cultures. Therapists compete heatedly to obtain positions in the prized training institutions, and for the rest of their lives they do not hesitate to let people know where that was. For their patients they advertise it by way of their diplomas, a constellation of which discreetly covers a wall in most therapist's offices. They bear silent testimony to the therapist's skill in being accepted by The University, The Medical or Graduate School, The Residency, The Professional Society, etc. They even are often in Latin, compounding the respect they inspire. This is social sanction for the therapist in a broad sense, and reputation in a narrow sense. The patient relaxes in his chair, knowing he is in good hands.

Therapists in other cultures also use training systems to increase their reputations. These systems vary widely, but almost all cultures have some expected course that therapists are supposed to undertake. Even therapists who receive their powers hereditarily must have it supplemented with an apprenticeship.[24]

Just like Western cultures, aspiring therapists elsewhere will often travel long distances to train under famed masters of their trade.[25] In Haiti a master therapist's fame is reflected in his pupils, and pupils are proud to have studied with the master. The training period varies from two years, for a Yoruk Indian shaman,[26] to seven years among Blackfoot Indians and Nigerian *babalawos*.[27] The training course includes such things as a memorization of a vast body of literature and associated rituals, learning specific healing techniques, mythology, and learning a special language for healers.[28] It also includes practicum like water-gazing, divining, and how to impregnate charms with various spirits, as among the Ashanti in Ghana.[29]

I was pleased to learn that some of the training of witch-doctors is just as irrelevant as some of mine was. For instance, Eskimo shamans must learn and be able to name ". . . all the parts of his body, every single bone by name in the sacred shaman's language."[30] Shades of anatomy in the sacred language of Latin! I felt a kinship with my Eskimo brother, and hoped that he was working toward curriculum reform.

Another interesting aspect of the training of therapists in some other cultures is the emphasis on self-control and self-knowledge as part of the training. Blackfoot Indian medicine men, for instance, used much of their seven-year training period to train their mind to have complete control over their body.[31] Ute Indian shamans underwent individual dream analysis as part of their training:

> "Since dreams were also the agency through which shamans ob-
> tained individual supernatural curing power, the shaman in his
> own development learned much about his own past unconscious
> motivations . . . By his encounters with the supernatural, the
> shaman not only learned much about the rituals of driving out
> evil spirits in patients, but he came to understand himself bet-
> ter."[32]

We will return to the use of dreams in the next chapter.

There are various ways of signifying the end of the therapist's training in other cultures. Yoruk Indian shamans can finish the minimum "core curriculum" in two years. After that they can take an optional course culminating in a "pain-cooking dance." The extra study is expensive but gives them a higher reputation and the right to charge higher fees.[33] Among some American Indian groups, there were as many as four separate degree levels, only a select few therapists attaining the highest one.[34]

A few cultures other than Western cultures have a regular examination at the end of training. The Association of Nigerian Doctors, for example, both holds an examination and grants a certificate to be a witchdoctor.[35] The best description of such a system is anthropologist George Murdock's account of Tenino Indian shamans:

> "To practice, it was not sufficient merely to have accumulated the
> requisite number and variety of spirit helpers. The prospective
> shaman also had to pass the equivalent of a state medical board
> examination conducted by the shamans who had already been ad-
> mitted to practice."[36]

The purposes of this board examination, according to Murdock, was to disqualify false shamans who did not really believe in their own power and ". . . to review carefully the entire life of the candidate." He concludes that ". . . their decision as to whether or not to admit him to practice seems clearly to have rested on their collective estimate of his personal characteristics, of his fitness to be entrusted with the exercise of great power."[37]

One other aspect of the training of therapists in other cultures is interesting in comparison with our own—it is often very expensive and includes privation. In reference to Menomini Indian medicine men, Maddox says:

> "Frequently the collections of skins, peltries, and other goods that have to be purchased involved a candidate hopelessly in debt; but so great was the desire on the part of some Indians to become acknowledged medicine men that they would assume obligations that might require years of labor in hunting to liquidate; or, if they failed, then their relatives were expected to assume the responsibility thus incurred."[38]

And privation was often thought to be good for the candidates, improving their knowledge of the spirits.

Besides training, therapists have other means for increasing their reputations. Sometimes these are outright advertising, as a sign in Nigeria that reads: "We cure mad fellows in 21 days."[39] Or it may be a testimonial letter from a grateful patient posted on the wall of the therapist's examining room; this I observed in the office of an acupuncturist in Hong Kong.

More dramatic methods sometimes used to enhance the reputation of therapists in other cultures are legerdemain and "miracles." These are, of course, regarded as nonprofessional by Western therapists. Eskimo shamans frequently used tricks like ventriloquism to impress their patients. They would also appear to do things like grinding a stone into sand with their bare hands.[40] And a shaman in Tibet was known to be able to wash his face in boiling oil without getting burned.[41]

Divination is the other technique commonly used by therapists, especially in Africa, to impress their patients. Nigerian *babalawos*, for instance, do not take a history from their patients. Rather a patient whispers his problem to a handful of palm nuts;

the *babalawo* then casts the nuts and from their position makes a diagnosis.[42]

Other methods of divination include throwing "bones" (wooden blocks with markings), feeling the patient's pulse, constant gazing at water, star-gazing, watching the flickering of an oil lamp, listening to the wind, and watching the trembling of the hands. It should be emphasized that these procedures, frequently ridiculed in Western descriptions of other cultures as proof of their "primitiveness," are methods used by the therapist to increase his reputation and, thus, increase the patient's faith and expectations. Often the therapist is in possession of accessory information that allows him to make an accurate diagnosis.

chapter 5

Techniques of Therapy:
Electric Eels
and Electroshock

People willing to cede the fact that witchdoctors share with psychiatrists the first three components of psychotherapy often do so in the belief that they hold a trump card—the techniques of therapy. Whatever similarity may exist among therapists in their utilization of shared world-views, of personal qualities, and of patient expectations, it is thought that the scientific techniques used in Western therapy will sharply and conclusively separate witchdoctors from psychiatrists.

However the therapy game is in no-trump. The techniques of therapy all over the world are found to be the same. There is no technique used in Western therapy that is not also found in other cultures. There *are* techniques, however, used in other cultures that are only rarely used by Western psychotherapists. Cultures, as we will see, often favor certain types of therapy or particular techniques, but the difference is one of quantity—how often they are used. These differences in the quantitative use of techniques are directly related to particular values of each culture. Overall the similarities in the techniques used by witchdoctors and psychiatrists far outweigh the differences.

Before beginning the discussion of specific therapies, four warnings should be sounded. First, the division between techniques of therapy and the personal characteristics of the therapist is artificial. The two reinforce each other and are really inextricably intertwined. Certain therapists choose certain techniques which are compatible with their personalities; for instance an authoritarian personality may choose suggestion or hypnosis. Second, it is easy to confuse techniques used to increase the expectations of the patient (such as hanging diplomas on your wall or magical divination, discussed in chapter 4) with the techniques used for therapy per se. This too is an artificial division, but one which will have to be adopted to break up the massive subject into digestible units.

Third, the reader is reminded of the discussion in chapter 1 regarding magic and science. With few exceptions the techniques used by both witchdoctors and psychiatrists are on exactly the same scientific—or prescientific—plane. And given their theories of causation, the treatment techniques of therapists elsewhere are just as logical as ours. Parenthetically it should be noted that therapists everywhere believe that *their* techniques are "scientific" and that other therapists use "just magic." The disparaging appraisals that I have heard of one witchdoctor's work by another are the equal of anything I have heard among therapists in Western professional circles.

Finally, although the techniques of therapy have been separated into categories below, it should be emphasized that all therapists usually employ more than one category simultaneously. In other words both witchdoctors and psychiatrists use physical, psychosocial and group-milieu therapies in combination or together.

Physical Therapies

DRUGS

Since the wide introduction of tranquilizers in the 1950s, drugs have become a mainstay of Western psychiatric therapy. No other culture, past or present, has developed such an array of sophisticated and powerful drugs. But other cultures have used drugs which are quite similar for thousands of years. The Aztec and Toltec Indians of Mexico, for example, had a highly developed empirical pharmocopoeia.[1] Western pharmacology has been slow to appreciate the contributions of other cultures.

Rauwolfia root is a good example. This drug, with the trade name of Reserpine, was introduced into Western psychiatry in the 1950s as a major tranquilizer. At the time it was recognized as having been used in India for centuries as a tranquilizer. Later it was found also to have been in wide use in West Africa for many years. In 1925, in fact, a famous Nigerian witchdoctor was summoned to England to treat an eminent Nigerian who had become psychotic there.[2] Armed with his rauwolfia root, the witchdoctor had better medicine to offer the psychotic patient than did any English psychiatrist of that period. Rauwolfia remains a favorite among West African witchdoctors as an initial treatment for acutely disturbed patients, often to make them more amenable to the psychosocial therapies. This is the same way major tranquilizers are often used in the West. Rauwolfia has also been used to produce prolonged sleep therapy in Nigeria, a type of treatment popular in French psychiatry.[3]

Major sedative drugs are used by therapists in all cultures. In the West usually barbiturates or tranquilizers are used. Little work has been done to explore the types of sedatives used in other cultures but they are almost always present. There are references to their use in China in the twelfth century B.C.[4] One sedative that has been explored is *Kava*, a widely used drug in the Pacific Islands. Although there is controversy about exactly what it does, it appears to be a sedative and not an antipsychotic.[5] Another sedative drug, derived from cactus, is used by Indian witchdoctors in Peru to encourage the patient to express his inner thoughts; this is analogous to the use of amobarbital "truth serum" in Western cultures.[6]

Another important group of drugs used by Western psychotherapists are the antidepressants. They are relatively new, and their efficacy is still being assessed. It should be noted that opium has been in use as an antidepressant in many cultures for centuries. Its poppy seeds have been found in Stone Age sites 4,000 years old, and Homer testified for its utility in curing sadness and worry. It is still used, in much the same way as our antidepressants, by the Yemeni *mori* to treat severely depressed patients.[7]

Just as it is difficult to get out of a modern psychiatrist's office without being given some kind of minor tranquilizer—often Miltown or Librium—so it is difficult to see therapists in other cultures without being given medications. Their pharmacological armamentarium for less severely disturbed people usually consists of roots, leaves, and herbs in various forms of preparation. Some of these preparations have mild sedative properties. Since drugs like Miltown and Librium have no demonstrated value beyond mild sedative properties, the "primitive" concoctions of the witchdoctor are probably at the same level.

In both cases it may be that the element of suggestion and being given something by the therapists is the really important ingredient. The Western psychiatrist hands the prescription to his patient with a strong suggestion: "Take these three times a day and you will feel better. They won't solve your problem, but they'll help you to deal with it. We'll talk again next week." And they do make the patient feel better, even if they are just sugar pills. The patient symbolically takes part of his therapist home with him for the week, and in fact does deal with his problem more effectively.

The witchdoctor does this with even greater finesse. Rather than merely writing out a prescription, he often gives the medicine in a ritualistic way. For instance in Nigeria he makes a series of shallow razor cuts on the scalp and rubs the medicine in. And all astute witchdoctors know, as do Western therapists, how much more effective it is to give medicine by injection than by mouth, even though both should theoretically produce the same result.

One of the most common criticisms of witchdoctors is that they use harmful, even fatal, drugs. As is true for many of the stereotypes we are dealing with, it is probably that we overestimate the harmful techniques of other therapists and underestimate the harmful aspects of our own techniques. Put another way, we overvalue our own techniques and undervalue the other techniques.

It is certainly true that therapists elsewhere use drugs that are sometimes harmful; a certain drug they frequently apply to the eye, for instance, may cause serious inflammation.[8] On the other hand Western medications, including the drugs used in psychiatry, may also produce harmful results. The psychiatric literature is replete with descriptions of cases that went wrong because of side effects of the drug. In an interesting study done on over 1,000 hospitalized patients at an eminent American medical center, it was found that 20 percent of the patients suffered some complication of the therapy. Over half of these complications were moderately or very severe, and in 16 cases caused or contributed to the death of the patient.[9] It is doubtful if the morbidity caused by therapists elsewhere is much higher than this.

SHOCK THERAPY

Mild forms of shock therapy are widely used by therapists in many cultures. It is common, for instance, to spray or throw water in the patient's face, thereby producing a mild shock, raising the level of emotion, and encouraging the patient to give up his symptoms. Such an approach is widely used by Mexican *curanderos*.[10] This technique is rarely used in Western psychotherapy; only recently have we heard of an occasional therapist (usually nonprofessional) producing shock by water or a slap on the face during a group confrontation.

Major forms of shock therapy, by contrast, were until recently a very important technique in Western psychiatry. These forms of shock produce a convulsion and are believed to be effective in treating psychotic states and severe depression. They were developed in the 1930s and remained until the spread of major tranquilizers in the 1950s a therapeutic mainstay for Western psychiatrists. The shock and convulsion were produced by drugs such as camphor, picrotoxin, Metrazol, Indoklon, and insulin, or by an electrical machine.

Shock therapy is not new, however; the idea is about 4,000 years old. There are drawings of electrical fish on the walls of Egyptian tombs dated at 2750 B.C. The Greek name for these fish can be translated as "numbing," and authors such as Aristotle, Pliny, Plutarch, Cicero, Diocorides, and Galen discuss their medicinal properties. The first clear reference to their application to the head is by Scribonius Largus, a Roman physician and contemporary of Pliny who recommended their shock to cure severe headache. Ten centuries later a Muslim physician also recommended them to cure epilepsy.[11]

A clear reference to the use of electric fish to produce shock and cure psychiatric cases is found in a 16th century Jesuit missionary account of Ethiopia: "The superstitious Abassines [Ethiopians] believe that it [the electric catfish] is good to expel Devils out of the human body, and it did torment Spirits no less than men."[12] I find this reference especially interesting since during my stay in Ethiopia in 1964–66, electric shock therapy was being widely promoted by a psychiatrist there as a new technique. Modern psychiatry, he said in effect, was coming to Ethiopia to expel the Devils out of the human body.

This should not denigrate the discoveries of Sakel, Meduna, and Cerletti, the originators of modern shock therapy. Rather it should give needed historical perspective, and recognition of psychiatric techniques in times and in places other than our own. Cerletti himself became aware of these references to earlier uses of electric shock therapy after he had written his famous monograph, and paid them their due respect.[13]

Shock therapies are still in use by isolated cultures who have never heard of men like Cerletti. One rather remarkable account of the use of drug-induced convulsions to treat psychotics among the San Blas Indians (who live on a group of islands off the coast of Panama) follows:

> "In the course of our stay there Dr. Iglesias explained to me that they had their own method of prescribing shock treatment in selected mentally ill cases. This consisted of a presentation of a psychotic case to the Council of Chiefs. If the Council reached an agreement on the method of treatment the patient would be brought before the Council and so advised. Whereupon the patient would be taken by two tribesmen to an uninhabited island and instructed to drink a cup, of an especially prepared potion. There would apparently be no difficulty in having the patient comply with the instructions because of the inbred superstitions. Immediately upon consuming the medicine the patient would go into a series of convulsions. He would be left alone on the island for three days, and when the tribesmen returned for him he would be completely recovered. The name of the medicine could only be furnished in Cuna language, so could not be related in this way to any medicines known to us."[14]

What is especially interesting in this account is that the Indians deal directly with the ethical issue of administering shock therapy, i.e., review of the case by the Council of Chiefs. This is further than most Western mental hospitals have gone on the ethics of using electric shock therapy.

OTHER PHYSICAL THERAPIES

Except for drugs and shock therapies, other types of physical therapies have not gained very wide acceptance in Western psychiatry. Many of them are widely used in other cultures however. Massage is widely used to calm excited patients, in some cases simultaneously rubbing potions into the skin. Hot baths and thermal radiation were once popular treatments for neuroses in Europe, and are still found in other countries. An example is the Navajo sweat bath,[15] a sauna-like affair. Another example is the use of steam under a blanket with a disturbed patient, as used by Muslim *alfas* in Sierra Leone.[16] This raises the body temperature of the patient, and is reminiscent of therapy used for syphilis early in this century in Western cultures.

Acupuncture, the placement of narrow needles in the patient's skin, is used extensively to treat mental and physical illness among the Chinese. The rationale for its contemporary use is based on the theories of Pavlov; it is believed that mental disorders are caused by a disequilibrium between cerebral inhibition and excitation (*yin* and *yang* principles) and that proper stimulation of the peripheral nervous system with needles will rectify the imbalance.[17] Acupuncture has been in use for over 3,000 years, and is presently recommended for treatment of both neurotics and psychotics in China.[18]

Bloodletting is used relatively rarely for mental disease by therapists elsewhere, our stereotype notwithstanding. Usually it is done by making cuts on the body. Ndembu therapists in Northern Rhodesia are one group who do use it.[19] Dietary regulations are very commonly used by therapists in many cultures. Music therapy, an occasional ancillary aid in Western psychiatric hospitals, is of great importance in the healing ceremonies of other cultures. The music may be chanting, as in the Navajo curing ceremonies, or the rhythm of drums, as in African healing rites.

An important form of psychiatric therapy with proven efficacy that has not been emphasized by Western psychiatry is the spectrum of relaxation exercises and meditation. These can be considered as a form of conditioning as well as a physical therapy. They are used in many cultures, most commonly in India. First the patient assumes certain postures. Then he practices specified exercises. Gradually he learns to control his voluntary muscles, then his involuntary muscles. This produces symptom relief.

The next step is meditation, aimed at determining the causes of the bodily disturbance. The patient may need a *guru* or teacher to help him. Factors interfering with the meditation are explored, one by one, in a process quite similar to analytic psychotherapy. The object is to detach the self from the sources of conflict and examine them. In this manner the conflicts are resolved and the patient arrives at the end state, peace of mind.

Psychosocial Therapies

Psychosocial therapies have always held greater prestige than physical therapies among Western psychotherapists. Accordingly they are given greater emphasis and are used extensively. Therapists elsewhere also use psychosocial therapies, especially suggestion and confession.

Most psychosocial techniques begin with a history. In Western therapy a history is usually considered mandatory, and is one of the most sacred shibboleths of medical school training. It has become increasingly apparent to Western therapists that taking a history in itself is a technique of therapy, the act of ventilation by the patient and the art of listening by the therapist often being effective in producing symptom relief.

Some non-Western therapists ignore taking a history, in sharp contrast to Western psychiatrists. A few even pride themselves on being able to make a "blind" diagnosis of the patient's problems and treat him without the patient telling him a thing, a type of divination referred to previously. More often than not, however, the witchdoctor has surreptitiously gained access to the patient's history by other routes.

Many other therapists make history-taking an important part of their therapeutic procedure. Here, for instance, is an account of how a traditional healer in Ghana evaluates a case.

"The patient was a teacher in his early twenties, preparing for an entrance examination to an institution of higher learning. He was taken to the healer one evening by several friends in a state of violent upset and behavior disturbance. The first thing the healer did was to administer forcibly what must have been a (herbal) sedative, and when the patient fell asleep the healer found out what he could from the friends who had brought him. This was later followed by long talks with the patient himself, who stayed in the healer's compound. From this a picture of the case was built up . . ."[20]

A Sudanese *zar* doctor carefully asks the patient about such things as eating and sleep disturbances. On the basis of the answers this therapist decides whether or not the illness is serious enough to warrant a full *zar* healing ceremony.[21] Other accounts of history taking include the Yemeni *mori,* the Haitian *hungan* (who questions relatives as well as the patient), and Maya Indian healers in Mexico (who ask about dreams as part of their routine history).[22]

A history is also a focal point in Morita therapy. This is a Japanese form of therapy emphasizing a daily diary kept by the patient, initial bedrest, and subsequent occupational therapy. The therapist and patient review the patient's diary on a daily basis.[23]

CONFESSION

Confession and suggestion are the two most important psychosocial therapies used by therapists in other cultures. In Western psychiatry they are less emphasized in theory, though in practice both may be very important components contributing to the efficacy of the therapy.

Confession may be by private prayer, to another person such as a friend or therapist, to supernatural beings or ancestors via an intermediary (such as a priest), or it may be public. Confession to a therapist and the public confession of group therapy are both relevant for Western psychiatry. Most psychotherapists will attest to the symptom relief that accompanies the patient who says he feels "so much better because I've finally been able to tell someone." The patient has shared his guilt. What part this plays in therapy can only be speculation; my own experience is that it is very important.

Confession is acknowledged to be very important by non-Western therapists and often plays an integral part in therapy.

Weston LaBarre, an anthropologist, has done an extensive review of confession as used by the Indian groups of the Americas.[24] He describes confession to an appointed individual (an old man or shaman who first asks you, "Have you done bad?") as well as public confession. He concludes that the confession is clearly associated with emotional catharsis.

In addition to sharing the guilt and to obtaining emotional catharsis, confession may also produce a reliving of painful experiences (abreaction) that may be therapeutic.[25] This is frequently found among the peyote cults of the Navajo and other Indian groups. As one observer noted: "It is difficult to overestimate the importance of this feature."[26]

Confession is also used extensively by *curanderos* in Mexico and Guatemala. The Guatemalan *curandero* may ask the patient to confess everything bad he has done from childhood up to the present.[27] Mexican *curanderos* often center attention on the events immediately preceeding the onset of symptoms, and make the patient confess everything wrong he was doing or thinking.[28] These confessions are usually public to everyone attending the healing ceremony. Public confession is also used by therapists in many other areas including Sierra Leone, Burma, and Ethiopia.[29] In the last the confession may be made by the patient while she is possessed by her *zar* spirit. The spirit speaks through the mouth of the woman, telling those assembled all the evil things she has done.

Natural sequelae to confession are acts of atonement (penance) and absolution. Both are important parts of many therapists' armamentarium. In Catholic cultures the penance is often prayers, offering candles to certain saints, or visiting a sacred shrine. Abstinence from a favorite food or activity (such as sex) is found universally as penance. Another common prescription is the requirement that the patient wear certain kinds of clothing, or carry special objects, or avoid specific words or places. With all of these the therapist has given the patient something to do which, if he carries it out, will absolve him of his wrongdoing and remove his symptoms. Such restrictions and taboos also alleviate guilt, and may act as a substitute for a tic or a compulsion if the patient was afflicted by these.

One reason that confession, atonement, and absolution are not discussed as techniques of psychiatry in Western cultures is that they are part of religion. Any priest can testify to their efficacy in removing psychiatric symptoms. Psychotherapy and religious healing are very closely allied, as Jerome Frank describes very clearly in *Persuasion and Healing*.[30] In the West psychiatry and religion are distinct entities. In many other cultures the therapist may also be the religious agent, and use of the techniques of confession, atonement and absolution follows naturally.

SUGGESTION

Suggestion is the other major psycho-social therapy used by therapists in other cultures. And, like confession, it is not emphasized in theory by Western psychiatrists though it may play an important role in practice. As a therapeutic technique suggestion is closely bound up with the patient's expectations. The higher these expectations are raised and the greater the patient's desire to please the therapist, the more effective suggestion will be. Its effect can also be enhanced by concurrent factors like physical exhaustion, e.g., Luo patients in Kenya may be made to dance for hours before the curing ceremony begins.[31]

Suggestion may be of many types. The first of these is direct command. This may be an assurance that "you will get well" or an admonition to "stop behaving like a madman." Accounts of witchdoctors' activities in many cultures contain suggestion of this kind. Their use of suggestion has been likened by one observer to its use by Madison Avenue advertising men in a barrage—he is told to do it, he hears slogans and rhymes about it, he is told about the bad effects from not doing it, the suggestion becomes associated with music, etc.[32]

The use of symbolism is another form of suggestion. Water or other material is almost universally used in symbolic cleansing rituals, purifying the body of the causes of the mental disturbances. The most famous Mexican-American *curandero* of this century relied on a simple glass of water or a bath as his most potent technique.[33] Often the purifying liquid is drunk with much ritual, as by the Apache shamans who present the potion in a turtle shell, have the patient pass it to his lips four times before drinking, and mark the spot on the shell where he drank by a cross of pollen.[34] The more vivid the visual imagery used, the stronger the suggestion is: "As the river always flows forward and never back, so your illness will never return."[35] The use of purgatives or emetics to cleanse the patient by diarrhea or vomiting is a commonly used variant of this.

Another use of suggestive symbolism is in ceremonies of death and rebirth, such as are found in the treatment of mental disorders in New Guinea and the Sudan.[36] R. H. Prince, a Canadian psychiatrist who studied Yoruba healers in Nigeria, has described such a ceremony in great detail. It is done as a discharge ceremony, and the patient and therapist stand in the middle of the river with three doves. The doves are ritually killed, one by one, accompanied by much suggestion and incantation, and allowed to float away. The disease is gone and the patient emerges from the river reborn.[37]

Suggestive symbolism is also used by therapists to retrieve lost souls. The healer may make a brief imaginary journey, and then some apparent thumping in the next room signifies the return of the lost soul. Using a medicine branch to symbolically brush evil spirits out of a patient, a very common technique among Eskimo shamans, or brushing the soul back into the patient is also used: "With a large handful of plants, Manuel ushered the spirit in the door of the hut, brushed it along the floor, and into the patient's body."[38]

Another type of suggestion in wide use by witchdoctors is the giving of charms, amulets, rings, talismans, religious objects, effigies, or magical formulas written on a piece of paper to the patient. In many cases this is preventive psychiatry, given so that the illness will not recur. In much of the world almost all children, as well as many adults, have an amulet tied around their neck, usually containing a piece of paper with verses from the Bible, Koran, or other religious scripture on it. This is to prevent symptoms from the evil eye that can cause either physical or mental illness. Medical missionary lore is replete with stories of the "primitive native" who took the prescription the white doctor had written for him and wore it around his neck. What the missionary fails to realize is that for many of the drugs he is prescribing (such as minor tranquilizers) the patient probably gains more benefit wearing the prescription around his neck since that is more compatible with his belief system.

Another form of suggestion is a sacrifice. Commonly an animal is killed after first having the disease of the patient transferred to it. The Nigerian ceremony of rebirth described above is an example. I myself once had the assistance of such a sacrificial ceremony for a patient I was treating for both physical and mental symptoms in rural Ethiopia. After considerable preparation a lamb was passed over the patient's head three times. The patient then kissed the tail of the lamb and it was sacrificed. The patient was well a few days later; whether the lamb or any medicine was responsible I am not certain.[39]

A final therapeutic aspect of suggestion is that it provides an institutionalized and accepted way to express aggression. Not only can you symbolically divest yourself of your symptoms, but you can project and displace them onto others. In some cultures, for instance, the therapist instructs you to place an object (containing the symptoms) next to a path. The first unwary passerby then becomes afflicted with your symptoms.

It is many of these techniques of suggestion which have given witchdoctors their bad name in Western psychiatry. It is all looked upon as foolishness and superstition—mere magic for the ignorant. What is important to realize is that these treatment techniques are perfectly logical within the framework of the disease's causation. If the psychiatric symptoms are being caused by the intrusion of a foreign object, then exorcise it. If a lost soul is to blame, then coerce it back. If evil spirits are the cause, then appease them with a ritual or sacrifice. It is only because we have a different framework of causation that these techniques look foolish.

How often suggestion is used as a technique by Western psychiatrists is a matter of speculation; in my experience it is used much more often than is usually acknowledged. Each time the therapist assures the patient that he *will* get better he is using suggestion. Each time the therapist smiles, nods, and says "hmm-hmm" approvingly he is also suggesting to the patient that that is the way things really are. (He is also conditioning the patient.)

But suggestion as a psychiatric technique is suspect among many Western psychiatrists. Reputable psychiatrists, especially those analytically inclined, don't want to be caught in its company. Possible reasons for this are at least fourfold. First, suggestion is associated with symptom removal, a goal of therapy not held in high regard in many forms of Western psychiatry. The assumption is that new symptoms will just replace the old ones and the patient will not be any better off. This may or may not be true, as has been discussed previously.

A second reason for the low status of suggestion as a psychiatric technique in the West is that it is not compatible with the Protestant ethic. This ethic says that you get something worthwhile only by working hard for it. Suggestion promises relief of symptoms with a minimum of work, and as such it is not acceptable. The obverse side of the coin, of course, is psychoanalysis which classically may take 400 hours and cost $15–20,000. This is highly compatible with the Protestant ethic.

Another reason is that suggestion as a psychiatric technique is quite similar to some aspects of religion. In other cultures where psychiatry and religion are closely intertwined this poses no problem. But in Western cultures where they have recently separated, psychiatrists are suspicious of any technique that has overtones of religion. Thus Western patients must obtain their amulets (crosses, medals, etc.) from extrapsychiatric sources. Finally, the use of suggestion strikes too closely at our own magical thinking to be comfortable. Western psychiatric therapy is supposed to be rational and scientific, not irrational and magical. This is true despite the *theory* of Western psychiatry which gives great importance to the irrational and the unconscious.

HYPNOSIS

Hypnosis is simply the logical extension of suggestion, and like the latter it is an important part of therapy in most cultures. In Western psychotherapy, however, it has second-class status, probably for the same reasons that suggestion is held in disrepute. Hypnosis is used explicitly by some Western psychotherapists, and may be used implicitly in therapies like classical psychoanalysis (in an altered state of consciousness the patient may incorporate the analyst's frame of causation as self-hypnosis—"I *do* want to sleep with my mother," etc.)

Hypnosis is reported to have been used in therapy in China 3,000 years ago.[40] Modern descriptions of its users include a mystical group of *Sufi* practitioners in Afghanistan. These therapists learn about it in secret training (which may take as long as sixteen years!) and use it for physical and mental illnesses of all kinds. One report of a treatment session involving eighteen patients claimed fifteen immediate cures.[41]

It has also been described as a therapeutic technique used by Apache Indian shamans and Washo Indian shamans. One of the latter, at the turn of this century, even sent away for a book on it—"The Art of Attention and the Science of Suggestion"— from a mail-order catalogue. He then practiced his technique on rocks and trees until he had it perfected.[42]

Hypnosis is one aspect of the yoga techniques of therapeutic meditation described above.[43] It is also a large component of group therapies (possession cults, etc.) in other cultures. The trance phenomenon in Bali, for instance, which may be seen as a type of group therapy, is considered to be a variety of mass hypnosis.[44]

PSYCHOANALYTIC TECHNIQUES

The psychiatric techniques associated with psychoanalysis have held the highest status in Western psychotherapy since Freud popularized them early in this century. By some they are regarded as the only techniques, everything else being relegated to the realm of magic and "mere suggestion." Psychoanalytic techniques continue to be a hallmark of Western psychiatry, though their image has been slightly tarnished by newer additions such as group and community psychiatry.

Although there is no other culture in the world where psychoanalytic techniques are as important as they are in Western culture, these techniques do appear elsewhere. Dream interpretation, the pennon of psychoanalytic techniques, provides an illustration. Dreams can of course be used for purposes other than interpretation. For instance, they may be used to foretell the future, to ascribe social role status (as in becoming a shaman), or to gain power from the supernatural.[45] The concern here will be only with their use for interpretation to gain more knowledge of the patient's unconscious.

Probably the best study of dream interpretation in another culture was done by Anthony F. C. Wallace, a highly respected anthropologist who studied the seventeenth century Iroquois Indians. He observed:

> "The Iroquois looked upon dreams as the windows of the soul, and their theory of dreams was remarkably similar to the psychoanalytic theory of dreams developed by Freud and his associates. In brief, the Iroquois believed that the soul had wishes of which

the conscious intelligence was unaware, but which expressed themselves in dreams."[46]

And in another passage:

". . . Intuitively, the Iroquois had achieved a great deal of psychological sophistication. They recognized conscious and unconscious parts of the mind. They knew the great force of unconscious desires, and were aware that the frustration of these desires could cause mental and physical ("psychosomatic") illness. They understood that these desires were expressed in symbolic form by dreams, but that the individual could not always properly interpret these dreams himself. They had noted the distinction between the manifest and latent content of dreams, and employed what sounds like the technique of free association to uncover the latent meaning. And they considered that the best method for the relief of psychic and psychosomatic distress was to give the frustrated desire satisfaction, either directly or symbolically."[47]

Wallace concluded that Iroquoian and Freudian dream theory are not exactly the same, but that the differences are not more marked than the differences between, for instance, Jungian and Freudian theories of dream interpretation.

The Navahos are another Indian group that used dreams in this way. A Swiss psychoanalyst, Dr. Oskar Pfister, examined notes from Navaho curing ceremonies in the 1930s and decided that Navaho therapists were "instinctive psychoanalysts." He described what was occurring as follows:

"The shaman understood that the sterility of the woman had as cause an incestuous attachment to the father . . . it was necessary first of all, in order to overcome the frigidity, to bring about compromise with the incestuous attitude in Freud's sense. The sterile woman had to acknowledge that she really harbored incest wishes toward the father and had an attachment to him. The medicine man, as an incorporation of the father, performed the act symbolically, in a manner acceptable to society and therefore removed further repression."[48]

I don't agree with Dr. Pfister's interpretation of what the medicine man was doing, but he does show very nicely that the activity of this native healer can be looked upon as analytic therapy equally as much as that of Pfister's colleagues in Zurich. Another study of dream interpretation among American Indians was done by anthropologist Marvin Opler. In order to get valid data on the Ute Indian healers he became ceremonially adopted into the tribe and then underwent a shamanistic treatment for a feigned illness. He concluded that ". . . it was obvious that Ute shamans employed quasi-psychoanalytic techniques, independently invented in their culture." They used dream analysis as their chief technique: "Wishes, culturally geared motivations, and typical attitudes were dissected by shamans in dealing with the thematic material in dreams." Opler's observations on the non-directive methods of the shamans in eliciting material from the patient is especially instructive:

> ". . . no shaman divulges more of his own nature than is actually necessary in ceremonial practice. His neutrality and religious importance is parallel, perhaps, to the efforts of the analyst in evoking free associations and self-expressions from the patient before becoming involved in countertransference functions."[49]

The Diegueño Indian healers of Southern California also used dreams skillfully. "To the witchdoctor . . . dreams were significant because of their diagnostic value in the cure of neuroses and functional mental disorders, which he recognized as such and treated in a manner suggestive of psychoanalytic methods." The Diegueño therapists distinguished manifest and latent dream content, and believed that "dreams reveal to the dream doctor the patient's conflicts and desires, which are usually of a sexual nature.[50] Other parts of the world where dream interpretation is used by witchdoctors include Turkey,[51] Ghana,[52] Sierra Leone,[53] and the Philippines.[54]

Free association is another important psychoanalytic technique in Western therapy. It consists of the patient letting his mind wander freely from subject to subject, not restricting his thoughts but simultaneously verbalizing them to the therapist. This technique is used by some of the American Indian groups mentioned above as well as in group healing sessions in Ghana. A psychiatric observer of the latter notes that "the couch might be missing, and there may be many spectators, but the patient is given an opportunity to bring up anything that comes to his mind."[55] Aristophanes in ancient Greece also knew of free association as a psychotherapeutic technique. In *The Clouds* he has a character lie on the couch and express all his thoughts as free-association so as to dispel an obsessive fantasy he has about controlling the moon.[56]

CONDITIONING

Conditioning and behavior techniques have recently become popular in Western psychiatry, though they still are more used by psychologists and social workers than by psychiatrists. The major subtypes of conditioning are operant conditioning (reward), aversion therapy (punishment), desensitization (building up to the stress slowly), and extinction (repeating the stress many times until it no longer elicits a maladaptive response). Though these techniques are often written about in Western psychiatric literature as though they were new, they are about as new as the concept of a spanking. What *is* new is the incredibly complex terminology that its practitioners resort to in describing what they are doing.

Therapists in other cultures have long used the principles of reward and punishment. Praise, exhortation, threats, and punishment are commonly used by them. The exercises and meditation used in psychotherapy in India may also be seen as conditioning. Much of the ritual chanting of therapy sessions elsewhere may also be viewed as verbal conditioning.[57] An example of more complex conditioning techniques is found in Western Nigeria. In order to treat bedwetting there among male children a toad is tied to the penis of the child by a string. When the child wets the toad croaks and the child wakes up.[58] This is almost exactly analogous to a conditioning technique recently introduced in England where a bell rings each time the child starts to urinate.

Group and Milieu Therapies

GROUP THERAPY

Group therapy has become increasingly popular in Western psychiatry in the past 15 years. In some parts of the United States almost everyone belongs to some kind of group whether it be a confrontation group, T-group, sensitization group, psychodrama, group therapy, Synanon, or Alcoholics Anonymous. More research is being done on groups, and it is becoming clear that treatment of psychiatric patients in groups is an effective means of producing symptom relief and behavior change.

Therapists in other cultures also use groups. In fact the more widespread use of groups is one of the most marked differences between indigenous psychiatry in other cultures and Western psychiatry. Group therapy goes far back in history. Some of the earliest groups were associated with the Rites of Dionysius in Greece. The early Christian Passion Plays can also be considered group therapy, with catharsis occurring through acting out or through identification with the participants.

One of the most common types of group therapy occurring in other cultures is where some or all of the participants become possessed by spirits. These possession cults are found throughout the world, although the best-known ones are in the Caribbean area and South America. Among them are the *Voodoo* cult in Haiti, the *Shango* cult in Trinidad, the *Babalu* cult in Cuba, and the *Macumba* and *Umbanda* cults in Brazil. There are at least three good reviews of these cults which show them to be much more similar than dissimilar.[59]

Confession by group

Since there is a considerable body of literature on these cults and their social and psychological significance, I will review here only those aspects which are pertinent to being considered as techniques of group therapy. One of the foremost among these techniques is confession by the patient. This has been discussed above, but it is probably even more effective in relieving symptoms when done in a group setting. It is a common and important feature of these groups, functioning to relieve both guilt and anxiety.

Another psychiatric technique of these groups is acting out. They permit ". . . the sanctioned expression of behaviors which are otherwise socially unacceptable or unavailable."[60] The patient may, for instance, reverse roles and play the opposite sex, thereby giving vent to suppressed homosexual wishes.

Abreaction, the reliving of an emotional experience, is another important technique used in group therapies. Alexander Leighton describes it in Navaho ceremonials:

> "The ceremonial itself, or some parts of it, constitutes a symbolic reenactment of something which went wrong in the past and which is now being set right . . . The patient does it over again symbolically without a mistake, and so through the mediation of

the healer comes into harmony with great and mysterious forces within and without himself."[61]

Confession, role-playing, and abreaction are all integral parts of psychodrama, and so many of the group therapies in other cultures qualify as psychodrama. An observer of a Haitian *Voodoo* ceremony concludes: "It is a psychodrama which serves as a last resort against deeper mental illness."[62]

These possession cults play a cultural role that goes beyond group therapy of course. In Bali for instance, where I was able to observe it, group possession is integrated with art and is the major esthetic expression in the culture.[63] Other cultures do not necessarily compartmentalize things as we do into religion, psychotherapy, and dance. Conversely, Western psychotherapists often underestimate and fail to recognize the therapeutic aspects of our own plays, movies, dance, and other art forms.

The witchdoctor in these group therapies plays a variable role. More often than not he also becomes possessed by spirits. In Kenya the healer also goes into a trance during which he discusses the patient's problems ". . . in a way similar to psychoanalysts who intersperse abreactions with interpretations, in accord with Freud's teaching that abreaction without the release of strong emotions was without effect."[64]

Not all group therapy in other cultures includes possession as a component, however. An example of one that does not is Gibbs' interesting description of the *moot* among the Kepelle of Liberia. This is a gathering of neighborhood people to settle a dispute out-of-court. Gibbs shows how the *moot*, ostensibly a legal procedure, also functions as a form of group psychotherapy in this particular culture.[65] It illustrates clearly how the system of psychotherapy in other cultures may be closely intertwined with the legal, political, and religious systems.

MILIEU THERAPIES

Psychiatry in other cultures, to a much greater extent than in the West, utilizes environmental manipulation and social reintegration as important parts of the process of therapy. *Curanderos* in Mexico, for instance, almost always have other family members attend the healing session, and often charge them with carrying out certain aspects of the prescribed treatment. Witchdoctors in Nigeria are quick to tell the patient to take a new occupation or move to a new compound (because evil spirits are inhabiting the old one) if they believe that the stress will be relieved in this way. This account from Kenya also illustrates how a therapist may manipulate the environment for a patient:

> The repeated warnings to the patient and to the members of her home that they must maintain good and harmonious relations by behaving in a correct and charitable manner underline the importance of social factors in maintaining the mental health of the patient. All this behavior is sanctioned by the threat that another attack may be made by the spirits if the taboos are not observed."[66]

Social reintegration of the patient is very important in most cultures, often being regarded as of equal importance as removing his symptoms. In many African cultures the reintegration is effected by voluntary societies of ex-patients. These societies are social groups and function to give the patient a new set of social alliances. Examples are the Poro Society in Sierra Leone[67] and the Sopono cult in Nigeria.[68] One observer of these societies summarizes them as follows:

> "Treatment is not merely a 'doctor-patient' relationship but a form of social reintegration through the medium of social groups like the highly specialized N'jayei Society of the Mende. African medicine therefore plays a dual role designed to maintain the continuity of society as a functioning whole."[69]

A variant of this is found among the Pueblo Indians where the disturbed individual is adopted into a new clan in the tribe, thus acquiring a new set of social relations.[70]

In the process of manipulating the environment and reintegrating the patient socially, therapists in other cultures become deeply involved with the social stresses of their particular community. This is expected of them and is considered to be part of their proper job. Such involvement is more natural since the psychotherapist's role often overlaps with religious, legal, and political roles in the community. A Rhodesian therapist provides an example.

> "It seems that the Ndembu 'doctor' sees his task less as curing an individual patient than as remedying the ills of a corporate group. The sickness of a patient is mainly a sign that 'something is rotten' in the corporate body. The patient will not get better

until all the tensions and aggressions in the group's interrelations have been brought to light and exposed to ritual treatment. The sick individual, exposed to this process, is reintegrated into his group as, step by step, its members are reconciled with one another in emotionally charged circumstances."[71]

This extension of the role of therapist into a manipulator of social stresses underlies a contemporary debate in Western psychiatry. Is the therapist's role to treat his patient alone, or to treat the "sickness" in the society of his patient as well? What are the boundaries of community psychiatry? Most other cultures, it appears, have devised a very broad job description for their therapists.

The involvement of the family and the community in the therapeutic process accomplishes many things. The family often has to provide materials, labor, or finances toward the patient's treatment. Therefore they have a stake in the treatment, and are more likely to reinforce the changes that the healer is trying to make. This is found in Western psychiatry but in a much less developed form. The family and friends also reassert the importance of the continued participation of the individual in the group, and affirm the existence of a network by which the patient can re-establish social contacts.

HOSPITAL THERAPY

Hospitalization is used less in other cultures, but may be accomplished either by having the psychiatric patient move into the witchdoctor's compound or the reverse. Often one or more family members will stay with the patient. It is usually a last resort, and used only after outpatient therapy has failed. Occupational therapy is a common part of hospitalization; in Ghana, for instance, some hospitalized patients work on the farm or at the fishery owned by the therapist. Occupational therapy is also an integral part of Morita therapy in Japan. The underlying principle is that if a patient is made to work even though he feels he cannot, he will quickly learn that he can do the work and thus feel less handicapped.[72]

There is evidence that Western psychiatry has not yet arrived at the best method to hospitalize psychiatric patients. The multitude of experiments in the field, such as day hospitals and half-way houses, reflect a general dissatisfaction with the traditional custodial institutions. There too we may be able to learn something from other cultures. In Western Nigeria, for instance, Dr. T. A. Lambo, a Nigerian psychiatrist trained in England, has been developing a village hospital system for over ten years. The patients live in four villages surrounding the hospital rather than in the hospital itself. Preliminary evaluation shows a higher discharge rate and lower relapse rate of these patients and at lower cost.[73] Lambo has moved much closer to the concept of a true "therapeutic community" than anything yet developed in Western psychiatry.

Relation of Culture to Techniques

While discussing the therapeutic technique of suggestion I speculated on possible reasons why this technique is denigrated by Western psychotherapy. Briefly these reasons were that it only aims at symptom removal, it has overtones of religion, it is irrational, and it is contrary to the Protestant Ethic—you must work hard for what you get.

This provides a useful starting point for exploring the relationship between culture and the techniques of therapy. For while it should be evident from the foregoing discussion that all techniques of therapy are found scattered around the world, it is also true that they are not distributed evenly. Certain techniques occur much more often than others, and each culture appears to have its own preferences.

The reason is that techniques of therapy are intimately related to culture. They are related to the theories of causation of illness, the personality types valued, and the goals of therapy in the culture. The last is a reflection of more general cultural values.

The relation of theories of causation to techniques is obvious. If you believe that your sickness is caused by the loss of your soul, then you want techniques that will successfully retrieve the lost soul. A therapist who offers to explore your childhood experiences with you will be regarded as irrelevant, misinformed, and a quack. Maybe you will even call him a "witchdoctor." Conversely, if you believe that your sickness is caused by childhood experiences, then you want a therapist who will explore these experiences and not undertake a ritual to look for a lost soul.

Occasionally the same therapeutic technique will be used in different cultures for quite different reasons. For instance, confession might be used by a Western psychotherapist because he believes that the patient will relive the confessed experience and better understand it. Confession might be used by an Indian medicine man, on the other hand, because he believes that only thus will the spirit of the offended clan ancestor be liberated, permitting the patient to recover. Though the technique—confession—is the same, and the result—recovery—may be the same, nevertheless in both cases the technique is closely associated with the cultural belief about causation of the sickness.

Techniques of therapy are also related to the personality types valued by the culture.[74] If in a certain culture the therapist is expected to be a warm, gentle, empathetic, nonassertive individual, then the techniques of therapy favored by that culture are not likely to be directive ones like suggestion and hypnosis. Similarly, each individual therapist, consciously or unconsciously, selects those techniques which are most compatible with his personality. In one of the very few attempts to analyse this relationship, psychiatrist Ari Kiev attempted to relate the childhood experiences in a culture to the consequent adult personality type, and then to the techniques of therapy preferred by the culture. To illustrate he describes certain childhood experiences which produce guilt (as opposed to shame) in an adult; he then considers how this feeling relates to the use of bloodletting as a therapeutic technique in that culture.[75] This is an interesting beginning in an area where much more work needs to be done.

The goals of therapy are also culture-bound, and are related to the basic values of the culture. Possible goals of therapy include the following:

1. symptom removal, e.g., reduction in anxiety
2. attitude change, e.g., "right-mindedness" stressed in Eastern therapies
3. behavior change, e.g., stopping of compulsive handwashing
4. insight, e.g., understanding why you are depressed
5. improved interpersonal relationships, e.g., getting along

with your neighbors
6. improved personal efficiency, e.g., greater ability to accept responsibility
7. improved social efficiency, e.g., greater ability to do socially useful work
8. preventive and educative, e.g., increasing the ability to adapt and cope in future situations

Though many of these goals overlap, they are found differentially emphasized in different cultures. The choice of goals for any specific culture is related to values of that culture. The goals chosen then determine, in part, the choice of therapeutic techniques that will be used.

In the United States, for instance, cultural values held in high regard are work, achievement, independence, responsibility, and rational thinking. Goals of therapy which are usually considered appropriate for a patient in this culture are therefore insight, improved personal efficiency, and improved social efficiency. And the techniques of therapy which best achieve such goals are psychoanalytic, insight-oriented therapy, behavior therapy, drug therapy, and occupational therapy.[76] The importance of childhood experience is compatible with our strong assumption of cause-and-effect to explain everything. Therapy is rational, objective, intellectual, and "scientific." In harmony with the Protestant Ethic, you must work for success in psychotherapy and successful psychotherapy will help you to work.

In other cultures the values, goals, and techniques are often quite different. In Nigeria for instance there is much less stress on independence and rational thinking. Symptom removal and improved interpersonal relationships are considered desirable goals of therapy, and are achieved using suggestion, group therapies, and environmental manipulation. There is no attempt at insight and little attempt to change behavior. A psychiatric observer in Nigeria concluded: "Indeed, I have seen very little evidence in Yoruba psychotherapy of any attempt to change the individual."[77]

Another example is Navaho Indian culture where harmony within the community is an important cultural value and improving interpersonal relationships is the goal of therapy. The technique of therapy most used is a long curing ceremony involving the whole community. The forces of change are then set into motion:

> A significant implication of this view is that the patient does not need to reflect on his behavior or examine his motives, conscience, or reactions in order to be helped. There is no exhaustive analysis of intrapersonal dynamics; he need only place himself within the curing system, which, once set in motion, proceeds almost automatically . . . In one sense, all Navaho curing is psychotherapy. Looked at another way, however, none of it is psychotherapy as we know it. In the sense of verbal interaction between patient and therapist, with the goal of changing behavior through increased insight and self-awareness, psychotherapy hardly exists at all.[78]

Morita therapy in Japan provides still another illustration. Japanese cultural values are based upon ancient Oriental philosophy and patterned after Zen Buddhism. The ideal is a calm but happy acceptance of reality.

> "In such terms the goal and problem of psychotherapy for the Japanese is how to live in the midst of this sad transitoriness of all things—one does not struggle against this, but becomes one with it. There is no need to look backward as in Western psychotherapy to seek for past causes which no one can prove to have really taken place."[79]

The goal of therapy that is compatible with cultural values such as this is "right-mindedness," a change of attitude. The techniques used to achieve this goal are a particular combination of personal history-taking, rest, solitude, and occupational therapy. The techniques are closely interrelated with the goals and values, and Morita therapy is no more exportable to Western culture than psychoanalytic therapy is importable into Japan.[80]

Finally there is an important vertical dimension to the problem as well as the horizontal dimension we have been examining. There are not only differences in techniques of therapy between cultures, but also differences within the same culture over a period of time.

Anthropologist A. F. C. Wallace's study of Iroquois Indian psychotherapy provides a classic demonstration of this. Wallace documents how the preferred techniques of therapy changed from expressive, cathartic techniques centering on dream interpretation, to repressive, disciplinary techniques centering on public confessions and authoritarian commands. The shift occurred simultaneously with a change in Iroquois society from being powerful and politically independent at the end of the seventeenth century to being emasculated and politically dependent in the early nineteenth century.[81] He suggests that the system of psychotherapy is related to the political and sociocultural organization of the society at any given time. Since cultural values would also be expected to change with shifts such as the above, it would be reasonable to expect a temporal relationship between cultural values and techniques of psychotherapy. Different periods in the life of a culture may require different types of therapy.[82]

In the light of this, it is interesting to speculate about contemporary changes in Western psychotherapeutic techniques. Does the decline of classical psychoanalytic techniques and the emergence of brief therapies, group therapies, instant insight, "breakthroughs," etc., represent changes in Western culture? Some observers contend that we are moving from a production-oriented, work-oriented system of values to those that are consumption and leisure oriented. If this is true, what will future Western psychotherapy be like?

part II
Psychotherapists
Observed

chapter 6

Case Studies
of Therapists:
Ethiopia, Borneo,
and the United States

Up to this point in our study of witchdoctors and psychiatrists we have been building mosaics, borrowing pieces freely from widely varying sources. This produces a picture of a therapist who is whole but not real. He is like a momentary pattern on a shifting kaleidoscope.

This chapter is an attempt to fix the kaleidoscope, to look behind the mosaics at real people. These people are therapists in Ethiopia, Borneo, and the United States. They each help people who are disturbed in their particular cultures. It is relatively easy for us to know Western therapists as real people—we have seen and heard them. But therapists in other cultures, be they witchdoctors, medicine men, shamans, or whatever, lack substance in our minds. Attempts to picture them as real people constantly conflict with our deeply ingrained stereotype of masked, evil figures gathered around a pot full of boiling missionaries. This stereotype represents the Tarzan stage of Western understanding; it is time to grow beyond that.

An Ethiopian Spirit Doctor

Abba Wolde Tensae Ghizaw is the best known priest-healer in Ethiopia. His fame is such that fourth-grade schoolchildren a thousand miles away know who he is—they have heard their mothers discussing him. As a therapist he represents an important mental health resource in this African kingdom.

To reach his village from Addis Ababa, the capital, is a trip of an hour and a half by car. I made the trip often during my two years in the country. It takes you along the heart of the 8,000-foot plateau that occupies much of Ethiopia; in the distance are 13,000-foot mountains, eucalyptus trees, and fields of yellow daisies. The lush farmland is cultivated with simple tools and wooden plows. Centuries exist side-by-side here as the country attempts to leapfrog into the technological present.

His village, Ghion, is indistinguishable from dozens of others along the main roads of Ethiopia. The streets are mostly unpaved. Small shops form a perimeter for the large open marketplace near the center of town. Grains and spices and household supplies change hands there, especially on days of the big market when people come in from the countryside for miles around. They all know Abba Wolde Tensae, both as a priest and as a healer.

His house is a modest wooden structure with an aluminum roof, surrounded by well-kept gardens. It is like the houses of the school teachers, the successful merchants in town, and the government Health Officer who runs the medical clinic. Abba Wolde Tensae owns some of these other houses, for he is one of the largest landowners in town. But he does not like to discuss money or his investments—he says it is God's money which he has invested to carry out His work. At the edge of town are clustered many smaller dwellings made from a mud and straw paste that hardens like plaster. Aluminum or thatched leaves are used for the roof. Some of these people originally came to the village to be cured by the healer and then stayed on.

Abba Wolde Tensae is a priest in the Ethiopian Orthodox Church. This branch of Christianity broke off from the mainstream in the fourth century and since then has gone its own way. For centuries Ethiopia, cut off from the rest of the world by its mountains and canyons, developed by itself. It was only vaguely known to outsiders as the mysterious kingdom of Prester John. Ethiopian Orthodox Christianity became the core of Ethiopian cultures and values. The religion was embraced by the ruling Amharas as the official religion, and potential persecution by its Moslem neighbors on all sides solidified the bonds of Church and State.

Thus religion and culture are closely interdigitated in Ethiopia. For a priest like Abba Wolde Tensae to be also a healer is logical and consistent with the infusion of religion into all aspects of the culture. In the village of Ghion he occupies a place of importance religiously, therapeutically, politically (as an important Church figure), and economically (as a landowner).

As a therapist Abba Wolde Tensae is an important health resource. Ethiopia had, at the time of my stay there, just over 300 medical doctors for its 22 million people. Most of these are located in the cities, and a town like Ghion has none. Medical care is given at the government health station by a Health Officer (with four years of training after high school) and dressers (equivalent to nurse's aides). Some Health Officers try to work cooperatively with priest-healers like Abba Wolde Tensae; others scorn them as representing everything "uncivilized" that educated Ethiopians want to eradicate. There were only three Western-trained psychiatrists in the country, all of them Europeans concerned primarily with running the single mental hospital in the capital.

Abba Wolde Tensae and other healers like him fill the gap in mental health services. He knows what is wrong with patients who come to him—they are afflicted with *zar* spirits. These spirits may attack an individual in a variety of situations, especially if he is alone near a river, in the forest, or in a cave.[1] Most patients who come to Ghion for treatment are found to be possessed by them. In making the diagnosis Abba Wolde Tensae is confirming a belief in *zar* spirits that is very widespread among Ethiopians. Even students who have been educated in Europe or America will often cling to their belief in *zar* spirits, especially as the cause of mental illness. It is a belief encouraged by the culture generally and by the Church specifically. The following statement by a high Church official is representative:

"There are many kinds of diseases. It is man himself that brings disease on himself. We believe evil spirits are the cause of some diseases. . . . . Most mental illnesses are caused by devils. Most of the time doctors say that mental cases can be cured by prolonged treatment, but we usually see them cured by going to the holy water."[2]

Thus the naming process is easy as long as the therapist shares these conceptions of causation with his Ethiopian patients.

In regard to classifying illnesses, Abba Wolde Tensae does not make many of the distinctions that Western classificatory systems do. The important things are whether or not the disease is spirit-caused, what parts of the body the spirits are in, and how many spirits are present. The Western dichotomy into physical and mental illness is approximated by a division into non-spirit and spirit-caused diseases, but there are many points of divergence. Thus a tuberculous abscess of the spine may be treated as a local collection of *zar* spirits, whereas tuberculosis of the lung is referred to the Health Center. In one analysis of cases seen by Abba Wolde Tensae, one-quarter were clearly psychiatric, one-quarter were clearly somatic, and half were admixtures.[3] Like most therapists in the world he does make a distinct category of "insanity," corresponding approximately to those mental diseases that Western classificatory systems label as psychosis.

Abba Wolde Tensae is an impressive and imposing person. At age 47 he carries his 200 pounds on a large frame. He appears strong and athletic, and moves with a certainty that implies confidence and success. He has a long black flowing beard that is streaked with white hairs. Usually he wears all black robes at his work with a white sash and sometimes a white skullcap. Often he wears black sunglasses as well.

His main personality characteristics are his confidence, genuineness, fatherliness, and interest in his patients. His underlying warmth is partly masked by an authoritarian manner. Those around him speak highly of him, and appear totally dedicated to assisting him in his work. When discussing his work he is humble, declining to take any credit for his cures and insisting that he is only God's tool. At the same time he is proud that his healing ability is so well known, places important people who visit him in the front row of his healing ceremonies, and delights in having pictures taken of him at work. Overall he appears well adjusted and Ethiopian friends assured me that they did not consider him to be psychiatrically deviant.

His relationship with his patients is one of a father with his children. He knows what is best for them and does not hesitate to tell them so. He expects respect and obedience on their part; he has little time for those who disagree. During the healing ceremony there is considerable bodily contact through the laying-on-of-hands as he exorcises the evil *zar* spirits. Most patients are seen once or twice during a healing ceremony. Difficult cases, however, may remain as patients near his compound for weeks or months, being cared for by relatives. His fee is whatever donation the patient wants to leave.

Abba Wolde Tensae came to his healing profession partly through heredity and partly through supernatural designation. He originally learned how to heal from his father, and when he entered the priesthood his healing powers increased through divine sanction. He attended the first six years of public school, then entered the traditional Church training school for the priesthood. He speaks Amharic, the official language, as well as Gaez (the Church language), and a little English and Arabic. During World War II he fought against the invading Italians. He has been at his present location in Ghion for twelve years. Prior to that he was in another part of the country. It is rumored that he had to leave his former post because he was run out—he carved a large cross on a tree sacred to Moslems in the area. Whether true or not the story is an accurate reflection of this man's zeal.

Patients come to Ghion from all over Ethiopia. Some have traveled for several days to reach it. In a survey of patients only 14 percent were found to be from the Ghion area itself.[4] The actual edifice in which Abba Wolde Tensae conducts his healing ceremonies is not an imposing structure though it can be immediately pointed out by anyone in the village.

Patient's expectations are raised by this healer's imposing appearance and self-confidence as well as by his reputation and the pilgrimage they have made to see him. He conveys an air of absolute certainty that he knows what is wrong and how to make it right again. He has been observed by at least two other Western-trained psychiatrists, and both were also impressed by his genuineness and belief in himself.[5]

Healing ceremonies are held in a large room with a rough-hewn wood floor, aluminum roof with skylights, and wooden benches. On a weekend the room is crowded with 200 to 300 people. One of the walls of the room is full of proofs of his powers—canes and crutches thrown away by healed cripples, jars of worms representing spirits he has exorcised, and mementos of gratitude from healed patients. Abba Wolde Tensae begins the service on a raised pulpit that contains some Orthodox Christian inscriptions, pictures of Jesus, colored lights, a wreath, and a telephone. Since telephones are still uncommon in Ethiopia its presence is impressive; moreover when a call comes during a service the question of where it might be coming from adds a distinct aura of mystery.

The ceremony begins like many religious ceremonies with reading from Holy Scriptures. It is usually not long before the reading "strikes home" with an offending *zar* spirit present, the person cries out, and collapses on the floor. This patient is helped to an open area immediately in front of the pulpit with a chair in the middle for the patient. Often the patient begins writhing and screaming and has to be held by assistants. Abba Wolde Tensae slowly descends from the pulpit, approaches the patient, and begins a rather standardized dialogue in Amharic:

> ABBA WOLDE TENSAE: "What is your name?"
> SPIRIT SPEAKING THROUGH PATIENT: "Buda."
> ABBA: "What kind of devil are you?"
> SPIRIT: "*Zar* devil."
> ABBA: "When did you take possession of this woman?"
> SPIRIT: "Three years ago near a river while she was washing clothes."
> ABBA: "Why?"
> SPIRIT: "Because she did wrong. She did not care for her baby properly. She left it uncovered to the Evil Eye."
> ABBA: "I command you to leave this woman now."
> SPIRIT: "No."
> ABBA: "You will. Howl like a hyena and leave her."

At this point the woman cries out and falls to the floor writhing. After one to two minutes she lies still and is carried away by assistants to slowly recover in the next room.

During the dialogue Abba Wolde Tensae carries a large

wooden cross in his left hand. His right hand is in a bucket of holy water held by an assistant. Alternately he throws handfuls of the water in the patient's face and then hits her forcefully with the cross. Often the spirit is reluctant to leave, and so he becomes more and more forceful in his exhortations and accompanying actions. The whole cure usually takes less than ten minutes. He then returns to the pulpit and resumes the reading of Scripture until the next patient's spirit cries out. During a single service he exorcises spirits from ten to twenty patients.

Abba Wolde Tensae also sees individual patients in his office. In addition to the techniques of therapy used in the public ceremony—suggestions, confession, and aversive conditioning—he employs a type of hypnosis and environmental manipulation. In private consultations he also often adds specific advice about how to live and how to behave. In other parts of Ethiopia a classical group therapy is used by *zar* therapists.[6] The techniques that he uses are certainly compatible with his fatherlike, authoritarian personality.

How effective is this therapist? Judging from his reputation and the personal testimonials that I heard I would say very effective. He claims to have treated over one million people in the past fourteen years though in actuality it is probably about 100,000. Because of the large number of *zar* spirits he has exorcised some people in the town have encouraged him to move elsewhere; they fear that all the free *zar* spirits will constitute a public health hazard. He keeps careful records of all his patients, and recent entries showed approximately 500 patients a month. The number of repeaters is relatively small, less than 15 percent.[7] In regard to psychosis he claims to have cured 786 cases of it. Clearly he is an important mental health resource in Ethiopia.

An Iban Therapist in Borneo

The Iban are a group of people who live on the other side of the world from Ethiopia. Part of the group live in the Indonesian part of Borneo and about 250,000 live in the Malaysian part called Sarawak. It was the latter group that I visited in 1969.

The Iban, also known as Sea Dayak, are the original head-hunters of Borneo. (I had hoped to find that they also shrank their captured heads and thus make contact with the original headshrinkers. Alas, they did not, shrinking apparently being confined to groups in New Guinea and South America.) Once renown for their fierceness and their use of blowpipes with poisoned darts in warfare, the Iban gave up headhunting early in this century. Now they are industrious, cheerful, and peaceful, making their living by cultivating plots of rice and sago and tapping rubber trees beside the tributaries of the Rejang River.

Therapists among the Iban are called *manangs*. One of the *manangs* whom I visited was Digat Anak Kutak. He lives in a longhouse beside a river one day's drive from the capital, Kuching. The road is unpaved. I was accompanied by Mr. Paul Beavitt, an English anthropologist who knows the Iban people in this longhouse and who also acted as translator. The drive winds between low rolling hills, rice paddies, and orchards of pepper trees belonging to the Chinese, Land Dayak, and other inhabitants of Sarawak. It is sparsely populated, with less than one million people in the whole country.

Digat's role as a therapist and healer is an important one, for Western-trained therapists are in short supply. There are less than twenty doctors in the whole country, none of them psychiatrists. The single 300-bed psychiatric hospital is in Kuching. It was set up by a psychiatrist who has since left, and is being run by a general practitioner and a psychiatric nurse. They do an impressive job, but with the scattered population of the country and the limited transportation it is obvious that they see psychiatric cases only when they have become severe and need confinement. Once a patient is discharged there is usually no follow-up since the scattered government clinics are often distant from the patient's home.

In order to assess the relative importance of *manangs* like Digat in treating cases of mental illness, I spent time at the psychiatric hospital interviewing Iban patients confined there. All eight patients I interviewed had seen a *manang* during the onset of their illness, and seven of the eight reported improvement from the contact.

In contrast to the scattered government clinics, *manangs* are usually close to the patient. Digat sees patients from two nearby rivers in addition to his own, but he is especially well known. The ratio of lesser-known *manangs* to the population is about one for every two hundred people, so an Iban can always reach one within a few miles on the River.[8]

Another asset that makes the *manang* an ideal mental health resource is that he speaks the same language as his patients. Sarawak has twenty-two separate languages, and Ibans form only one-third of the population. Consequently even if Western-trained therapists were desirable and available, they would not be able to communicate with Iban patients as Digat can.

Digat, like most *manangs*, usually has no difficulty diagnosing a case of mental illness. He knows what is wrong immediately— the patient's soul has been lost. This is part of a world-view shared by all Iban. The world is divided into the realm of men and the realm of spirits. The latter may be either helpful or harmful. A helpful one, for instance, may be an ancestral spirit; if you get lost in the forest this spirit might masquerade as a small deer and lead you back to safety.

Evil spirits, on the other hand, are always trying to steal souls. Most commonly they steal them during sleep. Dreams are thought to be the wanderings of the soul and are one of the two main lines of communication between the world of spirits and that of men. (The other line of communication is through the call of birds.) Thus dreams are accepted as the primary validation for their world-view by the Iban. An Iban *knows* his theories are correct because his subjective experiences during dreaming prove it and because when the *manang* captures a lost soul during treatment the patient usually gets well.

A person's soul is most likely to be stolen by evil spirits under certain conditions and it is these conditions which determine the classification of Iban mental diseases.[9] One such condition is when a person violates a taboo such as eating an animal forbidden by the mandate of an ancestor. Another possible condition is a failure to fulfill a command from the spirit world communicated by way of a dream or a bird call. The person may have been ordered, for instance, to hold a feast, sacrifice an animal, or even to become a *manang*. Other conditions which are thought to weaken the soul and make it susceptible to being stolen by spirits are frustrated love, heredity, poor circulation, retained placenta at childbirth, and becoming a Christian.

As a therapist Digat is not an imposing man but he is impressive. Like most Iban men he is short, about five feet four inches. He is in his mid-forties and has a wiry build reflecting his long days clearing land and planting his rice. He has receding hair and his skin is covered with the decorative tattoos commonly found among the Iban. Usually he wears long loose pants, no shirt, and goes barefoot. There is nothing in his appearance that marks him as a *manang*.

His manner is intense. He listens carefully, purses his lips, and nods frequently. He gives a strong impression of total attention directed toward the speaker. When he has an idea his eyes light up, he becomes excited, and suddenly smiles widely revealing two gold teeth. He says very little until he has had time to listen carefully. When he finally does speak he conveys the impression of having thought the problem carefully through.

As a *manang*, Digat's relationship with his patients is that of a technological expert rather than a father. He has special knowledge about lost souls and how to retrieve them. Other *manangs* have this knowledge too—he is just especially skilled at it. Consequently there is relatively little aura of mystery and charisma about him. He does not have to accept cases that come to him for help but can simply tell them to find another *manang*. Other accounts of Iban *manangs* imply that they are quite selective in the cases that they will undertake.[10] Digat, like most *manangs*, will undertake only one case at a time. The fee charged is usually set before treatment begins and is not dependent on a successful cure. It varies with the difficulty of the case, the length of the journey necessary to see the patient, and the reputation of the *manang*. It may be paid in cash, goods such as rice, or valued items like Chinese jars.

Digat was commanded to become a *manang* by spirits in a dream. Failure to carry out this command would have meant sickness or death. Other *manangs* migrate toward the profession either because their fathers are *manangs* or simply because they want to. Another *manang* I met in Sarawak had never had a command; he simply was interested in the work and apprenticed himself to a *manang* as a boy.

Digat's major asset for raising patient expectations is his reputation. And much of this rests upon his training. Digat is a *manang mensau*, a higher level of therapist than most of his counterparts nearby. The lower level of *manang* is called *manang mata*—"he can repeat many of the incantations used and he assists others in their cures."[11] But he cannot undertake difficult cases like mental illness without being a fully-trained *manang mensau*. Training to become a *manang* may take as long as eight years of part-time study. He must learn a vast volume of lore, songs, and incantations. And, even more important, he must come to understand and be able to control his own guardian spirit. Only after he has done these things can he be considered for initiation. This decision and ceremony are in the hands of fully trained *manangs* in his area, who gather together and admit him to the profession. The lengthy initiation ceremony includes application of medicine to his skin to protect him, gold dust sprinkled on his eyelids to help him find lost spirits better, a small fishhook placed in his fingertip to help him grapple with evil spirits more successfully, "and lastly they pierce his heart with an arrow [symbolically] to make him tender-hearted and full of sympathy for the sick and suffering."[12] Pigs are then sacrificed and he is declared to be a *manang mensau*.

There is yet one higher grade of *manangs* among the Iban, the *manang bali*. They are *manangs* who assume woman's dress, manners, and may even take a "husband." They become transvestites, they claim, at the command of the spirits. *Manang bali* have always been rare[13] and presently are almost nonexistent. I was unable to find anybody who had ever seen one, though rumors of their existence were abundant. Their function may represent a socially-sanctioned role for sexually deviant Iban men, though their total number apparently never was a large percentage of *manangs*. Most *manangs* are not sexually deviant, and in fact are looked upon as stable community leaders, second in respect and political authority only to the chief.[14]

Manang Digat almost always sees his patients in their longhouse. He journeys there after a day in the rice paddy, performs a healing ceremony during the evening, and usually returns the same night. Because he must farm like other men he is able to see only about ten patients each month.

A typical case for Digat is that of a young widow who complained of generalized weakness and inability to do her work.[15] Fearing that her soul had been lost her relatives called Digat. He came to her longhouse at dusk and sat down with her relatives in the common corridor that runs the length of the longhouse and connects the twelve separate family dwellings which open onto it. Her longhouse is raised off the ground about eight feet; beneath run chickens and pigs. Kerosene lanterns provide light as all the families in the longhouse slowly gather to watch the ceremony. Outside small monkeys at the jungle's edge chatter at the Southern Cross, then disappear.

Digat has decided that this woman is not too sick and only requires a small ceremony. For a more serious case he would use a full-scale ceremony, involving preparations by all the members of the longhouse and lasting sometimes all night.

His first job is to make a positive diagnosis. For this purpose he gets out his private medicine bundle. This bundle is highly valued, and marks him as a *manang* more than any single thing. Digat was reluctant to show it to me on my visit. Finally I offered him a small supply of my most powerful medicine for "madness" (chlorpromazine) in exchange for an examination of his medicine bundle. He consented.

The most important item in it is a piece of quartz with the horns of a large beetle attached. This is Digat's "stone of light" which he uses to make a positive diagnosis. By holding it up to the light and looking at the patient Digat can tell whether her soul is missing and, if so, how far it has gone. Other items in the bag include a wild boar's tusk (to help retrieve the soul), large pebbles, roots, and pieces of cotton. The last is to symbolically plug up holes so that the soul will not leave the body again once it has been retrieved.

Having ascertained the location of the lost soul, Digat then begins chanting and goes into a trance. While in a trance he falls to the floor and is covered with a special blanket by his assistant. The blanket is reserved only for special ceremonies like this. It is thought that while Digat is beneath the blanket he goes on a trip to the realm of the spirits to retrieve the lost soul of the patient. His own special guardian spirit guides him on the way.

Retrieval of the lost soul may involve many obstacles and dangers, but he is almost always successful. Some *manangs* in large ceremonies go into an adjoining room and emerge with a bloodied dagger, proof that they killed the offending spirit who was responsible. Once the soul is recaptured Digat comes out of the trance and blows it back into the woman's body through the fontenelle in her skull. Finally, Digat charges the patient, and often the family or community, with certain taboos to prevent relapse.

The principal therapeutic technique used by Digat in healing ceremonies such as this is suggestion. There may be some confession by the patient in front of her relatives and neighbors but this is not necessary. Analysis of the patient's dreams is common, and they are used in attempts to decipher messages that have been sent by the spirit world. Bad dreams, in fact, are valid reasons for consulting a *manang* in and of themselves. Drugs made from local herbs are also used frequently, though there is another healer in the culture, the *dukun*, whose main function is to treat patients with drugs. Often a *manang* and *dukun* will help each other, and in Digat's longhouse this was the case.

It is also clear that Digat and other *manangs* utilize environmental manipulation to an important degree. All healing ceremonies involve at least the family of the patient and often the entire longhouse. They become directly involved with the patient's problem, may have responsibilities for preparations needed for the healing ceremony, and often must observe certain taboos after the ceremony to keep the patient well. It is also in their best interest for the patient to get well since a community as interdependent as a longhouse misses any sick member. In the above case Digat suggested a redistribution of labor among the widow's relatives to help her through the prolonged mourning period.

The question arises whether *manangs* are "honest" in what they do. Early missionary accounts especially ridicule them as frauds and expose the tricks they use to get blood on the dagger, etc. My conversations with three of them convinced me that while they are not above trickery, they use it in the belief that they are helping the patient. They have absolutely no doubt that the patient's soul is lost, and they believe that anything which will assist in its retrieval is not dishonest. Other observers confirm this view of their authenticity.[16]

How effective are Digat and other *manangs* as therapists? It would appear that for treating a depressed woman like the one above they are quite effective by virtue of their mobilization of the patient's resources and through the technique of suggestion. For more serious cases of mental illness like psychosis their effectiveness is not known. In a country where there are no alternative resources for most mentally ill patients *manangs* are the first, and often the only, line of defense.

A Psychiatrist in California

The Californians are a group of people who live on the West Coast of the United States. Most ethnographers consider them to be part of the dominant Anglo-American culture found throughout the United States, though a few consider them to be a distinct subculture.[17]

The most common type of psychotherapists in this culture are called psychiatrists. There are estimated to be 20,000 of them and as such they constitute an important mental health resource. One of the better-known psychiatrists is Dr. William Boyce who lives in the town of Palo Alto (translation: high stick). The town is an affluent, intellectual town wedged between rolling green hills and the San Francisco Bay. The main commercial area is 30 miles to the north in San Francisco.

Dr. Boyce is well known in California. Although most of his patients come from towns in the immediate vicinity, occasionally they travel several hours from more distant towns for an appointment. Patients come to see him once or twice a week on a regular schedule, and treatment usually lasts several months. When hospitalization is needed it is carried out in the nearby Stanford Medical Center. Whereas there is no single "typical" psychiatrist in American culture any more than there is in any other culture, Dr. Boyce's activities can be considered as representative of three-fourths of the psychiatrists in this culture.

Dr. Boyce and his patients share a common world-view about what is wrong—the patients have been made ill by bad childhood experiences. Sometime during their early years the patients have had relationships that were pathological, and these have in turn infected their adult relationships. Most often the offending agents are either the mother or father, though other agents are possible as well. Dr. Boyce and his patients are able to validate this theory of causation by examination of the patient's dreams. Further validation arises from the fact that when these early relationships are explored the patients often get well. There is a complex system for classifying mental disorders in this culture but it is largely ignored by Dr. Boyce and his patients except for use on official documents. The personal qualities of this therapist which stand out are his self-confidence and his professional manner. There is a hint of warmth underneath, but it is not in direct evidence in his day-to-day contact with patients. Rather it comes out most strongly when he is at home playing with his three small children. Similarly his professional manner might be mistaken by some as aloofness; on the tennis court or Saturday, however, it is conspicuously absent and replaced by exuberance. He devotes total attention to his patients, and listens both carefully and thoughtfully. Occasionally he interrupts with a question, but more commonly he reserves his thoughts and interpretations for the long pauses when the patient has stopped talking.

He is a distinctive-looking man, almost six feet tall, with heavy glasses and a full beard. He is usually dressed in a suit with a colored shirt, and generally is not as orthodox in his demeanor as the healers in the other medical specialties in town. Because of these personal qualities he possesses a certain aura of mystery which his patients find attractive. His fee is $40 for each visit and is payable only in money. The fee must be paid whether or not the patient gets well.

Dr. Boyce became a psychiatrist through self-selection and through academic selection. Following secondary school he went to college, medical school, and internship for a total of nine years. This course of study was required by the culture as a prerequisite for admittance into the profession of psychiatry. He then attended a psychiatric residency for three years during which time he learned the theories and lore of his profession, control over his own thoughts, and how to treat patients. His teachers were older psychiatrists who had previously been accepted into the profession. Two years after he finished his residency he was officially initiated into the profession after passing an examination given by the older psychiatrists in his area.

Patient expectations are raised by Dr. Boyce's impressive office. Situated in a new steel-and-glass building, the office is richly carpeted and furnished. A couch, the requisite paraphernalia of his profession, stands against one wall. Modern paintings grace the other walls and bespeak refinement, intelligence, and success. The collecting of them is one of his favorite hobbies. Furthermore, the office is situated adjacent to the Stanford Medical Center, thereby accruing further patient expectations that spill over from this eminent institution. Dr. Boyce maintains a teaching position on the faculty there and does not hesitate to identify himself as a faculty member when asked by a patient.

But Dr. Boyce's major asset in raising patient expectations is his reputation. Much of this comes from the fact that he was trained at the leading psychiatric center on the East Coast and then went to Europe where he studied briefly with one of Freud's leading disciples. Framed pieces of paper on the wall attest to these facts. He returned to start practice and although he never completed a classical analysis himself he is regarded by his colleagues as being well trained in the classical psychiatric tradition. His reputation has since been enhanced by his publications of four scholarly papers on psychiatric history.

The techniques of therapy used by Dr. Boyce are predominantly psychosocial. He takes a careful history, concentrating on the patient's childhood experiences and relationships with his mother and father. In the process of giving the detailed history the patient often confesses things he has done. Dr. Boyce encourages the patient to make interpretations of his childhood experiences and try and relate them to the present difficulties. Dreams and free association are often utilized to accomplish this. Sometimes the therapist will help the patient make these interpretations, and he will also help the patient see his own resistances to getting well. Dr. Boyce also operates on the assumption that his patients will relate to him in the same way that they previously related to their mother and father; occasionally he points this out to the patient. Other techniques of therapy which are used occasionally are drugs and group therapy for patients for whom they appear to be indicated.

Dr. Boyce sees approximately 40 different patients a month; usually 10 of them are new patients. Regarding his effectiveness, his former patients freely extol his virtues. And insofar as patient satisfaction and a long waiting-list for appointments correlate with effectiveness, he must be viewed as one of the better psychotherapists in the Anglo-American culture.

chapter 7

The Efficacy
of Witchdoctors,
Psychiatrists,
and Untrained Therapists

The four components of psychotherapy delineated in part one are presented as the important components of psychotherapy everywhere. Witchdoctors, psychiatrists, and all other varieties of psychotherapists are hypothesized to use them for their effectiveness. A witchdoctor who does not share a world-view with his patient, does not have personal qualities deemed therapeutic in his culture, cannot raise patient expectations, or has no command over therapeutic techniques will be equally as ineffective as a psychiatrist with similar inadequacies. Conversely, a witchdoctor who fulfills those qualifications should be just as effective as the psychiatrist who does, each in his own culture.

These postulates, if true, should be reflected in studies of efficacy. Such studies should demonstrate that those therapists who most fully meet the four requirements are the most successful. Unfortunately studies on the efficacy of psychotherapists are scant. Those which do exist are mostly anecdotal, and as objective assessments are noteworthy for their methodological shortcomings. Nevertheless they are the only studies available, and as such it is useful to survey them. They may be considered as partial verification of the postulates if they indicate that:

1. Witchdoctors et al. get about the same therapeutic results as psychiatrists insofar as they use the four components of psychotherapy equally skillfully;
2. psychiatrists et al. get therapeutic results when psychotherapy is conceived of broadly in terms of all four components; and
3. untrained and partially trained psychotherapists get successful therapeutic results insofar as they innately possess and use the four components of psychotherapy.

Efficacy of Witchdoctors

Despite its anecdotal nature, the evidence regarding the efficacy of therapists in other cultures is instructive. It is almost unanimous in suggesting that witchdoctors get about the same therapeutic results as psychiatrists do.

Beginning with American Indian groups, anthropologists have remarked on the effectiveness of medicine men and shamans in several instances. M. K. Opler was impressed by the cures effected by Ute shamans[1] and M. E. Opler was similarly impressed by Apache Indian shamans.[2] A Yoruk Indian shaman is described by another anthropologist as follows: "Her psychotherapeutic skills are revealed not only in her treatment of psychosis, neurosis, and psychosomatic ailments, but also in her voluntary decision to limit child therapy only to behavioral disorders."[3] And Wallace, commenting on Iroquois Indian psychoanalytic psychotherapy, comments that "the effectiveness of the Iroquois dream-therapy was sometimes admitted even by the Jesuits, who had neither psychological insight nor religious sympathy for the primitive dream-theory"[4]

Elsewhere in the Western hemisphere, an anthropologist commented upon the efficacy of Guatemalan *curanderos*,[5] and his impression has recently been verified by a psychiatrist.[6] Another psychiatrist, Ari Kiev, reports a similar impression after observing Haitian *hungans*.[7]

In British Guiana a Guianese psychiatrist trained at the

Maudsley Hospital in London has begun a collaboration with local healers of the East Indian Kali Cult. Kali therapy is a semireligious type of healing based upon the motivation of the patient and similar to what in Western culture is called reality therapy. The first five patients taken from the mental hospital for treatment by the Kali Cult healer included a man with paranoid schizophrenia, a man with manic-depressive psychosis, a man with epilepsy, and two women with depression and schizo-affective schizophrenia. The healer rejected two others—a chronic schizophrenic and a senile woman—as unsuitable for Kali therapy. The five were treated for eight successive Sundays. The first patient escaped from the hospital and the other four all showed marked improvement.[8]

Rogler and Hollingshead, both sociologists, were impressed by the skill of Puerto Rican mediums in working with schizophrenic patients. Their observations afford a clear view of the principle of Rumpelstiltskin: "The medium understands their [the patient's] subculture; she knows how to placate the troubled by plausible interpretation of their troubles."[9] Spiritualistic sessions were described as having many of the therapeutic advantages of group psychotherapy. And occasionally a Puerto Rican family would bring a disturbed family member to a Western psychotherapist for one specific reason—they wanted the patient calmed so that he could be taken to a "genuine" therapist, a spiritualistic medium.[10]

Turning to African cultures, Canadian psychiatrist Raymond Prince provides the best assessment of the efficacy of psychotherapists on that continent. After spending 17 months studying 46 Nigerian Yoruba witchdoctors he concluded that "Western psychiatric techniques are not in my opinion demonstratably superior to many indigenous Yoruba practices."[11] He observed many quacks as well as many highly skilled therapists, and judged that the therapeutic results obtained are about equal to those obtained in Western psychiatric clinics and hospitals. Prince even occasionally referred refractory cases he had treated to the native healers. One such case, a man with psychotic-like symptoms whom Prince had treated unsuccessfully with chlorpromazine and sedatives for six months, was subjected to a series of sacrifice sessions by the *babalawo*, then initiated into a divination cult. The patient recovered and had no further relapses.[12]

The Federal Minister of Health in Nigeria verifies the utility of the native therapists. His willingess to send psychotic government employees to such healers has been frequently rewarded: ". . . many of these patients returned within a few weeks to see me, apparently completely cured and ready to fit themselves into society."[13]

Also in Western Nigeria is the village hospital system set up by Dr. A. Lambo, a British-trained Nigerian psychiatrist. Lambo uses traditional Nigerian therapists in his system ". . . to supervise and direct the social and group activities of our patients."[14] Lambo comments on their effectiveness:

> "We assessed the work of these healers and found their results in certain areas were better than ours. They understood the philosophy of the people and were especially adept at handling the African's dreams."[15]

Whether it is Lambo's hospital system per se, or the use of the native therapists, or some combination of these factors, is difficult to say, but the results for patients has been dramatic. The village hospital system, in comparison with a traditional Western-style mental hospital in Nigeria, has twice as high a discharge rate, a lower relapse rate, and a cost of only one-fifteenth per patient treated.[16]

Studies from Ghana provide indicators pointing in a similar direction. A psychologist in Accra did a careful study of five native therapists. He visited each one every ten days for a period of six months and analyzed 302 cases seen by the therapists. He concluded that these therapists were often very effective.[17] Another field study of 23 healers in Ghana produced a similar conclusion.[18] Also in Ghana Margaret J. Field, a physician and anthropologist, did an extensive study of healing shrines and the therapists who run them. Her book documents 146 case histories, including patients with depression, anxiety, obsessive-compulsive neurosis, involutional psychosis, and schizophrenia, to show the therapeutic effectiveness of these healers.[19]

Elsewhere on the African continent native healers have been successfully used in government clinics by psychiatrists in the Sudan.[20] A native healer in the Ivory Coast impressed two psychiatric observers: ". . . the therapy could succeed because of common psychocultural premises shared by the patient, the healer, and their community."[21] Psychiatrists in Liberia report in a similar vein[22] and finally a psychiatrist who made a broad survey of African medicine men in general concluded: "His counselling and curing is psychoprophylactic and psychotherapeutic activity of high relevance to the mental health of his society."[23]

Probably the most conclusive evidence for the efficacy of therapists and their techniques in other cultures comes from India. N. S. Vahia, director of psychiatry at a medical school in Bombay, studied traditional Indian meditative techniques for over six years in an attempt to determine their scientific validity and possible therapeutic utility. These techniques, consisting of exercises and meditation to bring about mind control over the body, were employed by Vahia and his associates on 30 psychiatric patients. Biochemical and electrophysiological studies were performed in conjunction with the treatment. Vahia concluded that the techniques were indeed effective, especially for psychoneurotic and psychosomatic disorders.[24]

Western psychiatry and medicine have always turned a skeptical eye toward these meditative techniques for one major reason—such techniques claim as a goal the voluntary control of the autonomic nervous system. This, according to Western scientific notions, is impossible. Recent findings are forcing a reevaluation of this impossibility. Experiments with rats have shown that they could be taught to voluntarily control autonomic nervous responses such as blood pressure and pulse rate. When rewarded for increased blood pressure the rats responded by raising it still further; conversely they were successfully taught to decrease it as well. The author of this report, in commenting on the extension of these findings to people, adds: "I believe that in this respect they are as smart as rats."[25] In short, it may well turn out that there is scientific validity behind traditional Indian therapists' claims to control autonomic responses and to cure patients in this way.

The other major Indian study was done on Ayurvedic therapists. These traditional healers use a combination of herbs, tonics, rubbing oils, enemas, and purgatives in complex combinations. They have been used in India since the first century A.D. when, according to one observer:

"... ayurvedic medicine had developed into a system that in some respects resembled and in others surpassed that of Hippocrates and Galen. Its most accomplished practitioners, usually resident at the royal courts, were learned in such basic subjects as anatomy, including dissection and physiology, pathology, and therapeutics. Pharmacology was relatively well developed."[26]

In 1959 N. C. Surya and his staff of Western-trained psychiatrists at the All-India Institute of Mental Health in Bangalore began a five-year study to determine the efficacy of ayurvedic treatments for schizophrenics. Ten beds were set aside for an ayurvedic unit, staffed by two physicians and two technical assistants all qualified in ayurvedic treatment. Each patient on this unit was then compared with 100 consecutive cases treated in the remainder of the hospital where drugs, electro-shock, and insulin therapy were used. Most patients on both units were diagnosed with schizophrenia.

The results are seen in Table I. The differences between the

TABLE I

Comparison of Western Psychiatric Treatment
and Ayurvedic Treatment of Schizophrenic Patients

		Psychiatric Treatment	Ayurvedic Treatment
cases		100	227
average stay (days)		65.8	59.6
	improved	85%	75%
discharge evaluation	partial	5%	15%
	not improved	10%	10%
cost (rupees per day)		2-3	1

two forms of treatment are negligible except for the lower cost of the ayurvedic therapy. There are several methodological shortcomings to the study, specifically in regard to staff ratios (higher on the ayurvedic unit), the inability of the ayurvedic unit to handle violent cases (24 patients had to be transferred), and the lack of follow-up due to difficulty locating the patients. Nevertheless the study is probably the best to date of a non-Western treatment system, and the authors conclude that ayurvedic treatment is as effective as Western psychiatric treatment methods for treating schizophrenia.[27]

Another major country where traditional therapists and therapies are being widely used is China. Since coming to power the communist government has extolled the ancient Chinese methods, especially acupuncture and moxibustion. The result is that about one quarter of all medical schools are specifically devoted to traditional therapy, and such therapy is integrated into the other schools as well.[28] An assistant professor of medicine at one medical school is a practitioner of traditional medicine.[29]

Unfortunately no accurate data are available to assess the efficacy of these traditional therapists and methods. There are claims that they are superior to electroshock and insulin for treating psychotics.[30] However, these claims are not supported with figures, and are thrown into question by other Chinese claims for miracle cures of such things as deaf-mutism using acupuncture.[31] It is hoped that the re-opening of China will provide hard data on the interesting and valuable innovations which are taking place in China using traditional therapists and ancient therapies.

We should not be too surprised to find that therapists in other cultures are as effective as those in our own culture. They can name the patient's disease and raise his expectations equally as well as we can. Their selection procedures for the profession are geared to attract as many individuals with therapeutic personality characteristics as ours are. And they use techniques of therapy as effectively.

It is this last, the techniques of therapy, that is most difficult for us to accept. How can witchdoctors, relying primarily on such techniques as suggestion and hypnosis, achieve as good results as Western therapists who use techniques so much more sophisticated? The answer is twofold. First, as we have seen, therapists elsewhere use on occasion the same "sophisticated" techniques as Western therapists do. Second and more important, we consistently underestimate the power of techniques like suggestions and hypnosis. Their low status in Western therapy blinds us to their real strengths.

A good illustration of what "simple" suggestion and hypnosis can do in producing therapeutic results is the story of Russian composer Sergei Rachmaninoff. Being depressed and unable to write more music Rachmaninoff turned to a therapist in Moscow who relied heavily on suggestion and hypnosis:

> "Consequently, I heard the same hypnotic formula repeated day after day while I lay half asleep in an armchair in Dahl's [the doctor's] study. 'You will begin to write your concerto . . . You will work with great facility . . . The concerto will be of an excellent quality . . .' It was always the same without interruption. Although it may sound incredible, this cure really helped me. Already at the beginning of the summer I began to compose. The material grew in bulk, and new ideas began to stir within me—far more than I needed for my concerto."[32]

The result was Rachmaninoff's *Second Piano Concerto*, an acknowledged masterpiece which he dedicated to Dr. Dahl. It should be listened to by anyone who doubts the efficacy of "simple" suggestion and hypnosis as used by therapists all over the world.

Efficacy of Psychiatrists

Psychiatrists should also be effective psychotherapists insofar as they meet the criteria for Western cultures of the four components of psychotherapy. Just as for witchdoctors, there is abundant anecdotal evidence to support this. In both the popular and the scientific literature there is a multitude of testimonials describing successful psychotherapy.

Verification of the efficacy of Western psychotherapy at more than the anecdotal level has been the subject of spirited discussion. Since 1952, when H. J. Eysenck published his classic paper purporting to prove that psychotherapy has no efficacy,[33] Western therapists have slung scientific arrows back and forth supporting, reviewing, criticizing, condoning, and condemning.

To a Martian psychotherapist, viewing the battle from on high, it must all look a little fatuous. The very existence of thousands of Western psychotherapists, all with full waiting rooms, is rather solid evidence that they are successfully doing *something* for their patients. Intelligent people will not voluntarily give up an hour a day or an hour a week, at a sizable fee, if they are not getting anything in return. Indeed if psychotherapy did not "work" it would have long since died off with the dinosaur and the dodo bird, not only in Western culture but in all cultures.

Eysenck and his subsequent supporters err in conceptualizing the psychotherapeutic process too narrowly. They focus on techniques and style of therapy, usually to the total exclusion of the other factors such as the naming process, the personal qualities of the therapist, and the expectations of the patient. Like one of the seven blind men they are holding onto the trunk of the elephant and describing a thin, round, flexible beast.

Eysenck's original paper, for instance, utilizes as "controls" patients who are in a state mental hospital. These people he designates as having received no psychotherapy. Such patients are of course subject to expectations inherent in their impressive edifice, and they also have contact with ward attendants and other personnel who may be therapeutic. Similarly in a paper by E. E. Leavitt the patients designated as "controls" were evaluated in a single session and then placed on a waiting list.[34] Since the initial evaluation included the possibilities of raising the patient's expectation, of personal contact with an individual whose personal qualities might have been therapeutic, and even of the naming process, these patients can hardly be said to have received no therapy.

A review of other studies attempting to prove that psychotherapy is not effective reveals similar shortcomings. "Untreated" control groups really have been subjected to a treatment process. And those patients not accepted for treatment in a formal psychiatric clinic seek and receive treatment elsewhere from informal psychotherapeutic resources. Moreover, those few studies which do focus selectively on components of psychotherapy other than techniques—for instance the studies on personal qualities in chapter three and those on patient expectations in chapter four—all point toward the conclusion that psychotherapy *is* effective.

To sum up, studies purporting to prove that Western psychotherapists are ineffective are invalid because they conceive of psychotherapy too narrowly. They are also at variance with anecdotal evidence suggesting that these psychotherapists are effective. Studies focusing on components other than techniques suggest that therapy is effective. What remains to be done is a broad study taking all four components into consideration, a Herculean task that would conclusively establish the efficacy of

Western psychotherapy.[35] Some of the following studies using untrained therapists are a start in this direction.

The Efficacy of Untrained Therapists

Untrained and partially trained psychotherapists should achieve successful results in therapy insofar as they innately possess and use the four components of psychotherapy. Their success may come despite that fact that they have had little or no training.

What, then, is the function of training? One function, as outlined in chapter four, is to raise the expectations of the patient. The more highly trained the therapist is in the patient's eyes, the greater will be the patient's expectations of getting well. Training may do other things as well. It may give the therapist more confidence that he can name what is wrong. It may teach him more about himself so that he can use his personal qualities more effectively (as, for instance, with a personal analysis of the therapist). And it may polish his skills (or teach him new ones) in the techniques of therapy. In all of these ways training almost certainly improves a therapist's efficacy.

But though training may improve the efficacy of a therapist, it is not necessary for successful psychotherapy to occur. An untrained therapist may be able to name what is wrong, may naturally have therapeutic personal qualities, and my innately use techniques of therapy skillfully. If he can also raise the patient's expectations in ways other than through his training credentials, then he may be a successful psychotherapist.

Western culture has recently provided a plethora of experiments using untrained and partially trained therapists. These experiments are often not planned, and emerge spontaneously from the disparity between inadequate numbers of trained therapists and the rising expectations of people for psychotherapy. Four structures in particular have provided foci for these experiments. It is instructive to examine these structures briefly, as well as specific programs which have attempted to evaluate the untrained and partially trained therapists.

First, untrained and partially trained therapists abound in the new varieties of group therapy and self-education—T-groups, encounter groups, sensitivity-training groups, and all permutations thereof. Sometimes the leaders of these groups have been trained, but often they are self-designated psychotherapists. No hard data are available on their efficacy to date, though their rapid spread and popularity suggests that some people at least are being helped.

Another roof now sheltering many untrained and partially trained psychotherapists is the community mental health center. There are currently over 250 of these centers in operation, all with staffing needs for psychotherapists. It is part of the irony of the community mental health center movement that its architects, most of whom held very traditional views about who should do psychotherapy, pushed legislation through to build the centers but failed to consider who would staff them. The result has been a manpower vacuum into which are flowing untrained therapists in large numbers. Already the percentage of the staff who are nonprofessionals in urban centers is 22 percent, in suburban centers 9 percent and in rural centers 33 percent.[36] Some of the studies of efficacy to be discussed below arise from this group.

A third source of experiments demonstrating the utility of untrained and partially trained psychotherapists has been the new careers movement. Individuals with limited educational backgrounds, usually from lower socio-economic status, have been pressed into service as aides in teaching, corrections, social service, community development, health, and mental health. In the last they are sometimes placed in the community mental health centers. They are variously designated as nonprofessionals, paraprofessionals, subprofessionals, mental health aides, mental health expediters, etc., but regardless of their label they usually are doing psychotherapy with their patients. Although hard data on their efficacy are still forthcoming, the preliminary impressions of professionals observing them has been almost unanimously one of respect and surprise that they are so effective.[37]

A final structure housing many partially trained therapists is the suicide prevention center. There are now over 100 centers in the United States utilizing about 7,000 staff members. These are often housewives who receive several hours of training in how to talk with acutely disturbed and suicidal patients. Since contacts with patients often include follow-up calls as the crisis is resolved it seems fair to label what they do as psychotherapy. Again hard data on their efficacy is not available, but most professionals who have had contact with them will vouch for it. Looking at specific programs which have attempted to assess the efficacy of lesser-trained psychotherapists, medical students are one such group. Although they may have had no experience or training as psychotherapists, they may be indistinguishable to the patients from trained psychotherapists. Because they are working in the medical center they are implicitly sanctioned by that particular institution and will be perceived as psychotherapists by their patients. One study using them as individual psychotherapists with outpatients reported that 82 percent of the patients felt improved as a result of the contacts.[38] Another study of 128 psychoneurotic outpatients and medical student therapists reported a 72 percent patient improvement after short-term psychotherapy.[39]

Several states have begun programs to use college graduates as psychotherapists in mental health centers. Course work is usually supplied by community colleges. Once they finish their training they are assigned to centers to do primary psychotherapy. Florida, for instance, began such a program in 1954, and initial results have been reported as very promising.[40]

Rioch's attempts to train housewives to do psychotherapy over a two-year period has been widely quoted and carefully evaluated. The first 16 women have been very favorably rated as psychotherapists both on tapes (rated blindly by outside professionals) and by their supervisors on the job. Rioch concluded that "the experiment demonstrated that a college degree is not a necessary prerequisite for training as a Mental Health Counselor . . ."[41]

Another project took college graduates and trained them for one year in both didactic and clinical psychotherapy. They were then placed on the back wards of mental hospitals to do "socio-environmental treatment of chronic mental patients." Most of their work consisted of group therapy, and the impressions of their efficacy by psychiatric professionals were favorable.[42]

College students have successfully been used as psychotherapists. Their utilization as "case aides" in state mental hospitals has grown so that in 1966 there were over 7,700 student volunteers in these jobs. One study of them showed that they helped 31 percent of chronic psychotics to leave the hospital.[43] Another study claimed that, on subjective evaluation, 71 percent of the chronic mental patients with whom they worked showed improvement.[44]

Other programs have successfully used college students to do "affiliative therapy" and "companionship therapy" with preadolescent and adolescent disturbed boys.[45]

A particularly interesting study using college students as group therapists was done by Poser. For comparison he assessed the results of the students against those obtained by professional psychiatrists and psychiatric social workers. The students got better results than the professionals. Two patients were also used as therapists in this study, and got results comparable to the professionals but not as good as the college students.[46]

A study that was primarily concerned with a different problem utilized one therapist with no formal training in psychotherapy but ten years experience and nine therapists with formal training and varying lengths of experience up to 25 years. In the scoring of tape-recorded interviews for an "ideal therapeutic relationship" the untrained therapist scored higher than the other nine.[47] An army psychiatrist in Ft. Devens, Massachusetts, found the solution to his overwhelming case load by using medical technicians as psychotherapists. He gave them six weeks of on-the-job training, then called them "social work consultants" and let them go to work. With good supervision they did individual and group therapy, consultations for the dispensary physicians, and even saw suicide attempts as the primary therapist. He reports the results as very favorable.[48]

Using people with a high school education or less as "mental health aides" in low-income communities is becoming relatively common. The prototype of such programs was at Lincoln Hospital in the South Bronx. There neighborhood residents were recruited, trained up to one year to administer "psychosocial first aid," and used to staff Neighborhood Service Centers where people could drop in and get help with all shades of social and psychological problems.[49] Despite administrative and political problems the use of these indigenous psychotherapists has been successful. Other mental health centers in low-income neighborhoods have begun similar programs, one of which cut the psychiatric hospitalization rate by 50 percent.[50]

Hospital aides in mental hospitals have been used in several studies as untrained and partially trained psychotherapists. In one such program Truax, Carkhuff et al., following out the implications of their research on personal qualities of the therapist to their logical conclusion, took hospital attendants and tried to teach them how to be genuine, warm, and empathetic in less than 100 hours of training. They report that with five attendants so trained the levels of these three qualities "meet or exceed those obtained on the average from a group of more experienced therapists in the Wisconsin program." They conclude that the hospital attendant training program "clearly suggests that lay counselors, trained and supervised can do anything that professionals can do and sometimes more."[51]

Aides were also used as therapists in a controlled study for 327 schizophrenic patients at a Veterans Administration Hospital. Assessment of the aides revealed a high ability to communicate with patients, an innovative approach to therapy, and effective rehabilitation of the patients.[52]

Two other experimental programs have used hospital aides as therapists. One of them, using the aides for inpatient schizophrenic patients, concluded that ". . . the psychiatric aide as therapist can effect significant behavioral changes in chronic patients and do so as effectively as other more costly types of approach."[53] And a program allowing the aides to do brief psychotherapy with schizophrenic patients discharged from the hospital reported that ". . . the treatment results of the nonprofessional personnel compared favorably with the results of the psychiatrists."[54]

Finally it should be noted that patients themselves have been used occasionally as untrained psychotherapists. In one such program in a state mental hospital eight patient-therapists were "given a brief orientation, including material on behavior dynamics, and were told that their role was a professional one." They saw 200 patients over a two-year period, usually working a 40-hour week. They employed techniques ranging from simple encouragement to socializing their patients to operant conditioning. The program was reported to have ". . . won the approval of both staff and patients as an effective treatment force."[55]

chapter 8

Psychotherapists
in a Mexican-American
Subculture

There are approximately five million Mexican-Americans in the
United States, forming the second largest minority group and
constituting an identifiable subculture. If, as has been maintained,
the components of psychotherapy are universal in principle but
culture-specific in application, then the psychotherapists of dominant Anglo culture should be irrelevant for subcultural Mexican-
Americans. This thesis provides a focus for the chapter, which
will examine the case of the Mexican-Americans in some depth.

It is of course both simplistic and naïve to generalize about
a Mexican-American subculture. Mexican-Americans range from
braceros who come from Mexico to pick crops, to middle-class,
activist *chicanos* who are proud of their heritage, to wealthy,
totally assimilated professionals who are Mexican-American in
name only. The relative proportions of the unassimilated, transitional, and highly assimilated segments of the spectrum are estimated in one study to be one-fourth, one-half, and one-fourth.[1]
Nor do generalizations about the subculture take into consideration the facts that Mexican-Americans come from different parts
of Mexico with distinct cultural differences, that they may be of

more Spanish or more Indian descent, or that one group of "Mexican-Americans" in Southern Colorado settled in the United States directly from Spain and were never technically Mexicans at all. Such facts set limiting boundaries on generalizations about the subculture, and these boundaries should be kept in mind.

To provide a more precise focus for examination, the Mexican-American subculture in Santa Clara County, California, will often be referred to. I became familiar with this group over a two-year period, and have specifically tried to examine the system of psychotherapists utilized by Mexican-Americans there. The county is a fertile crescent of one million people around the southern tip of San Francisco Bay, and includes the city of San Jose as well as wealthy suburban and rural areas. Ten percent of its population is Mexican-American, the same percentage as in the state of California as a whole. The county provides a full range of Anglo psychotherapists both in private practice and through an extended network of community mental health centers.

Underutilization of Anglo Psychotherapists

If Anglo psychotherapists are really irrelevant for Mexican-Americans, then it would be expected that they would be under-utilized. This is exactly what occurs. Private Anglo psychologists and psychiatrists, of which there are 150 in the county, claim they rarely see Mexican-Americans as patients. Fees of twenty to thirty-five dollars an hour are one obvious explanation for this since Mexican-Americans are over-represented in the lower income brackets.

However, fees cannot explain a similar underutilization of the community mental health centers where fees are on a sliding scale adjusted to the patient's income. During a recent year only 4 percent of the patient visits to the main center were by Mexican-Americans. Of these 15 percent were for the drug abuse program, meaning that visits for traditional psychotherapy were below 4 percent.

Partly because of this underutilization, a satellite center was opened closer to the Mexican-American part of San Jose. In spite of the fact that most census tracts in that area have Mexican-

American populations of over 25 percent, during its first nine months of operation only 11 percent of patient visits were by members of this subculture. There is also evidence that those Mexican-Americans who do begin therapy with Anglo psychotherapists there terminate or are terminated earlier than Anglo patients; Mexican-Americans made an average of 2.6 visits per case whereas Anglos made an average of 5.8 visits.[2]

This pattern of underutilization of Anglo psychotherapists by Mexican-American patients has been substantiated elsewhere in California. In a recent year they constituted only 2.2 percent of State mental hospital admissions, 3.4 percent of State Mental Hygiene Clinic admissions, and 0.9 percent of Neuropsychiatric Institute outpatient admissions.[3] They should constitute about 10 percent of these based upon expectations from the population. Mexican-Americans have also been shown to be kept in therapy a shorter time than Anglo patients and be less likely to be offered individual or group therapy.[4] A study of Mexican-Americans in Texas confirmed their underutilization of inpatient psychiatric facilities.[5]

Possible Explanations for Underutilization

One explanation for the underutilization of Anglo psychotherapists by Mexican-Americans is that Anglo psychotherapists utilize the four components of psychotherapy geared for Anglo culture and do not adapt them for the Mexican-American subculture. The Anglo therapists are thus irrelevant for Mexican-American patients. This is, I believe, the most important explanation of why Mexican-Americans underutilize Anglo mental health services. Much of this chapter will be taken up in an exploration of it. Before proceeding to that, however, it is first necessary to explore alternate and ancillary explanations for the underutilization and also to describe the psychotherapists whom Mexican-Americans *do* use.

Some of the alternate and ancillary explanations are as follows:

Mexican-Americans have a lower incidence of mental illness. When faced with the figures of underutilization mentioned above, some authorities have concluded that Mexican-Americans must have a lower incidence of mental illness.[6] I believe this is probably false. Although there is no worthwhile comparative study of Mexican-American mental illness, one attempted study of neurosis among adults in Mexico City arrived at the incidence of 44 percent for women and 32 percent for men.[7] In Santa Clara County indicators of stress and maladaptation such as the numbers of welfare recipients, juvenile delinquents, and neglected and dependent children are all disproportionately high for Mexican-American areas.[8] And most studies of groups who are either poor[9] or in the process of acculturating[10] show a high incidence of mental illness; many Mexican-Americans are both poor and acculturating.

Mexican-Americans do not use Anglo psychotherapists because of language considerations. This certainly has some validity. Of the 120 psychotherapists in Santa Clara County community mental health centers only four speak Spanish. Even the signs in the main center are in English only, in marked contrast to the county hospital next door where all signs are bilingual. The message is easy to read: traditional mental health services are for English speakers only.

The majority of Mexican-Americans in Santa Clara County are bilingual. Spanish is the language for home and English for elsewhere. However, the last thing a person learns in a second language is to express his feelings. It is not an uncommon observation for a bilingual individual to forget his second language altogether when he becomes sufficiently disturbed. The result is that even bilingual Mexican-Americans may find it very difficult to undertake psychotherapy in English.

Language considerations alone are not sufficient to explain the underutilization, however. As should be apparent from the discussion of cognitive anthropology in chapter two, the language shapes the thought. A Mexican-American often needs not only somebody who shares the Spanish language, but somebody who shares a Mexican-American world-view as well. There must be more than just linguistic congruence; there must be cognitive congruence for successful psychotherapy.

Mexican-Americans use physicians rather than Anglo psychotherapists for mental health problems. This explanation has been favored as an important one by Karno and his co-workers in their extensive survey of Mexican-Americans in East Los Angeles.[11] It has some validity to it; most groups with low incomes in the United States probably use family physicians for emotional problems rather than going to a professional psychotherapist. However it is at most a partial explanation for the underutilization by Mexican-Americans specifically; Karno's own survey revealed that the difference between utilization of family doctors by Mexican-Americans and Anglos in the same area was only the difference between 75 percent and 66 percent.[12]

Mexican-American family structure makes it less likely that members will seek psychiatric help. This also has some validity as an ancillary explanation for the underutilization. Mexican-American families are often close and interdependent. They are expected to provide mutual support in crises and not to seek outside help. Taking problems to someone who is not a family member constitutes loss of face for the whole family. Furthermore, it is said that such families tolerate a greater degree of deviant behavior and therefore make psychotherapeutic help less necessary.

Mexican-American Psychotherapists

Coincidental with the fact that Mexican-Americans underutilize Anglo psychotherapists is the fact that they do use their own psychotherapists. These therapists include a broad range of individuals from housewives to traditional *curanderos* (female: *curandera*) to community leaders who function as mental health ombudsmen.

The first level of traditional healer is the housewife. Knowing what herbs to treat certain illnesses with is part of her job. If her home remedies fail she usually next turns to relatives and close friends. If they also fail she may seek out a *señora*, usually an older woman in the neighborhood who is an expert in home remedies. The next step is to go to a *curandero*, the most commonly used term for Mexican-American folk healers who will be discussed in more detail below.

Variants of the *curandero* are the *adivino* who just diagnoses the illness but doesn't treat it,[13] the *albolario* who relies mostly on herbs for treatment,[14] the *medico* who also relies on herbs,[15] and the *magico* who combines herbs with spiritualism.[16] Herbalists alone may form a separate category of curers in some areas.

Similarly spiritualists may be looked upon as a separate category, and are also called *mediums*. Some people distinguish spiritists from spiritualists, the second being thought of as much more religious.[17] Spiritualists often have diplomas from schools in Mexico (they may be obtained by correspondence courses), converse with spirits of the dead, and use trances; they usually charge higher fees than *curanderos*.

All of these healers may either be "general practitioners," treating the whole range of human ills, or they may be "specialists." The latter may specialize either in a specific disease (e.g., *susto*, a Mexican-American disease category to be discussed below) or in a specific technique (e.g., holy water). It should also be stressed that there is great geographical diversity in how these healers are conceptualized and named. A *curandera* in San Jose may correspond to a *señora* in San Antonio, a *medica* in New Mexico, an *albolaria* in parts of Mexico, and a *parchera* in parts of Guatemala.

Returning to *curanderos*, the best known type of indigenous Mexican-American therapist, they usually come to their profession by divine election. The election may be revealed by way of a dream, voice or vision, and occurs at an early age. Alternatively or in addition they may apprentice themselves to an older *curandero*. Most people express a preference for older *curanderos*.

The major characteristic of a *curandero* is his religiosity. "His knowledge, intuition, humility, and interest in people may be important, but his religious demeanor, untrammeled by the authority of the Church, is his paramount virtue."[18] Most of them do not charge a direct fee, but expect a small offering or gift instead. The average cost of such a visit is one to two dollars.

The *curandero* works at his profession only part-time, and sees patients either in his own house or in theirs. The setting invariably includes religious objects. Usually the patient is accompanied by his whole family. Diagnosis of the illness is made by the history, symptoms, and retrospectively by the response to treatment. The patient's complete recent history of interpersonal relations is inventoried in search of etiological factors. Occasionally *curanderos* simply take the patient's pulse and announce a diagnosis.[19]

The techniques of treatment used by *curanderos* are many,

but there are a few things they do *not* do. They do not become possessed, nor exorcise spirits, nor prophesy, nor communicate directly with a guardian spirit. They also do not do witchcraft. Because Anglos often confuse *curanderos* with witches, many *curanderos* refuse to treat cases of people who believe they have been bewitched.

The techniques they do use are as follows: massage, cupping, "cleansing" rituals (using herbs and eggs), herb remedies (now being replaced by vitamins and antibiotics), magic potions, religious vows and promises (such as votive candles or a visit to a shrine), prayers, holy water, rules and advice (e.g., about diet), confession, and reassurance. Some *curanderos* tend to specialize in one healing technique alone, as was the case with the most famous *curandero* of all, Don Pedrito Jaramillo, who used holy water for everything.[20] One enterprising *curandero* even used a stethoscope for curing, though not for diagnosis.[21]

The family of the patient is present throughout the curing session and becomes intimately involved. They may be specifically told how to help the patient, or to make votive offerings. This enables the *curandero* to make extensive use of family and social manipulation if he wishes. "Thus treatment is not merely the result of the doctor-patient relationship but is instead a form of social reintegration through socially recognized methods."[22]

In Santa Clara County *curanderos* continue to exist and provide a mental health resource for Mexican-Americans. How important a resource they provide is not clear. Most Mexican-Americans vehemently deny their existence because they associte *curanderos* with being superstitious and backward. *Curanderos*, for their part, are loath to discuss their practice with an Anglo because of a deep fear (not without reason) of the medical society and the Internal Revenue Service. The more I came to know the Mexican-American subculture in the county, however, the more convinced I became that *curanderos* are still important (though declining) mental health resources.[23]

One study of the utilization of these healers by 75 Mexican-American housewives in a southwestern city found that half of the housewives had been treated by a *señora* and one-fifth had been treated by a *curandero*.[24] In an effort to determine the utilization of *curanderos* by more seriously ill people I interviewed seven Mexican-American patients from Santa Clara County at a nearby State Hospital. All had been diagnosed as having schizophrenia. Three of the seven admitted to having been treated by *curanderos* for their illness and a fourth had been told to go to one because she believed that she had been bewitched by her husband's mistress. One of them had been treated by a *curandero* a total of nine times and used the *curandero* as his main mental health resource between hospital admissions. He felt he was greatly helped by these visits.

An example of a *curandero* in Santa Clara County is Mr. R. He is a 75-year-old man who lives with his wife in a modest but well-kept house in San Jose. There is no sign outside. He became a healer at age 10 in Mexico, and came to the United States at age 22. He sees five to ten patients a day for a wide variety of reasons including physical illness, mental illness, social and domestic problems, and divining the future. He also claims to be able to influence the release of prisoners and pick winning numbers in Reno. His fee is whatever a patient wants to give. His techniques include suggestion and practical advice (obtained from his contacts with the spirits) as well as occasional herb medicines from Mexico.

Because Mr. R. would not discuss his practice directly with me, I sent a research assistant to him as a patient. This woman had been brought up in South America so she speaks fluent Spanish. She feigned depression and anxiety ostensibly due to domestic problems. On the first visit he listened to her history, went through a ritual of alternately feeling her pulse and then a crucifix, told her to return with a picture of her husband, and promised to commune with the spirits about her problem three evenings hence. On the second visit he told her who her husband was having an affair with (which was not true), asked whether she wished to keep her husband or divorce him, and went through another ritual using "holy water" and a crucifix on her hand. On the third visit he claimed that he had "cured" her husband's purported philanderings and offered her specific advice on how to act at home to alleviate her domestic problems.

I have interviewed two other patients who have sought help from Mr. R. The pattern of treatment was similar in each case. Both told about other friends who had been treated by him. One woman wanted a divorce from an alcoholic husband who was beating her. Each time the woman suggested divorce the husband threatened to kill her if she persisted. Mr. R. told the woman to get the divorce, and that his spirits would protect her. Another woman was said to have come to him with domestic problems. Mr. R. told her to go home and she would find her husband in bed with a neighbor. She did and found exactly that. Returning she demanded of Mr. R. what he was going to do next. He countered by asking what *she* was going to do. She filed for divorce.

There is another group of people who often call themselves *curanderos* but who are not mental health resources. These are fortune-tellers. One of them, a woman who advertises herself as a *curandera* on her business card and offers "advice on love, health, and business," speaks practically no Spanish. All of them that I have had contact with had starting fees of five to ten dollars, and were most concerned with extracting as much money as possible from their patients. They should not be confused with true *curanderos*.

Another type of psychotherapist used by Mexican-Americans are what I have called mental health ombudsmen. These are at least as important mental health resources in Santa Clara County as *curanderos* are, though I am not aware of descriptions of them elsewhere. They are the community leaders to whom people turn with problems. In some cases these individuals overlap the political leadership as well. Their role is similar to the all-understanding ward bosses of the past who were politically important but who also served as a listener, adviser, legal counsel, social worker, and referee for individual and domestic problems of all kinds.

In East San Jose I have identified about twenty such individuals. They are the people named when you ask a Mexican-American the question: "If you had such-and-such a problem, who would you go to?" All of them are Mexican-Americans themselves. They are of both sexes. Most have regular jobs, and supply mental health services during their off-hours. None of them would consider accepting payment for their services. Many of them are aware that what they are doing is "psychotherapy" in the Anglo frame of reference. Most of them tend to specialize in certain types of problems. They see the entire range of mental health problems except for psychoses.

An example is Mr. J. He is a middle-aged man who is outgoing, warm, positive, sensitive, and energetic. During the day he works as a blue-collar worker. During evenings and weekends he often sees adolescents with drug and/or school problems. He averages three calls a week. Usually they come to his home, but sometimes he makes the visits. He provides support and practical advice in his attempts to solve the person's problem. He often takes books out of the library on psychology and counseling in an attempt to improve his ability to help people. He has had opportunities to join the Anglo establishment in a "community liaison" capacity but fears that he would lose his credibility within the Mexican-American community if he did.

Another example is Mrs. P. She is a quiet but warm middle-aged woman who gives freely of her own feelings and conveys confidence. She has worked intermittently for several Anglo agencies, and has averaged three calls a week for primarily domestic problems over many years. She usually visits the home. She has allowed me to come with her on several calls, including problems such as a mentally retarded girl's reported disruption of a family (she was being scapegoated), a woman with anxiety and obsessive thinking, a woman with multiple sclerosis and mental deterioration, and a couple with severe marital discord.

Mrs. P. describes her technique as listening and ventilation:

> "I listen mostly. Then they often feel better. Sometimes they understand what's going on better just by telling me. I also encourage them to express their feelings. They're scared to. I tell them I know it will be hard at first."

Some of Mrs. P's empathy is a product of her own past domestic difficulties. At one point she sought traditional Anglo psychiatric help. Its failure typifies the reason why she is a major mental health resource for the Mexican-American community:

> "I couldn't talk to him. All he ever did was ask me about things way in the past. My problem was in the present. I couldn't talk to him at all."

It should be noted that *not* included as significant psycho-therapeutic resources for Mexican-Americans are the community "caretakers" described by Lindemann and Caplan for Anglo middle class communities—the clergy, teachers, probation officers, police, etc.[25] It was the existence of this group, in fact, that led to community consultation being included as one of the five essential services for community mental health centers. For

Mexican-Americans, however, these "caretakers" are identified with the establishment and are to be avoided whenever possible. The only exceptions are a few Catholic priests and a rare teacher or welfare worker. To go to the police with a problem would be accepted as prima-facie evidence by Mexican-Americans that the person *must* be psychotic. Thus not only the formal Anglo psychotherapists are rejected by Mexican-Americans but the informal ones are rejected as well.

Mental Illness and the Mexican-American World-View

Having described the psychotherapists that Mexican-Americans do use, what can be said about this preference in the light of the four components of psychotherapy? Is the congruence between Mexican-American patients and Mexican-American psychotherapists, and lack of same with Anglo psychotherapists, sufficient to explain the underutilization of Anglo mental health services by Mexican-Americans?

Beginning with the world-view of the Mexican-American subculture (and keeping in mind the limitation of generalizations about five million people), there are many cultural values and potential areas of conflict which would not be readily apparent to an Anglo psychotherapist but which are shared by a Mexican-American therapist and his patient. These potential areas of conflict are points of stress, and the more aware of them the therapist is the more effective he is likely to be. It is useful to review some of these points of stress, bearing in mind the possible difference between how an Anglo and a Mexican-American psychotherapist might perceive the situation.

The first point, often overlooked, is that most Mexican-Americans by definition are culturally deviant in terms of striving for economic advancement. This is the main motivating factor which brings Mexicans to the United States, yet economic advancement of the individual is a cultural value held in low esteem in traditional Mexican culture. The result is that first generation Mexican-Americans as a group are motivationally estranged from their parent culture, and psychiatrically one would expect conflicts in direct proportion to their acceptance of Mexican cultural values.

The second point of cultural stress is the role of women. Girls are valued primarily for their virtue, and an unmarried girl's honor is equated with that of the family. Young women are expected to get married and the maternal role is very highly valued. Women are late to mature, often because the grandmother lives with them and competes in maternal care of the grandchildren. There is a concomitant undervaluation of the sexual and companionship roles of women; sex is prudishly accepted by "nice women" only as an obligation. If a woman enjoys sex she may be suspected of being a prostitute. The net result is a submissive, masochistic woman who feels inferior and unable to live up to the ideals of her culture.[26] She tends toward depressive reactions, and is more acutely and affectively disturbed than her counterpart in Anglo culture.[27] One study which confirms this association of the status of women with psychiatric symptomatology suggests "that women whose status approaches that of men in the same community report fewer symptoms."[28]

The expectations of men constitute another major point of cultural stress. Virility is measured primarily by sexual potency (exercised by the double standard), and secondarily by strength, courage, and audacity. There is a belief in the biological superiority of man, and the traditional Mexican family is founded upon absolute authority of the man and absolute self-sacrifice of the woman. The result is an exaggerated ideal of *machismo* or masculinity. Some authors have suggested that this idea may be a logical reaction formation to the Oedipal dynamics of Mexican families, but this remains to be demonstrated.[29] What *is* certain is that "to be labeled 'homosexual' is the ultimate debasement in the sphere of male behavior."[30]

Out of this cultural stress one would expect men to have problems with authority and submission, sexual potency, and relations with women generally. It might also be anticipated that a man would act out his aggression, and in fact Mexico does have the highest reported murder rate in the world.[31]

These problems become worse as men get older. The discrepancy widens between what they feel they should be and what they actually are. "As they grow older they lose their dominant position and the older adults appear disturbed, impulsive, and anxious. They seem to be losing the grip on society that the older women are taking over."[32] This is also suggested by Jaco's study which found that the incidence of psychosis rose more for male than female Mexican-Americans with increasing age.[33] Viewing the world as hostile and having extremely poor interpersonal relationships are other major points of cultural stress. Life in general is seen as a struggle between good and evil, with health and prosperity maintained only by sustaining the delicate balance between the forces. The saints are on the side of the good, but devils and witches are opposed. An individual views himself as a passive victim of forces in his environment.[34] Projection comes easily.

Interpersonal relationships are seen from this same vantage point. There is a general distrust of extrafamilial social bonds, interpersonal relationships are unstable, there is fear of intimacy, and a general lack of social cohesion. Rubel, in describing the Mexican-Americans of San Antonio, says: "The themes of invidious sanction and malevolent intent are incessant in Mexiquito, and the means by which such hostile intentions are believed to be projected are manifold."[35] Mexican-Americans see themselves as being unable to get along with each other and the main stresses as intragroup; this contrasts sharply with Black Americans who view their main stresses as intergroup. Rubel, in an interesting thesis, tries to associate these poor interpersonal relationships with the strong nuclear family, and draws an analogy from the Mexican-Americans to the Ojibwa Indians.

The projection which commonly ensues from this hostile environment and from poor interpersonal relationships is best summarized by one author: "The Latin does not think he missed the bus because he arrived too late. He blames the bus for leaving before he arrived."[36] The corollary of this projection is that personal failures or short-comings are not easily admitted in Mexican-American culture, not even to trusted friends.

Another aspect of these poor interpersonal relationships is the importance of "correct behavior" and the suppression of emotions. Relationships are characterized by restraint and constriction, and role behaviors clearly marked in the traditional culture. There is a premium on self-control, and great fear of behaving incorrectly. "The Mexican grows up with much fear of his emotions, particularly hostile and sexual ones, and of the things that arouse these emotions."[37] Emotions are guarded against as having a power of their own.

Finally, perhaps the greatest point of cultural stress in Mexican-American culture is the process of acculturation itself. All of the above points must be seen primarily in the light of contrast between traditional Mexican culture and Anglo culture. The ambivalence about economic striving is seen in the college graduate who returns to his father's grocery store to work as a clerk. The different and changing Anglo role expectations of both men and women often contrast sharply with traditional Mexican culture, from simple dating patterns to the increasing difficulty unskilled Mexican-American men have obtaining jobs and maintaining their supreme role as provider for their family. Other cultural values clash when the collectivism of the Mexican-American *barrio* meets the individualism of the city, or when fatalism and resignation meet achievement, progress, and human perfectibility.[38]

Turning to that part of the world-view which involves the causation and classification of disease, it is found that here also Mexican-Americans often differ markedly from Anglos. And therapists trying to cure them may find it a difficult process unless these differences are recognized.

Within traditional Mexican-American culture there are three main causes of illness:

1. *Natural causes: Empacho,* the symptoms caused by a bolus of food lodged in the intestine, is an example.
2. *Emotional causes: Susto* caused by fright, *bilis* caused by anger, and *envidia* caused by desire are examples.
3. *Supernatural causes:* These may be caused either by God as punishment or by others. The latter category includes *mal ojo* (the evil eye) and *mal puesto* (witchcraft).

It should be added that Mexican-Americans, in addition to this group of indiginous disease beliefs, also accept most Western beliefs concerning the causation of diseases, e.g., bacteria and viruses.

Most mental illnesses in Mexican-American culture are conceptualized under the entities of *susto, mal ojo,* and *mal puesto.* Other causes of mental illness are also accepted, such as heredity, preoccupation with sexual activity, sexual frustration, immoral behavior, and overexposure to the sun. The majority of mental illnesses are subsumed under the three disease entities, however, and it is for this reason that each will be examined in more detail. Interestingly, the notion of God's punishment is rarely invoked to explain mental illness; the choice is rather to project the cause onto others.

To avoid confusion it should be added that there is extensive overlap of symptoms for these disease entities. No one symptom is specific for a given disease. The same disease may have different sets of symptoms and different diseases may have the same symptoms. The ultimate confirmation of the diagnosis is when the disease responds to treatment specifically prescribed for that disease entity. This retrospective method of diagnosis could be profitably used by mental health workers with Mexican-Americans.

Susto is known as the "fright disease," and is usually the result of a traumatic experience. The source of fright may be natural, e.g., an accident, or supernatural, e.g., a ghost. The latter category is often called *espanto*. Groups of individuals may develop symptoms at one time,[39] and it is more common in children. The result of the fright is that the soul is lost from the body. Rubel contends that *susto* occurs most commonly "as a consequence of an episode in which an individual is unable to meet the expectations of his own society for a social role in which he or she has been socialized."[40]

The symptoms of *susto* include fatigue, restlessness, decreased appetite, decreased interest, weakness, lack of interest in appearance or surroundings, somatic complaints, withdrawal, and sadness. In short, *susto* corresponds loosely to the clinical entities of anxiety and depression. The treatment for *susto* include prayers, votive offerings, herbs, and "sweeping" the patient with a branch by folk healers to draw the soul back.

Bilis and *envidia,* caused by anger and envy, are less common entities used to explain psychiatric symptoms. The belief in the former is that strong anger causes an overflow of yellow bile and produces diarrhea and vomiting.[41] It is clear that there exists a ready-made framework associating emotions and psychiatric illness in Mexican-American culture, and that this framework could be used to help explain symptoms in therapy.

Mal ojo, the evil eye, is commonly used to explain psychiatric symptoms. It is caused when a person with "strong vision" admiringly or enviously looks at another. "Any kind of special attention paid one individual by another . . ."[42] may cause it. Its causation is usually assumed to be inadvertent and the person is not held consciously responsible; implicit, however, is responsibility for unconscious desires. Here is another ready-made framework with which Mexican-Americans can accept and understand the unconscious. It is also another example of projecting the cause of illness onto others.

Clinically *mal ojo* occurs more often in the younger age groups. Headaches, crying, irritability, and restlessness are common symptoms, often accompanied by fever, diarrhea, or vomiting. It is usually of rapid onset and short duration. Psychiatrically it would appear to correspond with transient situational, neurotic, and personality disorders. Traditional treatments include prayers and "sweeping" or "cleansing" the patient with a raw egg. Another approach to treatment is to try and locate the person who inadvertently caused it (usually within the preceding 24 hours); if this person simply touches the afflicted the illness will be cured.

Mal puesto, witchcraft, is the most common explanation for all severe psychiatric illnesses. It occurs when a hex is willfully put on somebody by a witch, a healer specializing in witchcraft, or a layman who knows the intricacies of witchcraft. The witch or healer may be hired to do the job. The hex may be administered by torturing effigy figures of the individual, by magically putting foreign objects into the victim's stomach, by turning into an animal and attacking the person (nagualism), or by sprinkling magic potions on the victim or around his house.[43]

The major motives for *mal puesto* are envy, jealousy (especially sexual), and vengeance. The envy is most commonly "envy of the prosperous individual who indulges in conspicuous consumption to the discomfort of his less fortunate neighbors."[44] Belief in *mal puesto* is common in rural and uneducated Mexican-Americans, but its belief among all groups should not be underestimated. In a culture where projection is used easily, and where personal intercession by saints (and other forces of good) are common, it is only a short step toward blaming personalized forces of evil when things go wrong.

Clinically *mal puesto* is suspected whenever deviancy or severe psychiatric symptoms occur. Amnesia, hallucinations, ideas of persecution, hysterical symptoms, and mania are all suggestive.

Chronicity is a hallmark. *Miedo* is its early or milder form—"the victim is so frightened that he imagines seeing frightful things that do not exist and cannot be observed by normal people"[45] —and *demencia* is its full-blown form.

All chronic deviants from Mexican-American society may be considered as suffering from *mal puesto*. Schizophrenics, epileptics, those with organic brain disorders, psychopaths, and alcoholics may all qualify. Diagnosis is made by looking for the major motives that a person might have for causing it (e.g., unrequited love) and identifying the witch. Treatment is removal of the hex either by countermagic or by destroying the magical paraphernalia used for the hex (e.g., the doll image).

It is apparent that *mal puesto* is a major mechanism for explaining deviancy and projecting the blame for it onto others. It strengthens the nuclear family "as a social device by means of which members of one household perceive others outside it as attempting to influence and sanction their behavior."[46] And it functions as a "leveling mechanism," like gossip and ridicule, to enforce adherence to prescribed behavior. "Those most likely to be victims are those who, by abnormal physical, social, or psychological behavior, deviate from accepted Mexican-American norms."[47]

These are the major disease entities under which Mexican-Americans conceptualize psychiatric illnesses. There are several others of lesser importance. For instance, *mal aire*, an imbalance between hot and cold, may be due to relationships or emotions which are not in balance. *Empacho*, when the intestine is blocked by a bolus of food, may be caused by "permitting another individual to override one's personal autonomy."[48] And *caida de mollera*, fallen fontanelle in an infant, is partly caused by neglect of the mother, a serious charge in a culture that values the maternal role so highly.

Some of the social implications and meanings of these diseases have been mentioned above, but it would be useful briefly to tie them together. First, these illnesses frequently enable the patient to avoid the precipitating crisis, e.g., a student who is afflicted by *susto* on the way to take an important examination. If the illness begins after the crisis it may provide relief from guilt or social disapproval, for example, *mal ojo* or *mal puesto*, caused by others, may be invoked to explain the abnormal behavior. This affords an excellent rationale for otherwise unsanctioned social behavior. At a very practical level these illnesses focus attention on the individual and let society know that something is wrong; this is often the first step toward cure.

Perhaps the most important function of these Mexican-American disease entities is to re-emphasize Mexican-American values and customs. As such they are a resistance to culture change. They give you a way to "prove" that you are still Mexican, for Anglos never get these diseases. A Mexican-American who has serious cultural conflicts may resolve them by being diagnosed with these illnesses.[49] "Mexican folk medicine thus plays a dual role, for it is designed to maintain the continuity of society as a functioning whole as well as to reintegrate individuals into society."[50]

It is frequently assumed by Anglos who know about the Mexican-American disease system that belief in it is confined to *braceros* recently arrived from Mexico. Two studies have shown that this is not the case. One study of 75 Mexican-American housewives (two-thirds of whom had been born in the United States) asked about belief in five common indigenous diseases (*susto, empacho, caida de mollera, mal puesto,* and *mal ojo*). The results were that 97 percent of the housewives knew of all five diseases, and that 95 percent knew of instances of one of the illnesses in themselves, a family member, or friend.[51] Another study of 250 Tucson Mexican-American families confirmed the high prevalence of belief. For *susto*, for instance, 139 expressed strong belief, 57 were doubtful, and 54 had no belief.[52]

In an attempt to confirm these differences in disease classification I administered a questionnaire to three groups of people: 10 psychiatric residents at Stanford University; 10 anthropology graduate students at Stanford University; 20 high school students at a school in San Jose. Of these 7 were Black, 7 Mexican-Americans, and 6 were Anglos.

Directions for the questionnaire were given verbally and were also printed on top of the page as follows:

"I am trying to understand how people think about being well and being sick. You can help me by taking the 10 words which are listed below in alphabetical order and dividing them up. Divide them into at least 2 but no more than 5 boxes. A box can contain as few as one word. Divide them in whatever way seems most logical to you. There is no right or wrong way to divide them—just the way that makes the most sense to you."

might be divided as follows:

For example:	blue	blue	cold	slow
	cold	red	hot	fast
	hot	yellow		
	red			
	slow			
	yellow			

Here are 10 words to divide:

compulsive	neurotic
crazy	normal
depressed	religious
frightened	tired
hears voices	withdrawn

The subjects were told not to put their names on the paper; I was able to identify the papers for division into groups by the way in which I collected them.

In spite of methodological shortcomings of the study, the results suggested differences in categorization of symptoms between the different cultures. For instance the words "crazy" and "hears voices" were associated by 90 percent of the psychiatric residents, 60 percent of the graduate students, 48 percent of the non-Mexican-American high school students, and only 16 percent (1 out of 7) of the Mexican-American students. Such a difference may indicate greater religious belief among Mexican-American students (although only 1 out of 7 made the association between "hears voices" and "religious") and/or it may reflect greater tolerance for hearing voices in the Mexican-American community. In either case, it is clear that an Anglo psychiatrist and a Mexican-American student share less of a frame of reference than the psychiatrist does with a graduate student (a common source of "good" psychiatric patients).

Another example to illustrate this was the association of "frightened" with some combination of "crazy" and "hears voices" by 86 percent of the Mexican-Americans but only 20 percent of psychiatrists and no graduate students. This may well reflect the pervasive cultural belief among Mexican-Americans in *susto,* the syndrome thought to be caused by a severe fright.

Anecdotal material reinforces such evidence. During a recent home visit to an anxious, depressed Mexican-American housewife I attempted to explore the origin of her symptoms within the context of her obvious domestic difficulties. Toward the end of the interview I offered her a mild tranquilizer to alleviate her anxiety. She nodded politely, but I knew I had not gotten through. I then went back into the symptoms and discovered that she was convinced they were the result of *susto*. After telling her that the tranquilizer was especially good for *susto* she brightened up and smiled. Obviously my medicine could not help her until I understood what was really wrong with her.[53]

There is one other important aspect of the Mexican-American world-view in addition to the points of stress, concepts of causation, and system of disease classification. This is the existence of caste. An Anglo psychotherapist, from a Mexican-American point of view, is a member of a different caste than himself. Although the concept of caste overlaps the distinctions of both class and culture, it differs in implying a more rigid segmentalization of society with hereditary positions of dominance and submission. These positions implicitly are part of the divine order and dictate such things as social intercourse and occupation as well as the use of mental health facilities. Caste goes beyond income level, and value systems; it is The Order of Things.

Just as surely as the Blacks in our society have been treated as a lower caste, so have the Mexican-Americans. They receive reminders of their place every day. A recent illustration is the remarks of a juvenile court judge in Santa Clara County at the trial of a 16-year-old Mexican-American boy accused of incest:

> The County will have to take care of you. You are no particular good to anybody. We ought to send you out of the country—send you back to Mexico. You belong in prison for the rest of your life for doing things of this kind. You ought to commit suicide. That's what I think of people of this kind. You are lower than animals and haven't the right to live in organized society—just miserable, lousy, rotten people.

> There is nothing we can do for you. You expect the county to take care of you. Maybe Hitler was right. The animals in our society probably ought to be destroyed because they have no right to live among human beings. If you refuse to act like a human being, then, you don't belong among the society of human beings.[54]

These remarks are unusual only in that they became part of the court record and received publicity. Until recently Mexican-Americans have been used to hearing them. After all, this is The Order of Things.

Inevitably the psychotherapists and mental health facilities set up by the Anglo caste become associated with perpetuating this order. A widely circulated story in the local Mexican-American community concerns the fate of three Mexican-American county employees who went to Washington for the Poor Peoples' March. Upon their return they were ordered by their superiors to have psychiatric examinations. It is also common for the Welfare Department to order psychiatric examinations to get recipients classified as psychiatrically disabled and thus off the general welfare roles. If they refuse their check is withheld. Little wonder that for Mexican-Americans the psychiatry of the Anglos is looked upon as just one more way to degrade them.[55]

Therapist Qualities, Patient Expectations, and Techniques

As a further attempt to explain the underutilization of Anglo psychotherapists by Mexican-Americans and their simultaneous use of their own therapists, what can be said about differences in the personal qualities of the therapist, the patient expectations, and the techniques of therapy?

Regarding the first, it was mentioned above that traditional Mexican-American *curanderos* are selected by divine grace. This is very important, for it confers on them the accepted mantle of authority. In the case of mental health ombudsmen, they are self-selected for their roles. The community confirms the validity of this selection by seeking them out and using them. From a Mexican-American point of view the selection of both *curanderos* and mental ombudsmen stands in contrast to the purely academic selection of Anglo psychotherapists who have "just learned things."

The personal qualities of *curanderos* are supposed to be marked by religiosity, as previously outlined. Once accorded such sanction, however, there seems to be room for a variety of personality types. An active and authoritarian manner is common[56] and there is less value placed on being warm and empathetic. Their sincerity must be above suspicion if they hope to be accepted, and as proof of this quality most do not charge high fees.

Patient expectations of traditional Mexican-American psycho-therapists also rest heavily on their religiosity. The physical setting for healing almost always includes religious objects, usually crosses, icons, and pictures of Saints. Mr. R's living room is full of these interspersed with momentos and gifts from grateful patients. These also increase the patient's expectations.

Curanderos traditionally work out of a single office and expect patients to come to them. Often patients come long distances; the semireligious character of the *curandero* makes the journey into a true pilgrimage.[57] Mexican-American therapists are not tied to this model exclusively however. Mental health ombudsmen frequently make home visits and from my own experience I can attest to the usefulness of this.

A Mexican-American therapist's ultimate reputation, and consequent ability to raise the patient's expectations, rests on the degree of his religiosity. The *curanderos* studied by one psychiatrist in San Antonio varied from an illiterate man to the son of a physician; all were alike, however, in being considered very religious.[58] Since healing is a gift of God, Mexican-Americans wonder how a man can hope to heal anyone if he denies or has no relationship to the source of the cure. It is clear that ". . . the validity of a *curandero's* claims rest in large part on the extent of his basic devoutness and piety."[59]

Finally, the techniques of therapy used by Mexican-American therapists show a different emphasis than those used by Anglo therapists. The predominant techniques are those of suggestion, confession, family therapy, and environmental manipulation. These are in accord with such goals in therapy as symptom removal and improved interpersonal relationships (especially those within the family). The use of religion with the techniques also helps achieve the goal of a change in attitude of the patient; he is encouraged to accept God's suffering and to believe that it has a purpose. These techniques and goals are consistent with values in the Mexican-American culture, and should be contrasted with the techniques of Anglo psychotherapists who are more inclined to strive toward insight, improved personal efficiency, and improved social efficiency.

part III
Toward the Future
of Psychotherapy

chapter 9

The Implications
of Comparing Witchdoctors
and Psychiatrists

The observation that witchdoctors and psychiatrists are cultural variations of the same person should not be simply relegated to the realm of believe-it-or-not, or placed on a platter of hors d'oeuvres at a cocktail party. It should be held, studied, criticized, polished, and used in the conceptualization and delivery of mental health services. This chapter will attempt to examine the general implications of the data on the four components of psychotherapy, then look at the specific implications for psychotherapists in Western cultures, subcultures, and developing countries.

A shared world-view, the first component of psychotherapy, is necessary for a therapist and his patient. Ideally the therapist should share the patient's world-view by virtue of sharing his culture, i.e., by having been brought up in the same culture. This is not to rule out the possibility of a therapist learning another world-view and thus becoming an effective therapist in another culture. But it is an arduous process to learn another culture's values, points of stress, theories of causation, and system of disease classification. While possible, it clearly is a second choice to utilizing therapists who are indigenous to the culture concerned.

Also implied by this relativistic approach is the admonition that one culture has no right to impose its concepts of causation or system of classification upon another. The only exception is when there are relevant data that are scientifically proven (as opposed to being just empirically validated) and could be helpful to the other culture. An example of this would be the scientifically proven relationship between the metabolic abnormality of the disease phenylketonuria and subsequent mental retardation in the child. It is known that a certain kind of diet, if begun early enough in the child's life, will minimize or obviate the mental retardation. Western cultures have an obligation to share this kind of data with other cultures and encourage them to use it. It does not, by contrast, have the obligation to impose the concept that sexual deviancy is caused by a traumatic childhood experience. Such a concept may be true, may be false, or may be culture-bound, but in any case rests upon data which is on exactly the same scientific plane as the idea that sexual deviancy is caused by a lost soul or a broken taboo.

The same can be said about systems of disease classification. Since different cultures divide diseases in different ways, the cross-cultural comparison of the incidence of mental diseases should be seen for the nearly impossible task which it is. Similarly the efforts of the World Health Organization to establish a universal code of mental disease classification, while commendable in its aim to improve cross-cultural communication, should be recognized as largely an exercise in futility.

Since a shared language is a first step toward a shared world-view, the use of the patient's first language is mandatory if the therapist hopes to be effective. This importance should be reflected in recruitment and selection of psychotherapists everywhere. The utilization of translators in an established program of psychotherapy is always a last choice, and should never be used if there is an alternative.[1]

Another implication of a shared world-view is the necessity for community control of mental health services. In order for these services to be relevant they must be organized by those who have a world-view similar to the prospective patients. This is especially true for services aimed at subcultures in the United

States, but applies equally to the many subcultures in developing countries that will eventually have to be planned for. In other words Anglo mental health services should not be imposed on Mexican-Americans any more than Yoruba services should be imposed on Hausas in Nigeria. The Mexican-Americans and the Hausas should conceptualize their own services.

It can be validly argued that efforts of one culture to impose their mental health services on another culture are antithetical to mental health. It is psychiatric imperialism. The dominant culture disparages and discredits the beliefs and techniques of the other, effectively rendering them useless yet offering nothing to take their place. The beliefs and techniques of the dominant culture fail to take root in the new soil, composed as it is of elements of a different world-view. Mental health services are suspended in mid-air; anxiety is inevitable, and the culture as a whole suffers.

Turning to the second component of psychotherapy, the implications of the data on personal qualities of the therapist are profound. Quite clearly more studies are needed in this area, but if they substantiate the emerging trend in the studies done to date, then radical changes in the selection of therapists will be in order. If certain personal qualities are therapeutic in a given culture, then therapists should certainly be chosen from individuals possessing such qualities.

It is also possible that certain personal qualities will be found to be therapeutic for specific kinds of problems. There is already some evidence to support this.[2] The future result would be specialization of therapists based on their personal qualities. The breakdown of the specialization would of course vary from culture to culture. No longer would a single psychotherapist be expected to treat a range of problems from neuroses to schizophrenia to sexual deviation to alcoholism. Rather they would be specialized to deal with specific problems.

Training would also be expected to undergo changes if the implications of research on witchdoctors and psychiatrists were implemented. If the main function of training is to raise patients' expectations, cannot that be done in far shorter time? Given the same training program, why can't a person with only a high school education learn about the naming process and techniques of therapy as readily as a person with a Ph.D. or an M.D.? One component of training programs which does emerge as a valid universal principle is the desirability of maximum personal self-knowledge by the therapist. If his personal qualities are an important component in the therapeutic process, then presumably the better he knows himself the more effectively he can use his therapeutic qualities.

The importance of patient expectations, the third component of psychotherapy, implies first of all that the building and room used for therapy are important. If mental health services are relegated to austere or unimpressive edifices then the results in therapy will also be unimpressive. One of the major, although unintentional, assets of the community health center movement may be that sufficient funds were allocated for new buildings. The resultant array of new edifices may therefore be partly responsible for what positive therapeutic transactions have occurred in them.

To increase patient expectations it has been postulated that the therapist's belief in himself is important. Selection and training of therapists should reflect this; insecure, uncertain, or skeptical therapists should be deselected. Since individuality is also seen to be part of raising patient expectations there should be wide latitude left in all selection and training programs for the nonconformist.

In order to insure the highest possible standards of selection and training, and thus maintain patient expectations in the reputation of therapists in their culture, there should be a highly-developed system of surveillance within the psychotherapeutic profession in each culture. It should be clearly advertised which therapists are accredited and which are not, and no psychotherapist should be allowed to practice unless he has met certain minimal standards of competence. In this way patients will gain increasing faith in witchdoctors and psychiatrists all over the world.

The data on the fourth component of psychotherapy, techniques, implies primarily that Western psychotherapists should be more humble. Our assumption that *we* are using advanced, scientific techniques and that *they* are using primitive, magical techniques has been shown to be completely without foundation. Also suggested by the data is the possibility that Western psychotherapists can learn from psychotherapists elsewhere about techniques such as meditation, and that techniques such as suggestion, hypnosis, and confession might be under-rated in the West. Quite clearly more data are also needed on the relationship between techniques, goals of therapy, and values of a culture, and priority should be given to work in this area.

Implications for Western Psychotherapists

Turning to specific implications for Western psychotherapists, it should be apparent that many people other than traditional therapists can be usefully authorized to do psychotherapy. And these people can be authorized with pride and assurance based upon the available evidence, not with apologies and trepidation as is usually the case. In fact, the evidence is such that Western psychotherapy should be apologetic when it does *not* use indigenous psychotherapists, not when it does use them.

Official sanction has already been given to experiments for using indigenous therapists in Western psychotherapy. The Joint Commission on Mental Illness and Health of the American Psychiatric Association and the American Medical Association, in issuing its final report in 1961, said:

"Nonmedical mental health workers with aptitude, sound training, practical experience, and demonstrable competence should be permitted to do general, short-term psychotherapy—namely, treating persons by objective, permissive, nondirective techniques of listening to their troubles and helping them resolve these troubles in an individually insightful and socially useful way."[3]

More recently the head of the American Psychiatric Association, in his 1969 presidential address, called for an increased emphasis on using paraprofessionals in psychiatry. So it is not the lack of official sanction that has delayed more widespread use of indigenous therapists, but rather the resistances to be discussed in chapter 11.

Where might some new psychotherapists for Western culture come from? One large reservoir is the pool of middle-age housewives who have successfully raised a family and are wondering what to do with their next 20 years. Rioch and her associates, as mentioned in chapter 7, have shown that there are mature, empathetic women among this group who become excellent psychotherapists.

Another potential source is college graduates, discharged Army medics, and others who want to go into the burgeoning human services industry but do not want to (or cannot) get a Ph.D. or M.D. If selected for therapeutic personal qualities, many excellent psychotherapists could be obtained from this group. It has been suggested that such individuals could become a new profession of "psychiatric assistants."[4] Training programs in community colleges for such individuals, leading to an Associate in Arts degree as a "mental health technician," began in 1966; there are over 50 programs in operation. It is customary for professionals to minimize the amount of patient responsibility these people have. In fact they should have, and often do have, almost complete responsibility.

Good psychotherapists may also be found among the pool of 96,000 psychiatric aides in state and county mental hospitals. A sociologist, arguing along the lines of the shared world-view, has suggested that such aides inherently make better therapists than professionals because they are closer to the patients and understand their world better.[5]

Finally there is a large potential source of psychotherapists among the bartenders, barbers, hairdressers, pharmacists, foremen, probation officers, and housemothers of Western culture.[6] These are often empathetic, insightful people who have therapeutic personal qualities, are able to name what is wrong, and innately use techniques of therapy skillfully. With a little training and social sanction they could also raise patient expectations to get well. When I made the suggestion in print previously that such individuals could be used as psychotherapists[7] I received many confirmatory letters in reply, one of which read as follows:

". . . I am one of those who without a degree or any conscious effort seem to attract the troubled, the lonely, the drinker, the ex-convict, the handicapped, and others. . . . I term the disease the 'you know' symptom. People who only want someone to listen, and consequently emphasize every sentence with a 'you know.' "

There are many people in Western culture with the "you know" syndrome. It is time that we utilized our knowledge and provided them with therapists.

Implications for Subcultural Psychotherapists

Psychotherapists working within a subculture should first of all be free to develop their own job description. The functions of psychotherapists vary across cultures, and the job expectations of the dominant culture should not be imposed on the subculture. For instance, most psychotherapists in Western cultures confine their functions to seeing mentally ill patients in their office. This is the job expectation of the culture. A psychotherapist in a subculture, however, may deem it appropriate to include a greater degree of religious, political, or judicial function in his job. Moreover, the arguments given above for community control certainly apply to the services given by psychotherapists in subcultures.

The relationship between psychotherapists in the dominant culture and the subculture should be one of cooperation, coordination of services, and mutual referral where appropriate. An example of this is "root workers" who do psychotherapy within the subculture of rural Black America. Using a combination of elements derived from Haitian voodoo and fundamentalistic Protestant religion, they treat patients with many kinds of symptoms who believe they have been hexed. Good "root workers" are highly respected and charge low fees. Although almost totally ignored by therapists in the dominant American culture, the few "root workers" who have been used have been so successfully. For instance, an internist at a large northern medical center used "root workers" to bring severely disturbed psychiatric cases on whom the "working of roots" failed to bring about a cure.[8] In fact, it would seem reasonable to expect that all community mental health centers whose constituencies include rural Black Americans should have a working relationship with the local "root workers" and may even have one on the permanent staff.

An example of an exciting effort in the direction of cooperation with subcultural psychotherapists is occurring at the Neighborhood Medical Care Demonstration, an O.E.O. Health Center in the South Bronx. There anthropologists on the medical team have identified the herbalists, faith healers, and mediums in the Puerto Rican community being served.[9] Simultaneously a medical student working with the team compiled a pharmacopoeia of herbs used by the Puerto Rican indigenous therapists.[10]

It has been shown that up to two-thirds of Puerto Ricans believe in spiritualism, and that these spirits can be influenced and manipulated by the intervention of a skilled medium.[11] Therefore it seems logical to cooperate with these therapists. The first such referral in the South Bronx took place recently when arrangements were made for a medium to treat a Puerto Rican woman diagnosed with chronic undifferentiated schizophrenia who was hospitalized at Bronx State Hospital. Since the hospital staff found it difficult to carry out the medium's orders the patient was transferred to the medium's home for two weeks of further treatment. The patient improved slightly.[12] More such efforts at cooperation are needed with the necessity of simultaneous close evaluation.

Another subculture where indigenous psychotherapists can and should be used is that of the American Indian. In early 1970 there were less than 20 Western psychotherapists (psychiatrists and clinical psychologists) providing mental health services for 400,000 Indians, a ratio of approximately one therapist for every 20,000 people. By contrast among one group of Indians, the Apaches, there was a ratio of one Apache shaman for every 100 people.[13] Clearly manpower considerations point toward the utilization of these indigenous therapists. Moreover the need for mental health services is acute if the extraordinarily high Indian suicide rate is an indicator.[14]

An exciting beginning in using more Indian therapists occurred in 1969 with the federal funding of training for 12 Navaho medicine men.[15] These therapists will be trained for a three-year period by the older medicine men who are rapidly dying out, having been disparaged and discredited by Western therapists. The efficacy of the Indian therapists can perhaps be best summed up by psychiatrist Alexander Leighton:

> "If an Indian is told to take digitalis every day he will probably munch a few tablets and then forget about them. If he is told that this green medicine comes from the leaves of the foxglove, that his body must never be without it any more than his mind without a good song, and that he must take it every morning of his life when the first brightness of the day is in the east, one stands a much better chance of having the instructions carried out."[16]

Even this valuable program for Navaho medicine men is done apologetically however. An official summary of the project reads: "This program provides mental health relevant manpower for that proportion of the Navaho Nation still nonlingual [sic] and unable to benefit from Anglo forms of therapy."[17] The implication is that if they don't speak English then Navahos are considered "nonlingual"; alternatively they are the first tribe of mutes ever known. And the implication of the "unable to benefit" clause is clearly that when Navahos become more like us, more civilized or whatever, then they won't need the services of a medicine man. This ethnocentrism permeates even the best attempts to promote utilization of subcultural psychotherapists.

Implications for Psychotherapists in Developing Countries

There is no shortage of mental health problems in developing countries. Urbanization, industrialization, familial disorganization, and overpopulation combine with rising expectations of the people to produce frustration and often chaos. Psychotherapists to meet these conditions are needed in large numbers.

Even if it were desirable (which it is not), there is no possibility that Western psychotherapists could even begin to meet this need. The handful of Western or Western-trained therapists in these countries at present must be used administratively. What is clear, however, is that these countries have an extensive system of indigenous psychotherapists. Ethiopia and Sarawak, as described in chapter 6, have *zar* priests and *manangs* to do psychotherapy. Ghana has over 10,000 native therapists, approximately one for every 540 people.[18] India has between 150,000 and 200,000 *vaid* and *hakim* type therapists, serving the needs of four-fifths of the Indian population.[19] Ceylon has only 17 Western-trained psychiatrists but approximately 10,000 practitioners of ayurvedic medicine.[20] And a remote Japanese village of 380 people has no Western-trained therapists but a total of 15 shamans.[21]

It is also clear that people in these developing countries believe in and use their own therapists. And this is not confined simply to the lowest classes; in fact there is evidence that use of indigenous therapists in some developing countries is becoming most widespread among the newly emerging middle class. A study among Nigerian families in Ibadan indicated no difference in usage of native practitioners between families with children in secondary school and those without such children.[22] Two-thirds of patients in a Western hospital in Nigeria were found to be simultaneously receiving traditional therapy.[23] A study of Nigerian students in Britain found that over 90 percent of them showed evidence of traditional African beliefs in witchcraft.[24] And the people consulting native healers in Ghana were found to be 65 percent literate, and of these the majority were in white-collar jobs.[25]

Indigenous therapists in these countries, then, are believed in and used. And they are also thriving. In Field's excellent analysis of healing shrines in Ghana over half of the shrines studied had come into existence within the past 10 years.[26] The traditional healers have also shown a good ability to adapt themselves to the changing social structure and new jobs; three traditional Walbiri doctors among the Australian aborigines were found to be working regularly as a mechanic, a miner, and a carver.[27]

The problem is how to integrate these therapists and their techniques with existing medical services and the evolving social structure. An excellent illustration of how this can be done successfully is the use of "terpsichore trance therapy" (T.T.T.) in Brazil. This is an adaptation of traditional Brazilian trance and possession cults and is described as follows:

"Weekly therapy sessions lasting two hours take place in an auditorium of the State of Guanabara Telephone Workers Union. The technique is as follows. Middle and upper-middle class patients referred from the clinic are instructed to assemble in the auditorium wearing informal clothing. They are joined by an orchestra, the therapist, and his assistants. Patients stand shoulder to shoulder with their eyes closed, as samba-like music is played. They are told to think exclusively about their most pressing problems or the things they wish for the most. The 'mono-idealism' is intended to encourage trance induction. The orchestra plays slowly and softly at first and increases its pitch and tempo as the session proceeds. The same music is played at the start of each session. The therapist induces trance in each patient in turn, using a method derived from the Umbanda sect. The patient bends forward and the therapist causes him to rotate with increasing speed until he enters a trance, at which point he is slowed down and encouraged to dance to the rhythm of the music. He is then left to continue on his own while the therapist repeats the procedure with the next patient. Some patients are able, after a few sessions, to enter into a trance state by themselves, the stereotyped opening music acting as a signal stimulus to trance induction for these individuals. Although verbal communication is not encouraged in T.T.T., some use is made of creating lyrics to music drawn from Umbanda ritual. The lyrics focus on themes such as living more happily, solving problems, and other intensely personal and individualistic goals."[28]

The results of this modified form of group therapy are reported as very favorable, especially for patients with hysterical, neurotic, depressive, and psychosomatic problems. T.T.T. is employed most frequently as an adjunct to supportive psychotherapy and drugs. A detailed investigation of the method and results of this treatment is underway, and includes the use of measurements recorded by electrocardiographs and electro-encephalograms.

Another country where exciting attempts at integration have been occurring is India. The government there established a Central Institute of Research in Indigenous Systems of Medicine in 1952. And in a subsequent report the Health Survey and Planning Committee stated:

"An integration of Modern and *Ayurveda* is eminently desirable and all steps toward achieving that end should be promoted. Such integration should result in the development of a system of medical knowledge and practice based on all the best that is available in Modern Medicine and Ayurveda."[29]

The result has been that in ayurvedic medical schools much time is now devoted to studying modern medicine, and legislation has been introduced to set up a central council that would draft uniform standards of instruction and examination for practitioners of indigenous medicine.[30] Similarly in Ceylon there has recently been founded both a research center and a government medical college to train more indigenous practitioners.[31] These beginnings of integrating indigenous therapists should be encouraged, expanded, and closely evaluated.

chapter 10

Models
for Future Mental Services:
Eskimos
and Mexican-Americans

While it may be easy for us to agree that Zambia or Burma ought to incorporate indigenous therapists in their mental health services (agreement is very inexpensive at a distance of 10,000 miles), it is more difficult to see the implications for subcultures closer to us where agreement may cost status. For this reason I will sketch some possible models for future mental health services for Alaskan Eskimos and Mexican-Americans. I am aware that the very process of outlining such mental health services violates one of the most important implications in the previous chapter—community control of conceptualizing the services. The following outlines, then, do not represent the way such services *should* be, but rather one way they *might* be. I honestly do not know what mental health services would look like if they were turned over to members of these subcultures for planning. One thing is certain—it would be an interesting and exciting process to watch.

Mental Health Services for Alaskan Eskimos

There are about 26,000 Eskimos in Alaska. Combined with the 17,000 Indians and the 7,000 Aleuts they constitute the "native" population of the state, one-fourth of its total. They live at a subsistence-level, by hunting and fishing, spread through about 150 villages in the northern and western reaches close to the Bering Sea.

Like most subcultures in the United States the Eskimos have received less than their share of services. Until recently they have lacked legal representation and consequently have been exploited. The Bureau of Indian Affairs school system has been both irrelevant and colonialistic. Medical services have been better, with seven hospitals, eight health centers, and a system of native village health aides.[1]

Mental health services for Eskimos, however, have been less progressive than medical services. Until 1963, when a state psychiatric hospital was opened in Anchorage, any Eskimo who was thought to be sufficiently mentally disturbed to require hospitalization was sent by a general physician to a private hospital in Portland, Oregon. If an Eskimo from rural northern Alaska was not disturbed before being sent to Portland, he almost certainly was afterward. The first psychiatrist was assigned to the native health service in 1966. Prior to that, psychiatric consultations were done by psychiatrists in private practice in Anchorage. The two with whom I was personally acquainted in 1962 had little knowledge of Eskimo culture other than the misinformation and prejudices instilled by the mass media.

Up to the present, then, mental health services for Eskimos have just been drifting along in the wake of developments of American psychiatry, though keeping at a respectable distance. The present mental health team of a psychiatrist, psychologist, and social worker do a creditable job given a population of 50,000 inhabitants spread over an area one-fifth the size of the United States. Clearly innovations are in order. Following the line of thought developed in preceeding chapters, future mental health services for Eskimos might be based on the following three principles.

1. *Individual and group psychotherapy should be done by*

indigenous therapists. The indigenous therapists in Eskimo culture are shamans. Up until the turn of the century they exerted great power in Eskimo society. However, when the white whalers broke all the sacred tabus and still caught whales and when the missionaries arrived with their medicine the influence of the shamans began to wane. Today very little overt shamanism exists, though it has not died out completely. At Gambell, a small village of about 250 Eskimos on St. Lawrence Island, there were eight identifiable shamans in 1955, two of whom were in active practice.[2] Even where there are no shamans in actual practice those people who once were or are thought capable of being shamans are feared and respected.[3]

Even where they are dying out the concept of the shaman as a psychotherapist could be revived. Traditionally in the past a shaman was divinely selected through a "calling" to practice his profession; this could be used as the keynote in recruitment. Since both males and females were shamans there would be equal opportunity employment. A few shamans in the past were severely disturbed individuals; these would be screened out in the recruiting process. That many others were stable, intelligent, empathetic individuals is verified by Jane Murphy in her study of shamanism on St. Lawrence Island; in fact she says that the best shamans appeared to be exceptionally healthy. She concludes that "the full-fledged shaman who is capable of dealing with the crises of illness and death and of offering psychological support to the individuals taken into his spiritual custody displays qualities that can hardly be separated from those of leadership, responsibility, and power."[4] These are our indigenous therapists.

Once identified and recruited, the shaman would have to be trained. Training could in part be done by older shamans, but initially a Western psychotherapist should probably participate as well. This would be consonant with traditional apprenticing of a shaman to "old masters." In the past he also had to go through a five-day trial period of endurance before he became fully accredited; as part of his self-analysis a marathon group-therapy session might substitute for this.

His training would teach him what types of cases to treat (e.g., psychoneuroses, psychosomatic disorders, etc.) and which ones to refer (e.g., epilepsy). Practices like bloodletting would not be permitted, whereas the common technique of "brushing" the disease (e.g., a phobia) onto a nearby inanimate object would be utilized. Although the traditional arctic pharmacopoeia is rather sparse it does exist, and chlorpromazine and imipramine could be easily added. It may not be necessary to stock amulets and walrus urine in the hospital pharmacy, though the possibility exists (and makes as much sense as does stocking meprobamate. The end result would be a modern-day shaman, employed by the native health service to provide mental health services. Probably he should also have a Civil Service rating. He could serve a group of small villages or one larger village. If assigned to a village with a government hospital or health clinic he should have an office in that building in keeping with patient expectations. By taking mental health services back to the village level he should be able to maintain marginal psychiatric cases in their village and reduce the hospitalization rate markedly. Referrals could be made to him by other members of the health service, teachers, and community agencies.

Turning to group therapy, this is associated in Eskimo society with the *karigi*, a "men's house" that was the meeting place during the long, dark winter months. It is there that the shaman effected many of his cures while a large group watched. Especially important group activities were the Messenger Feast and the Spring Whaling Ceremony.

When trapping replaced sea-mammal hunting in the 1920s the *karigi* began to lose its importance. Instead of living together during the winter the Eskimos began living alone in distant cabins. Some of the functions of the *karigi* were slowly lost to the church, school, store, and movie theater, and in 1960 it was difficult to find a functioning *karigi* remaining (there were two at Point Hope being used as clubhouses).

The *karigi* provided a setting for group therapy, and was a highly integrative structure in the society.[5] In terms of mental health needs for Eskimo society it would be desirable to have such a structure today, and there is no reason why a modern-day *karigi* could not be built as part of newly developing villages (e.g., around government and oil installations). It might include the functions of clubhouse and gymnasium, but would also give the shaman-therapist a place to meet with groups from the community. For instance he might meet with groups of mothers to discuss traditional Eskimo child-rearing practices leading to friendliness and cooperation, the advantages of these practices over some Western methods, etc. He could also meet with groups like alcoholics and juvenile delinquents. Other group therapy sessions could be held at the Anchorage Hospital for hospitalized tuberculosis patients, and in the boarding schools as "T" groups.

2. *Cultural concepts of disease causation and classification should be used, modified where necessary to correspond with known facts.* The efficacy of the traditional shaman was dependent upon acceptance by the population of his concepts of causation. Similarly, if the new shaman-therapist described above is to be effective, the population must accept his more modern concepts. It is possible to modify these concepts to correspond with known scientific facts on the causes of mental illness yet keep them based within the Eskimo cultural system.

Eskimo culture has five principal theories of the causation of mental illness.[6] In the training of the new shaman-therapist and in the education of the population as a whole each of these must be discussed, modified, or refuted.

Breach of tabu. Traditionally Eskimos believed that mental illness could be produced if a person broke one of the many sacred tabus, most of which concern the hunting of sea mammals. For instance, one should never allow dogs to chew on the bones of the whale. The illness caused by this breach could be translated into more modern terms as the result of guilt for having done something one should not do. Abreaction and public confession would be just as therapeutic now as they were in the past.

Soul loss. The theory that illness was caused by one's soul wandering off (or being sneezed or frightened "out") was very prevalent. The soul could then be captured and held by evil spirits. Translated into psychiatric terms the evil spirits could be unconscious neurotic conflicts which hold the soul; release would come when these conflicts were resolved.

Object intrusion. The idea that a physical object had intruded to cause disease would have to be refuted, but it is a short step toward seeing the "object" as an undesirable or unpermissable thought (e.g., a compulsion to steal). This thought could then be extruded or expelled by the shaman-therapist.

Sorcery. The idea of sorcery and witchcraft would have to be modified considerably. First of all there would no longer be any evil shamans; all shaman-therapists would be regarded as benevolent. Therefore there would not be any shamans to do sorcery. Therapeutically, however, it might well be possible to use some of the "homework" assigned by traditional shamans to counteract sorcery to correspond with the "homework" of behavioral therapy to treat analagous problems of mental illness.

Spirit intrusion. This is the most common Eskimo explanation of psychosis. It could be modified as necessary to a chemical basis, e.g., the "spirit" would be thought of as some metabolic intruder in the nervous system.

Other concepts of causation could also be modified and used constructively. For instance the Eskimo theory of disease transmission could be adopted to show how a disturbed, rejecting mother can produce a disturbed child. Similarly the concept of preventive mental health and anticipatory guidance is inherent in the Eskimo idea of a disease being impotent if it encounters an "immunized system" like that of the shaman. Many beliefs of course would have to be rejected altogether (e.g., that epilepsy is caused by the spirit of a fox), and the appropriate theory substituted (e.g., an abnormal electrical discharge in the brain caused by damage at birth).

Before a shaman-therapist could be really effective there would have to be a general re-education of the population. This could be accomplished through a required course for all native health service personnel and teachers. Mass media would also be useful; even the northernmost village of Point Barrow now has television.

There are two areas where re-education would not be necessary but rather a reinforcement of already existing beliefs would be sufficient. In both of these areas Eskimo cultural beliefs can be said to be ahead of Western ideas. The first is tolerance of deviant behavior, the individual not being ostracized as "crazy" but being accepted only as "different." The other is the continuity of the spectrum of physical to mental illness. It makes absolutely no sense to Eskimos to treat tuberculosis in Anchorage but send a schizophrenic to Oregon. Any dichotomy between physical and mental illness has been introduced by Western influence. It is only within the past few years that the psychiatric ward has been returning to the general hospital in the United States. In planning services for Eskimos there should be no dichotomy, with the psychiatric patients hospitalized in the general hospitals wherever possible and the shaman-therapist working out of an office in the same hospital. He would simply be part of the medical team.

3. *Non-Eskimo psychotherapists should be used for primary, not secondary and tertiary, prevention.* Discussed in theory for many years, the principles of preventive psychiatry have recently been codified and tentatively explored in several pilot programs.[7] Primary prevention is an attempt to reduce the number of cases of mental illness that develop, both by strengthening the individual's coping strategies and by influencing environmental factors that may be operating to produce or encourage mental illness. Secondary prevention, on the other hand, aims at early case finding and treatment of already existing cases of illness. Finally, tertiary prevention attempts to rehabilitate cases who have been treated and return them to society.

It seems reasonable to assume that some non-Eskimo psychotherapists will be included in Eskimo mental health services at least for the immediate future. They will be needed at a minimum to effect the transition of the services to Eskimo therapists. Based on the principles in part one of this book, it is logical to use these non-Eskimo therapists who are employed for primary rather than secondary and tertiary prevention. This is because primary prevention involves less direct patient contact (where Eskimo psychotherapists would do better) and also because primary prevention often includes dealing with other organizations within the established framework of services. Non-Eskimo therapists may be more effective in dealings with these organizations initially, though Eskimo therapists should replace them as quickly as possible. There has been a trend in Alaska toward using the present lone psychiatrist, psychologist, and social worker for primary prevention in this manner; it should be extended even further.

A plan for using non-Eskimo therapists for primary prevention might encompass the following activities.

Enhancing individual coping strategies: Such a therapist, when sent to the Bureau of Indian Affairs boarding school at Mt. Edgecumbe, would not see disturbed children but rather would spend his time giving anticipatory guidance seminars to the newly arrived students. He would emphasize the psychological problems that they may expect being a thousand miles from home, in a different climate, and so forth. Similarly he might spend his time with secondary-school teachers developing a course on the effects of rapid cultural change.

Environmental manipulation toward mental health: In any culture at any given time there are certain environmental factors operating to encourage mental health and others operating to produce mental illness. The identification of such factors has just begun. A non-Eskimo therapist engaged in primary prevention would spend time trying to identify these factors and to influence the planning forces to make appropriate changes.

For instance Chance has shown in his study of Kaktovik on Barter Island that stability of income is an important factor in minimizing Eskimo psychopathology.[8] Kaktovik contrasts sharply with a village like Gambell on St. Lawrence Island clined sharply "resulting in a keen sense of frustrated expectawhere the total village income tripled in three years, then detions."[9] The Eskimo economy in the twentieth century has fluctuated wildly as baleen, ivory, fox pelts, and government jobs have rapidly come and gone. A therapist trying to achieve primary prevention of mental illness would act as a consultant to planning agencies and would try to promote a stable economy, immune from the vicissitudes of ecological cycles, the whims of fashion, or the Cold War. Perhaps he would lobby for a guaranteed annual wage or negative income tax. His voice would be just one, and might be drowned out by the economists, educators, and social scientists, but at least it would be a voice raised in the name of mental health that is not now being raised.

The effects of rapid acculturation might be another environmental factor taken under study. In his study of Kaktovik, Chance identified some of the factors producing a relatively smooth cultural transition with little psychopathology in spite of rapid change. Other studies have shown how psychologically disastrous rapid cultural change can be when new goals are introduced but then made unattainable, e.g., when many Eskimo girls are trained for clerical jobs which then are not available. A therapist doing primary preventive psychiatry could be useful as a consultant in this area.

Training and continuing education of shaman-therapists: It is the non-Eskimo therapist who would have to institute the program described under (1) and (2) above. Doctors, nurses, administrators, teachers, and the indigenous therapists themselves would all need education. Presumably it would be difficult to find the professional manpower to do this part of the job alone, and for that reason (as well as the fact that social psychiatrists have no exclusive claim on the behavioral science market) professionals other than psychiatrists can and should be used. Ideally the professionals to do primary preventive psychiatry should be an interdisciplinary team including anthropologists, sociologists, psychologists, and community organizers as well as psychiatrists.

The recurring theme throughout this description of a hypothetical model for Eskimo mental health services has been the reactivation of elements found in the traditional culture. This does not mean that the services are designed to be technologically retrogressive—indeed, such a system would be progressive by Western standards. What it means is that the mental health services would be those of Eskimos, not those of psychiatrists from another culture. If created and run by Eskimos themselves, such services would promote dignity, a commodity in short supply in subcultures. The promotion of dignity itself is a step toward a better self-image and thus better mental health. The goal is for an Eskimo to be proud that he is an Eskimo.

Mental Health Services for Mexican-Americans

Eskimos, although technically an American subculture, are still sufficiently distant that the incorporation of their shamans within mental health services is not too threatening to Western therapists. No so with Mexican-Americans. There are five million of them in the United States and they are not distant. Radical new approaches to mental health services for them would be visible to all. It is to such approaches that we now turn.

It was emphasized in chapter eight that Mexican-Americans include a broad range of individuals in various stages of acculturation. For this reason their mental health facilities might well include a broad spectrum of services. At one end of the spectrum there would be Western-trained psychotherapists of Mexican-American background, at the other end *curanderos* would be employed. Mental health ombudsmen would certainly fit in. Mexican-Americans in all stages of acculturation would be able to find a therapist with whom they felt comfortable. Included on the staff of a mental health center employing large numbers of *curanderos* and other nonmedically trained therapists might be a consulting psychiatrist whose job would be specifically to screen patients for mental illness. (*Curanderos* will occasionally diagnose tuberculosis, for instance, as a form of *susto*.)

There would probably be few who would quarrel with the employment of mental health ombudsmen in these mental health services. It is a tragic waste of manpower for Mr. J. and Mrs. P., described previously, to work in jobs where their psychotherapeutic talents are not used. They should be able to do psychotherapy as a vocation, not just as an avocation. Their fears of losing status and credibility in the community if they joined official mental health services would be nullified in this case because the services would be set up and sanctioned by the community itself.

Not everybody would agree with the use of *curanderos* in these services, however. Oscar Lewis, for instance, says that "the *curanderos* . . . are prejudicial to the health of the people and are a definite impediment to the realization of national health programs."[10] If the mental health services are to be truly relevant for all Mexican-Americans, however, I believe that *curanderos* must be included. Their relationship with traditional Mexican-American culture, described in chapter eight, should make this apparent.[11]

Two of the major problems of using indigenous therapists would be religion and witchcraft. The indigenous therapist in Mexican-American culture is wedded to the first, which would produce confusion about the relation of medicine and religion. This might be solved by leaving it individually up to the indigenous therapist. Similarly *curanderos* are often associated with witchcraft in the minds of Anglos. As the prestige of being officialized accumulated on the *curandero*, however, this association would be successfully broken.

Family therapy would be one of the most common types of treatment offered by the therapists. This is in accordance with the importance of the Mexican-American nuclear family as well as with patient expectations. The family may participate in the treatment of individual members, often helping to define the goals of treatment. Therapists working with Mexican-Americans must realize that, contrary to Western culture, it is the patient's family and not the therapist who is the ultimate authority in cases of disagreement.[12] Couples therapy would also be compatible with the Mexican-American family structure, though the male-female roles referred to previously should be kept in mind. Sexual problems, for instance, should be brought up by the therapist only when clearly indicated; at risk is the dignity of the woman and the implied inadequacy of the man. Group therapy, on the other hand, is totally incompatible because of Mexican-American distrust of strangers and their tendency to project. Adolescent and child services would be compatible.

The mental health services should be centered in a building which will raise patient expectations, though they need not be confined there. Home visits by therapists may be indicated on occasion, especially when the problem concerns the whole family. Emergency and walk-in services should be the most common type offered. One-interview diagnosis and treatment—real crisis intervention—should be encouraged. Follow-up visits should be left on an as-needed basis rather than arranged at a scheduled time. This is compatible with the patient's expectations and the present-time orientation of the Mexican-American culture. Fees should be modest but should be charged. Being given charity is contrary to the Mexican-American value system.[13] Fee-for-service should be utilized rather than prepayment in light of the present-time orientation.[14] Evening and weekend hours are desirable since many Mexican-Americans are paid by the hour and so lose money when they take time off. Ideally all personnel should be bilingual; this is especially true of therapists because transitional Mexican-Americans often can express everything in English except feelings and personal matters.

All techniques from psychoanalytic techniques to herbs should ideally be available, though suggestion and confession will be used most frequently. Physical treatment should be used freely. Drugs, diets, massages, baths, heat treatments, breathing exercises, muscle relaxation techniques, and sleep treatment can all be used. When prescribing drugs they should be prescribed for either three or nine days when a short time interval is being considered, as this corresponds to the time interval used for folk medicines. Similarly, before breakfast is the time most medicine is taken. When taken more than once a day the prescription should be for the parts of the day, not every six hours, etc.[15] Environmental manipulation may also be employed by the therapist when indicated and for this reason a close liaison between the mental health services and community agencies would be desirable. As outlined previously the goals of therapy would be tailored for Mexican-American cultural values and would not necessarily be identical with those of Anglo culture.

Hospitalization of psychiatric patients should be avoided whenever possible. "Next to prison, the hospital is the most dreaded as a place of isolation in an impersonal and enigmatic world."[16] Hospitalization confronts the individual with isolation from the family and impairs his ability to meet family responsibilities. In addition there are practical problems like diet and often being unable to communicate.[17] Home care, halfway houses in the patient's neighborhood, day care, and night care are all alternatives to hospitalization. It has been shown that about two-thirds of hospitalized psychiatric patients can be kept in the community if day hospitals are available.[18]

Finally, preventive psychiatric services could be developed for Mexican-Americans, though such services, being future-time-oriented, would not have as much appeal as they do in Western psychiatry. For instance, parents could be taught to prevent *chipil*, the symptoms of rage and depression in the small child displaced by a new baby, by extra love and attention. Perhaps the best preventive services generally would be to assign an anthropologist and Mexican-Americans themselves to work with all planning agencies for Mexican-Americans. In this way all services could be made more relevant, and the population would be more healthy because of it.

The Mexican-American system of disease causation and classification provides a useful framework into which new beliefs from Anglo culture can be fitted as necessary. Fitting Anglo theories into the Mexican-American framework reaffirms traditional beliefs and values. The idea of natural causes (e.g., a bolus of food in the stomach as a cause of *empacho*) could be extended to include biochemical theories of mental diseases. The concept of emotional causes offers a readymade entreé. For instance, the belief that *bilis* is caused by anger could simply be extended by saying that stomach ulcers and depression are also caused by anger when it is turned inward. And environmental and biochemical causes of mental illness are both compatible with the Mexican-

American tendency to project the blame for the illness onto others rather than accepting the blame for it themselves.

Thus it is relatively easy to add Anglo theories to the traditional framework. Mexican-Americans can incorporate the two. As long as Anglo theories are not offered on an either-or basis (either accept my beliefs or keep your traditional ones), integration can be effected easily. In a village in northern Mexico the same vehicle is used to take some sick people to a nearby hospital and others to a *curandero*.[19] And a *curandera* herself terminated an interview by saying: "I have to go take a nap now. My doctor says I need plenty of rest, and I don't want to disobey his orders."[20]

Just as with the Eskimos, the recurring theme throughout the hypothetical plan for Mexican-Americans is fitting services into the traditional framework. This is a radically different approach than that of saying: "We have scientific medicine. You must discard your beliefs and accept ours." It is the difference between dignity and denigration. "Each victory of a traditional means of coping behavior is a validation of the worth of the Mexican-American way of life."[21]

Moreover, when created by Mexican-Americans within their own cultural framework the services will be utilized and be successful. The history of Anglo health services imposed on Mexican-Americans is a dreary one of underutilization and failures.[22] When the mental health services are created by, and belong to, the Mexican-Americans themselves, then they can be proud of them. Over the doorway of the mental health center may be written "Viva La Raza!"

chapter 11

Problems and Resistances: The Tarzan Mentality

There are formidable problems and resistances to be surmounted before witchdoctors and other indigenous psychotherapists can be fully incorporated into mental health services. The acute need for psychotherapeutic services in all cultures, however, demands that we find ways to solve the problems and meet the resistances. Most of these problems and resistances can be catalogued under three principle disclaimers: "But they are not scientists"; "But they are not professionals"; and "But they are not doctors."

But They Are Not Scientists!

The crux of this resistance resides in our ethnocentrism. It can be called the Tarzan mentality. It is our strong underlying belief that we Western psychotherapists practice science in our houses of steel and glass whereas therapists elsewhere practice magic in their houses of straw and grass. Witchdoctors are assumed to swing through the jungle on vines and live in a simple world where me-Tarzan, you-Jane suffices to cover most psychological eventualities.

The fallaciousness of this dichotomy has been pointed out. Psychotherapists in our culture and psychotherapists in other cultures practice on the same scientific—or prescientific—plane. We want to believe that the facts are otherwise so we try to make them such. We don't want to believe that our techniques are not scientific. We look in the mirror and pretend we see a monster that isn't us; once labeled the monster becomes fearsome, primitive, and a convenient counterpoint for our own self-image. Compounding the Tarzan mentality is our Judeo-Christian heritage and the belief that Western culture represents The Chosen People. We believe that we are really the end-stage of evolution. We are secretly skeptical not only of Copernicus' claims that the sun doesn't revolve around the Earth; we wonder also if it doesn't revolve around Western cultures. All the rest of the world is darkness.

A corollary argument against promoting and integrating psychotherapists in non-Western cultures is that by doing so we promote belief in magic, retard acculturation, and even encourage stresses which increase mental illness. An observer in Africa states it thus:

> The activities and theories of these traditional healers is perhaps today the principal agent for reinforcing and perpetuating beliefs in witchcraft on the community; the persistence of which, together with the various taboos and complicated things to do and not to do to avoid trouble, probably constitutes a major psychological stress.[1]

I believe that this is not necessarily true. As was illustrated in chapter 10 it is possible to treat people within their own belief system and world-view without having to agree with it. In my conversations with witchdoctors I have frequently been asked whether I thought one of their beliefs was true or not. My reply has usually been: "I don't know whether it is true or not. In my culture we say that such a patient is reacting to his father's authority (or whatever). If your belief helps him get well that is the important thing."

The anti-acculturation argument also hides some seeds of ethnocentrism—it assumes that as people in other cultures become more acculturated they will automatically want to discard their own theories of causation and world-view and adopt Western concepts in their place. It is one of the great revelations of the latter half of the twentieth century for Western cultures that this is not always true.

Another way of posing the but-they-are-not-scientists resistance is to argue that psychiatry is where medicine and surgery were 100 years ago. But then medicine and surgery underwent a rapid scientific revolution to get to their present state. Just as you would not want to promote and accredit an indigenous surgeon to do brain surgery, so you should not promote and accredit an indigenous psychotherapist. The answer to this argument is that maybe Western psychiatry will undergo a similar scientific revolution and maybe it will not. Psychiatry is fundamentally different from medicine and surgery in many ways. And to argue against using indigenous psychotherapists on these grounds is equivalent to arguing that present surgeons really should not be allowed to practice because 50 years from now the field will be more complex and open only to supersurgeons.

An important segment of the response to the anti-science argument is more research and evaluation. Much more attention must be directed toward identifying the underlying principles. Psychotherapy is like toothpaste; too much energy is presently invested in efforts to distinguish and promote particular brands and not enough in looking at the process itself. What brings about symptom relief, behavior change, and complete personality change must be identified. Research and evaluation on psychotherapy programs must be given more than lip-service; they must be the *last* item cut from the budget rather than the first. Only then will psychotherapists in all cultures start to qualify as true scientists.

But They Are Not Professionals!

The stereotype of psychotherapists in other cultures as disturbed, psychotic, sexually deviant members of society has been examined in chapter 3. It was found to be without support; instead it appears that psychotherapists in all cultures encompass a broad segment of the personality spectrum. Thus the argument that by promoting and sanctioning indigenous psychotherapists we would be promoting and sanctioning quacks is simply not true.

There *is* a real danger, however, that such undesirable individuals might try to identify themselves as indigenous therapists and become part of the newly sanctioned group. It is the same constant danger that exists among psychotherapists in Western culture where self-made hypnotists, naturopaths, and scientologists demand official recognition. In the United States alone there are estimated to be 25,000 such quacks. The true indigenous therapists in other cultures are in danger of infiltration by quacks in exactly the same way as true psychotherapists are in Western culture.

The answer lies in selective sanction, accreditation, and tight control by a professional association of psychotherapists. Only those psychotherapists would be sanctioned who met the criteria set up by the association. At present this needs to be done not just for developing countries and subcultures, but for Western cultures as well. Only two states, for instance, have licensing laws for marriage counselors. The governing bodies for psychiatry, psychology, and social work need to coordinate their thinking on what psychotherapy is, who should do it, and with what kind of training. If the tenets of part one are true, then re-evaluation of the field of psychotherapy would produce criteria for accreditation that differs somewhat from that criteria presently in use, but this would be a step forward. The ultimate outcome would be a professional association of accredited psychotherapists in each culture.

In developing countries this needs to be done as soon as possible for charlatanism is on the rise. In the past, when developing countries were predominantly rural, a therapist was known in the community by his neighbors. Community pressure enforced professional standards on him, and an unethical therapist was simply ostracized. With urbanization, however, therapists can operate in the anonymity of the city and so the natural social checks against charlatinism are gone. The result has been a decline in prestige for native therapists in these countries. It has also made it difficult to attract competent new recruits to the psychotherapeutic profession.[2] The trend could be reversed by instituting a system of selective sanction, accreditation, and licensing.

This raises the question of what exactly *are* professionals.

What are we referring to when we say that we would be lowering the professional standards by sanctioning indigenous psychotherapists? The designation "professional" usually implies skill based upon training, accreditation by a governing body, integrity, ethical behavior, and status. Professional psychotherapists in Western cultures usually have all these things. If the system of sanction, accreditation, and licensing were carried out as outlined above, then psychotherapists in other cultures would be just as much professionals.

It may be argued that it would be difficult to regulate professional integrity and ethical behavior among witchdoctors and other indigenous psychotherapists. In fact it *would* be difficult but not impossible. It would be as difficult as it is to regulate these qualities among psychotherapists in Western cultures. Witchdoctors sometimes seduce their patients, but this is not unknown among psychiatrists. Witchdoctors sometimes charge exorbitant fees, but so do psychiatrists. Witchdoctors sometimes refuse to treat patients who cannot pay, or send them to other healers; so do psychiatrists. The maintenance of professional integrity and ethical behavior among psychotherapists in all cultures is a continuing problem. It cannot, however, be used as an argument to deny the rights of psychotherapists in other cultures to practice any more than it is so used in Western cultures.

Perhaps the largest impediment to recognizing other psychotherapists as professionals is that of status. This is clearly evident in programs in Western cultures in which untrained therapists have been used. Often present in these programs is a tendency for the professionals to see the "paraprofessionals" simply as clerks. It is like the relationship between a football player and a waterboy; because he has served so faithfully the waterboy is allowed to sit quietly in the locker room with the real players, but the two are never in danger of being confused.

This is illustrated by a questionnaire sent out by one state starting a training program for "mental health technicians." The questionnaire asked health departments, state hospitals, and school systems how such a person might be used in their organization. The most frequent replies were to help patients find living accommodations, arrange for transportation to the clinic, assist in referrals to occupational centers, check on broken appointments, and fill out forms and reports.[3] In short the "mental health technicians" were being asked to do all those jobs that the professionals do not like to do.

Another indicator of status is pay. In the programs referred to above the "paraprofessionals" are often underpaid. In 1969 the "paraprofessionals" constituted 22 percent of the staff of urban community mental health centers but received only 11 percent of the salaries. At suburban centers the analogous figures were 9 and 3 percent, at rural centers 33 and 18 percent.[4]

It is feared by professional psychotherapists in Western culture that an influx of new professionals will force their own salaries down. The fear is well founded. It is in fact the wide discrepancy between supply and demand for professional psychotherapists that has forced salaries up to their present inflated height. Certainly if a large number of therapists become available to meet the demand the salaries would go down. And newly emerging professional therapists have a disconcerting habit of asking older professionals exactly what they are doing to earn thirty-five dollars an hour.

Professional therapists are willing, then, to give indigenous psychotherapists "paraprofessional" rank but are not ready to consider them as true professionals. To do so would entail giving up some status which few people are willing to do voluntarily. We are willing to grant the less fortunate equal opportunity as long as they don't have equal opportunity for *our* job. We want others to have equal dignity as long as it is not drawn out of our account.

It is the dignity which brings about the real payoff. If we accredit indigenous therapists but relegate their pay and status to that of a janitor, then we must expect to get a janitor-level performance. Conversely if they are accorded the status of a professional then we will get a professional-level performance. The corollary of this is that the employers and professional association of psychotherapists have the right to expect a professional-level job from them. That means examinations, periodic evaluation, and professional integrity. This has too often been minimized in efforts to place "new careerists" in as many jobs as possible. A job that is make-work or that is without status is just another failure in an endless cycle of failures.

In developing countries the same issue of status is paramount. It is important to stress that accredited witchdoctors can be just as professional as accredited psychiatrists. There is slow realization presently occurring in much of the developing world that their culture and values are not inherently inferior to Western culture and values. It is the beginning of real dignity and self-esteem, the food without which a country can never develop. These countries can take as much pride in their psychotherapists as Western cultures take in theirs.

But They Are Not Doctors!

The third disclaimer echoed in opposition to the integration of witchdoctors and other indigenous therapists into mental health services is that they are not doctors. It is used principally by psychiatrists, for they themselves are doctors. Psychologists and the other types of Western psychotherapists who do not have an M.D. long ago realized that medical training was not necessary for a good psychotherapist.

It is not only in Western cultures that doctors oppose the accreditation of nonmedical therapists; in other cultures they are raising their voices in opposition as well. For instance, in response to the legislation introduced in India to license indigenous therapists the Medical Association of India set aside a day of protest. "On that day the physicians of India wore special lapel badges, participated in silent marches, and held public meetings to explain to the general public the danger of unqualified medical practice."[5]

The major point usually raised by doctors is that nonmedical therapists have no training with which to screen cases in obvious need of medical attention. Indigenous therapists, they say, try to treat infections, appendicitis, and pneumonia with the same techniques that they use for neurotic and psychosomatic disorders. When these patients finally do get to true medical facilities it is often too late. Such criticism is certainly not without foundation. All physicians who have ever worked in developing countries can document instances of native practitioners treating patients with obvious physical illness to the patient's detriment; I have observed it myself several times.

The answer to this criticism is threefold. First, many indigenous therapists in other cultures *do* already refer cases to medical facilities. They have learned, often the hard way, that it is to the detriment of their own reputation to treat cases with heart failure or pneumonia.[6] Abba Wolde Tensa, described in chapter 6, frequently referred cases to the local health center.

Second, I believe that indigenous therapists can be taught that tuberculous absesses are not caused by *zar* spirits and that pneumonia is not caused by a lost soul. They can be taught to not use techniques like bloodletting or putting a hot iron on an abdomen with acute pain in it. Because they get poor results in these cases they are *anxious* to learn where to send them and alternative methods of treating them.

Of course it must work both ways. Medical therapists can and should refer appropriate cases to indigenous therapists if they expect to get referrals. Since in most areas doctors are in deadly opposition to nonmedical therapists of all kinds this has been impossible in the past. The relationship between the two must be made amicable before mutual referrals are likely to take place.

Finally, a system for screening patients with medical problems could be instituted. Medical doctors in developing countries could establish an ongoing liaison with native practitioners in their area, making periodic visits to their place of work. Not only would potential medical problems be screened but psychoses due to organic factors, not uncommon in some developing countries, would be watched for. The relationship would clearly have to be between equals, and the medical doctor would have to be convinced that he had as much to learn from the native therapist as he had to teach him, which is true.

This raises the medical problem of the limits of competence. Exactly what should a nonmedical psychotherapist be allowed to do and what should be forbidden? It is a difficult problem and general guidelines can only be suggested. In the final analysis an answer will have to be worked out separately for each culture after assessing its medical resources and its indigenous therapists. First, nonmedical therapists can continue to treat the whole range of psychological, psychosomatic, personality, situational, and social problems that now constitute the bulk of their practice. Such problems also form the bulk of most medical practices; a general practitioner or internist in Western cultures spends only one-fourth to one-third of his time seeing patients who are really medically sick.

Second, it should be acknowledged by all concerned that some psychological problems are much more difficult to treat than others. There probably should be a gradation of indigenous therapists, some with more training, experience, and self-assessment who can be used for the more difficult cases. A third point is that purely medical problems (pneumonia, infections, etc.) should be treated only by the medical practitioner.

One thorny medical issue that always arises in such a discussion is that of medication. Should nonmedical therapists be allowed to prescribe and dispense medicine? Part of the answer is that they have already done so for a few thousand years. Many of the herbs and roots which they use have active ingredients, rauwolfia being one example. It would seem reasonable to expect them to continue this, refined and improved with the addition of Western medications. Tranquilizers and sedatives would then continue to play a role in the therapy of these practitioners. It is probable that doctors in the West have become inordinately possessive of the right to prescribe and that their interdictions should be re-evaluated.

The other facet of the medical resistance is that of leadership. Doctors are accustomed to being in charge and telling others on the medical team what to do. It is, in fact, one of the great agonies of contemporary Western medicine that doctors are having to learn that they are not necessarily the leaders of the medical team, but rather that they must share leadership with nurses, administrators, and other members of the team. Promoting nonmedical therapists can be expected to rekindle the ire of medical men not used to being challenged.[7]

Medicine can and will change. It can adapt itself to working with nonmedical therapists. Both these therapists and their techniques can be adopted and used to improve mental health services. The brew can be distilled, with the supernatant retained and the residue discarded. And this can be done despite the hoary traditions of medicine and psychiatry, feet firmly planted in the medieval guild system, voices echoing "You just can't do that!" with each footstep down the hall of innovation.

chapter 12

Conclusions:
Genus—Psychotherapist,
Species—Witchdoctor
and Psychiatrist

If prostitution is the oldest profession then psychotherapy must be the second oldest. The social and economic aspects of both have been known for centuries, but the technical details of what actually transpires behind the closed doors have been curiously relegated to the realm of whispers. Now that intercourse has been put under a microscope the least that psychotherapy can do is to follow suit.

It has been the purpose of this book to make a step in that direction. The focus has been on some of the relevant questions regarding psychotherapy. In an attempt to elicit fundamental principles a cross-cultural perspective has been utilized. The data have been presented in the form of tentative conclusions. These are not meant to produce closure, but rather to open up the questions for full debate.

Part one of the book analyzes the four components of psychotherapy: (1) a shared world-view that makes possible the naming process; (2) certain personal qualities of the therapist that appear to promote therapy; (3) patient expectations of getting well, which are increased by such things as the pilgrimage, the edifice complex, the therapist's belief in himself, special paraphernalia, and the therapist's reputation; and (4) the techniques of therapy. All appear to be universal components of psychotherapy, although each is colored by the specific culture in which it operates.

Part two of the book describes real psychotherapists and discusses the results they get. A *zar* priest in Ethiopia, a *manang* in Borneo, and a psychiatrist in the United States are compared and found to be remarkably similar. Data on the results obtained by psychotherapists all over the world corroborates this similarity when all four components of therapy are taken into consideration. Finally psychotherapists in a Mexican-American subculture are examined and found to further support the previous data.

The final part of the book examines the implications of this analysis of psychotherapists. The data would appear to support experimental and innovative approaches to the recruitment, selection, training, and accreditation of psychotherapists in all cultures. Some currently unused but potentially valuable manpower resources are suggested. Future mental health services for Eskimos and Mexican-Americans are outlined as case illustration of these implications. And the many problems and resistances to such innovations are described.

In summary, the data have revealed the genus of psychotherapist, of universal distribution, and the species of witchdoctors and psychiatrists. Since these two species are simply shorthand for the many individuals who do psychotherapy in Western cultures and other cultures respectively, it would seem that the next step is further description of the subspecies under each of the species. More work is also clearly needed on the relationship of each species to its culture.

Finally, and most importantly, the book is an appeal for open minds and hard data. It asks that we put aside our ethnocentrism and look carefully at both witchdoctors and psychiatrists. The world has become too small to accommodate arrogance. The attitude that is needed is well exemplified by a story Dr. Alexander Leighton, one of the senior men in American psychiatry, tells about himself. It occurred when he was interviewing a native healer in Nigeria:

On one occasion a healer said to me through an interpreter: "This man came here three months ago full of delusions and hallucinations: now he is free of them." I said, "What do these words 'hallucination' and 'delusion' mean, I don't understand?" I asked this question thinking, of course, of the problems of cultural relativity in a culture where practices such as witchcraft, which in the West would be considered delusional, are accepted. The native healer scratched his head and looked a bit puzzled at this question and then he said: "Well, when this man came here he was standing right where you see him now and he thought he was in Abeokuta" (which is about thirty miles away), "he thought I was his uncle and he thought God was speaking to him from the clouds. Now I don't know what you call that in the United States, but here we consider that these are hallucinations and delusions!"[1]

Notes

Chapter 1: Introduction

1. Y. Sasaki, "Psychiatric Study of the Shaman in Japan," in W. Caudill and T. Lin, eds., *Mental Health Research in Asia and the Pacific* (Honolulu: East-West Center Press, 1969). Another effort at generalization that failed was Loeb's distinction between seers as "noninspirational" medicine men, and shamans, who were supposed to be "inspirational." Loeb hypothesized that seers were older types and that shamans were newer types and confined to "higher cultures." In fact most cultures have both types. See E. Loeb, "Shaman and Seer," *American Anthropologist,* xxxi (1929), 61–84.

2. W. Z. Parks, "Paviotso Shamanism," *American Anthropologist,* xxxvi (1934), 98–113

3. See "Healer Offers Unique Brand of Psychotherapy," *Medical World News,* September 29, 1967, pp. 36–37, and F. Jahoda, "Traditional Healers and Other Institutions Concerned with Mental Illness in Ghana," *International Journal of Social Psychiatry,* vii, 4 (1961), 245–268.

4. A. Zempleni, "Traditional Interpretation and Therapy of Mental

Disorder Among the Wolof and the Lebou of Senegal," *Transcultural Psychiatric Research*, vi (1969), 69–74.

5. G. P. Murdock, "Tenino Shamanism," *Ethnology*, iv (1965), 165–171.

6. A. B. Bergman, S. W. Dassel, and R. J. Wedgewood, "Time-Motion Study of Practicing Pediatricians," *Pediatrics*, xxxviii, 2 (1966), 254–263.

7. A. B. Bergman, J. L. Probstfield, and R. J. Wedgewood, "Task Identification in Pediatric Practice," *American Journal of Diseases of Children*, cxviii (1969), 459–468.

8. H. K. Silver, L. C. Ford, and L. R. Day, "The Pediatric Nurse-Practitioner Program," *Journal of the American Medical Association*, cciv, 4 (1968), 298–302.

9. See E. A. Stead, "Training and Use of Paramedical Personnel," *New England Journal of Medicine*, cclxxvii, 15 (1967), 800–801; H. B. Wise, E. F. Torrey, A. McDade, G. Perry, and H. Bograd, "The Family Health Worker," *American Journal of Public Health*, lviii, 10 (1968), 1828–1838; and T. J. Harrison, "Training for Village Health Aides in the Kotzebue Area of Alaska," *Public Health Reports* lxxx, 7 (1965), 565–572.

10. For the full dismal picture, see G. W. Albee, "Myths, Models, and Manpower," *Mental Hygiene*, lii, 2 (1968), 168–180.

11. Among the very few general works on therapists are those by J. L. Maddox *The Medicine Man: A Sociological Study of the Character and Evolution of Shamanism* (New York: Macmillan, 1923), M. Eliade *Shamanism: Archaic Techniques of Ecstasy*, trans. W. R. Trask (New York: Pantheon, 1964), C. M. Edsman *Studies in Shamanism* (Stockholm: Almquist and Weksell, 1967), and A. Kiev (editor) *Magic, Faith, and Healing* (New York: The Free Press, 1964).

12. Cross-cultural psychiatry is also called trans-cultural psychiatry, ethnopsychiatry, and psychiatric anthropology. Most of the literature concerns concepts of etiology in various cultures, the incidence of specific diseases or of mental illness in general, how symptoms are related to the culture, culture-bound syndromes, acculturation, child-rearing patterns, and research methodology. There are comparatively few accounts of treatment methods and the therapists themselves.

13. A. Kiev, "Prescientific Psychiatry," in S. Arieti, ed., *American Handbook of Psychiatry*, iii (New York: Basic Books, 1966).

14. F. C. Redlich and D. X. Freedman, *The Theory and Practice of Psychiatry* (New York: Basic Books, 1966), p. 271.

15. *Ibid.*, p. 272.

16. In an interesting parallel, anthropologist A. I. Hallowell examines "primitive" religion as a rational, empirical system and finds that it is no less empirical than our own. See A. I. Hallowell, "Some Empirical Aspects of Northern Salteaux Religion," *American Anthropologist*, xxxvi (1934), 389–405.

17. D. Hill, *Magic and Superstition* (New York: Hamlyn Publishing, 1968).

18. Two good examples of this are E. Berne, "The Cultural Problem: Psychopathology in Tahiti," *American Journal of Psychiatry*, cxvi (1960), 1076–1081, and W. Bolman, "Cross-Cultural Psychotherapy," *American Journal of Psychiatry*, cxxiv, 9 (1968), 1237–1244.

Chapter 2

1. C. Levi-Strauss, *Structural Anthropology* (New York: Basic Books, 1963).

2. *Ibid.*, p. 193.

3. G. M. Carstairs, "Medicine and Faith in Rural Rajasthan," in B. D. Paul, ed., *Health, Culture and Community* (New York: Russell Sage Foundation, 1955), p. 120.

4. W. M. Mendel, "The Non-specifics of Psychotherapy," *International Journal of Psychiatry*, v, No. 5 (1960), 400–402.

5. H. Ezriel, "Experimentation within the Psychoanalytic Session," *British Journal of Philosophy and Science*, vii (1965), 25. Quoted by W. M. Mendel, *op. cit.*

6. R. Benedict, *Patterns of Culture* (New York: Houghton Mifflin, 1934).

7. P. J. Pelto, "Psychological Anthropology," in B. J. Siegel and A. R. Beals, eds., *Biennial Review of Anthropology* (Stanford: Stanford University Press, 1967), pp. 140–208.

8. G. W. Allport and T. F. Pettigrew, "Cultural Influences on the Perception of Movement: The Trapezoidal Illusion among the Zulus," *Journal of Abnormal Psychology*, lv, No. 1 (1957), 104–113; and M. H. Segall, D. T. Campbell, and M. J. Herskovits, *The Influence of Culture on Visual Perception* (Indianapolis: The Bobbs-Merrill Company, 1966).

9. A. K. Romney and R. G. D'Andrade, eds., "Transcultural Studies in Cognition," *American Anthropologist*, lxvi, No. 3 (Special Edition) (1964).

10. B. L. Whorf, "Science and Linguistics," in J. B. Carroll, ed.,

Language, Thought and Reality (Cambridge: The Technology Press of Massachusetts Institute of Technology, 1957).

11. R. W. Brown and E. Lenneberg, "A Study in Language and Cognition," *Journal of Abnormal and Social Psychology*, XLIX (1954), 454–462.

12. F. Boas, "On Grammatical Categories," in D. Hymes, *Language in Culture and Society* (New York: Harper and Row, 1964).

13. For another example of this, see C. O. Frake, "The Diagnosis of Disease Among the Subanun of Mindanao," *American Anthropologist*, LXIII (1961), 113–132.

14. H. Conklin, "Hanunoo Color Categories," *Southwest Journal of Anthropology*, XI (Winter, 1955), 339–344.

15. Personal communication, R. G. D'Andrade and E. R. Heider, 1969.

16. For a survey of these standards of sexual attractiveness, see C. S. Ford and F. A. Beach, *Patterns of Social Behavior* (New York: Harper, 1951).

17. See J. W. Whiting and I. L. Child, *Child Training and Personality: A Cross-Cultural Study* (New Haven: Yale University Press, 1953).

18. W. Goldschmidt in the Forward to C. Castaneda, *The Teachings of Don Juan: A Yaqui Way of Knowledge* (New York: Ballantine Books, 1969).

19. For a clear analysis of this see J. Henry, "The Inner Experience of Culture," *Psychiatry*, XIV (1951), 87–103.

20. For instance, see R. Prince, "Some Notes on Yoruba Native Doctors and Their Management of Mental Illness," in T. A. Lambo, ed., *First Pan-African Psychiatric Conference* (Ibadan, Nigeria: Government Printer, 1962).

21. M. P. Nisson and K. E. Schmidt, "Land-Dayak Concepts of Mental Illness," *Medical Journal of Malaya*, XXI, No. 4 (June, 1967), 352–357.

22. For example see K. Soddy, ed., *Identity: Mental Health and Value Systems* (London: Tavistock Publications, 1961).

23. G. Devereux, *Mohave Ethnopsychiatry and Suicide: The Psychiatric Knowledge and the Psychic Disturbance of an Indian Tribe* (Washington, D.C.: Bureau of American Ethnology Bulletin 175, Smithsonian Institution, 1961).

24. Castaneda, *op. cit.*

25. E. D. Wittkower, H. B. Murphy, J. Fried, and H. Ellenberger, "Cross-Cultural Inquiry into the Symptomatology of Schizophrenia," *Annals of the New York Academy of Sciences*, LXXXIV (1960), 854–863.

26. *Diagnostic and Statistical Manual of Mental Disorders*, Second Edition (Washington, D.C.: American Psychiatric Association, 1968).

27. For a good example see Nisson and Schmidt, *op. cit.*

28. W. Caudill and C. Schooler, "Symptom Patterns and Background Characteristics of Japanese Psychiatric Patients," *Transcultural Psychiatric Research*, v (October, 1968), 133–137.

29. D. L. Johnson and C. A. Johnson, "Totally Discouraged: A Depressive Syndrome of the Dakota Sioux," *Transcultural Psychiatric Research*, ii (October, 1965), 141–143.

30. B. Kaplan and D. Johnson, "The Social Meaning of Navaho Psychopathology and Psychotherapy," in A. Kiev, ed., *Magic, Faith and Healing* (New York: The Free Press, 1964).

31. H. Rin, "A Study of the Aetiology of Koro in Respect to the Chinese Concept of Illness," *International Journal of Social Psychiatry*, xi, No. 1 (1965), 7–13.

32. T. Kora, "Morita Therapy," *Transcultural Psychiatric Research*, ii (October, 1965), 101–103.

33. See G. Devereux, "Three Technical Problems in Psychotherapy of Plains Indians Patients," *American Journal of Psychotherapy*, v (1951), 411–423; and G. Devereux, *Reality and Dream: Psychotherapy of a Plains Indian* (New York: International Universities Press, 1950).

34. G. Seward, *Psychotherapy and Culture Conflict* (New York: The Ronald Press, 1956); T. Abel, "Cultural Patterns as They Affect Psychotherapeutic Procedures," *American Journal of Psychotherapy*, x (1956), 728–740; V. D. Sauna, "Socio-Cultural Aspects of Psychotherapy and Treatment: A Review of the Literature," in *Progress in Clinical Psychology* (New York: Grune and Stratton, 1966); M. M. Bishop and G. Winokur, "Cross-Cultural Psychotherapy," *Journal of Nervous and Mental Disease*, cxxiii (1956), 369–375; and J. A. Bustamente, "Importance of Cultural Patterns in Psychotherapy," *American Journal of Psychotherapy*, xi (1957), 803–812.

35. E. F. Torrey, F. J. Van Rheenen, and H. A. Katchadourian, "Problems of Foreign Students: An Overview," *Journal of the American College Health Association*, ixx, No. 2 (1970), 83–86; and F. J. Van Rheenen, E. F. Torrey, and H. A. Katchadourian, "Preventive Psychiatry: Group Work with Foreign Students," to be published.

36. O. Lewis, "The Culture of Poverty," *Scientific American*, ccxv, No. 1 (1966), 19–25.

37. See R. Riessman, J. Cohen, and A. Pearl, eds., *Mental Health of*

the Poor (New York: The Free Press, 1964); R. Prince, "Psychotherapy and the Chronically Poor: What Can We Learn from Primitive Psychotherapy," in J. Finney, ed., *Social Change, Poverty and Mental Health* (Lexington: University of Kentucky Press, 1968); A. B. Hollingshead and F. C. Redlich, *Social Class and Mental Illness* (New York: John Wiley and Sons, 1958); R. G. Hunt, "Social Class and Mental Illness: Some Implications for Clinical Theory and Practice," *American Journal of Psychiatry*, cxvi (June, 1960), 1065–1069; and Sauna, *op. cit.*

38. K. Davis, "Mental Hygiene and the Class Structure," *Psychiatry*, i (1938), 55–65.

39. O. R. Gursslin, R. C. Hunt, and J. L. Roach, "Social Class and the Mental Health Movement," in Riessman, Cohen, and Pearl, *op. cit.*, p. 63.

40. See, for example, H. A. Robinson, F. C. Redlich, and J. K. Myers, "Social Structure and Psychiatric Treatment," *American Journal of Orthopsychiatry*, xxiv, No. 2 (1954), 307–316.

41. Y. Sasaki, "Psychiatric Study of the Shaman in Japan," in W. Caudill and T. Lin, eds., *Mental Health Research in Asia and the Pacific* (Honolulu: East-West Center Press, 1969).

42. J. P. Hes, "The Changing Social Role of the Yemenite Mori," in Kiev, *op. cit.*, p. 371.

Chapter 3

1. See K. M. Colby, J. B. Watt, and J. P. Gilbert, "A Computer Method of Psychotherapy: Preliminary Communication," *Journal of Nervous and Mental Disease*, cxlii, No. 2 (1966), 148–152; K. M. Colby, "Computer Simulation of Neurotic Processes," in R. W. Stacey and B. Waxman, eds., *Computers in Biomedical Research* (New York: Academic Press, 1965); and K. M. Colby, "Computer Simulation of Change in Personal Belief Systems," *Behavioral Science*, xii, No. 3 (1967), 248–253.

2. H. F. Harlow, "The Nature of Love," *American Psychologist*, xiii (1958), 673–685; and H. F. Harlow, "Primary Affectional Patterns in Primates," *American Journal of Orthopsychiatry*, xxx (1960), 676–684.

3. Harlow, "The Nature of Love," *op. cit.*

4. For a further analysis, see G. G. Gardner, "The Psychotherapeutic Relationship," *Psychological Bulletin*, lxi (1964), 426–437; and especially S. K. Pande, "The Mystique of 'Western' Psycho-

therapy: An Eastern Interpretation," *Journal of Nervous and Mental Disease,* cxlvi, No. 6 (1968), 425–432.

5. T. S. Szasz, *The Ethics of Psychoanalysis* (New York: Basic Books, 1965), presents a clear exposition of the no-responsibility position.

6. G. Jahoda, "Traditional Healers and Other Institutions Concerned with Mental Illness in Ghana," *International Journal of Social Psychiatry,* vii, No. 4 (1961), 245–268; and J. Dawson, "Urbanization and Mental Health in a West African Community," in A. Kiev, ed., *Magic, Faith and Healing* (New York: The Free Press, 1964).

7. P. Singer, E. Araneta, and L. Aarons, "Integration of Indigenous Healing Practices of the Kali Cult with Western Modalities in British Guiana," *Transcultural Psychiatric Research,* iv (April, 1967), 65–67.

8. See, for example, J. F. Rock, "Contributions to the Shamanism of the Tibetan-Chinese Borderland," *Anthropos,* liv (1959), 796–818.

9. M. K. Opler, "Dream Analysis in Ute Indian Therapy," in M. K. Opler, ed., *Culture and Mental Health* (New York: The Macmillan Company, 1959).

10. R. Prince, "Indigenous Yoruba Psychiatry," in Kiev, *op. cit.*

11. T. A. Lambo, ed., *First Pan-African Psychiatric Conference* (Ibadan, Nigeria: Government Printer, 1962).

12. C. Lévi-Strauss, *Structural Anthropology* (New York: Basic Books, 1963), p. 170.

13. G. P. Murdock, "Tenino Shamanism," *Ethnology,* iv (1965), 165–171.

14. W. Z. Parks, "Paviotso Shamanism," *American Anthropologist,* xxxvi (1934), 98–113.

15. C. R. Rogers, "The Necessary and Sufficient Conditions of Therapeutic Personality Change," *Journal of Consulting Psychology,* xxi (1957), 95–103.

16. B. J. Betz, "Experiences in Research in Psychotherapy with Schizophrenic Patients," in H. Strupp and L. Luborsky, eds., *Research in Psychotherapy* (Washington, D.C.: American Psychological Association, 1962), pp. 41–60.

17. C. B. Truax and R. R. Carkhuff, *Toward Effective Counseling and Psychotherapy: Training and Practice* (Chicago: Aldine Publishing Company, 1962). The outpouring was such that during the period from 1961 to 1967 these researchers produced a total of 57 articles.

18. R. R. Carkhuff and C. B. Truax, "Training in Counseling and

Psychotherapy: An Evaluation of an Integrated Didactic and Experimental Approach," *Journal of Consulting Psychology,* xxix (1965), 333–336.

19. Truax and Carkhuff, *op. cit.*
20. *Ibid.*
21. D. N. Aspy, "A Study of Three Facilitative Conditions and Their Relationships to the Achievement of Third Grade Students," unpublished doctoral dissertation, University of Kentucky, 1965, summarized in Truax and Carkhuff, *op. cit.,* p. 116.
22. R. Dubos, *Man Adapting* (New Haven: Yale University Press, 1965), p. 408.
23. R. R. Holt and L. Luborsky, *Personality Patterns of Psychiatrists* (New York: Basic Books, 1958).
24. A. P. Goldstein, "Domains and Dilemmas," *International Journal of Psychiatry,* vii, No. 3 (1969), 128–134.
25. Rogers, *op. cit.*
26. R. Prince, "Some Notes on Yoruba Native Doctors and Their Management of Mental Illness," in Lambo, *op. cit.*
27. E. H. Erikson, *Observations on the Yoruk: Childhood and World Image* (Berkeley: University of California Publications on American Archaeology and Ethnology, 1943, p. 262. Quoted in S. H. Posinsky, "Yoruk Shamanism," *Psychiatric Quarterly,* xxxix (1965), 227–243.
28. J. M. Murphy, "Psychotherapeutic Aspects of Shamanism on St. Lawrence Island, Alaska," in Kiev, *op. cit.,* pp. 53–83.
29. Y. Sasaki, "Psychiatric Study of the Shaman in Japan," in W. Caudill and T. Lin, eds., *Mental Health Research in Asia and the Pacific* (Honolulu: East-West Center Press, 1969).
30. R. I. Levy, "Tahitian Folk Psychotherapy," *International Mental Health Research Newsletter,* ix, No. 4 (1967), 12–15. Abstracted in *Transcultural Psychiatric Research,* vi (April, 1969), 51–55.
31. M. Eliade, *Shamanism: Archaic Techniques of Ecstasy,* trans. W. R. Trask (New York: Pantheon, 1964).
32. D. Boghen and M. Boghen, "Medical Attitudes, Beliefs and Practices in Martinique," *Transcultural Psychiatric Research,* iii (April, 1966), 47–49.
33. See W. G. Jilek, "The Image of the African Medicine-Man," in N. Petrilowitsch, "Contributions to Comparative Psychiatry," *Bibliotheca Psychiatrica et Neurologica,* cxxxiii (1967), 165–178, for examples of this.
34. Holt and Luborsky, *op. cit.*
35. W. Freeman, "Psychiatrists Who Kill Themselves: A Study in Suicide," *American Journal of Psychiatry,* cxxiv, No. 6 (1967),

846–847; and P. H. Blachly, H. J. Osterud, and R. Josslin, "Suicide in Professional Groups," *New England Journal of Medicine*, CCLXVI, No. 23 (1963), 1278–1282.

36. W. Bogoras, *The Chukchee* (New York: American Museum of Natural History, 1907).

37. A. L. Kroeber, "Psychosis or Social Sanction," in *The Nature of Culture* (Chicago: University of Chicago Press, 1952), pp. 310–319. See also G. Devereux, "Dream Learning and Individual Ritual Differences in Mohave Shamanism," *American Anthropologist*, LIX (1957), 1036–1045; G. Devereux, "Shamans as Neurotics," *American Anthropologist*, LXIII (1961), 1088–1090; and J. Silverman, "Shamans and Acute Schizophrenia," *American Anthropologist*, LXIX, No. 1 (1967), 21–31.

38. L. B. Boyer, "Notes on the Personality Structure of a North American Indian Shaman," *Journal of Hillside Hospital*, X (January, 1961), 14–33.

39. L. B. Boyer, "Remarks on the Personality of Shamans," *Psychoanalytic Study of Society*, II (1961), 233–254.

40. L. B. Boyer, "Further Remarks Concerning Shamans and Shamanism," *The Israel Annals of Psychiatry and Related Disciplines*, II, No. 2 (1964), 235–257; and L. Boyer *et al.*, "Comparison of the Shamans and Pseudoshamans of the Apaches of the Mescalero Indian Reservation: A Rorschach Study," *Journal of Projective Techniques and Personality Assessment*, XXVIII (1964), 173–180.

41. See Sasaki, *op. cit.*; M. P. Nisson and K. E. Schmidt, "Land-Dayak Concepts of Mental Illness," *Medical Journal of Malaya*, XXI, No. 4 (June, 1967), 352–357; and Rock, *op. cit.*

42. For another example of this kind of cultural bias, see S. Fuchs, "Magic Healing Techniques Among the Balahis in Central India," in Kiev, *op. cit.*

43. Sasaki, *op. cit.*

44. Kroeber, *op. cit.*

45. Murphy, *op. cit.*, also mentions transvestites as occurring among Eskimo Shamans occasionally.

46. Opler, *op. cit.*, p. 98.

47. C. Kluckhohn and D. Leighton, *The Navaho* (Garden City, New York: Anchor Books, 1962), p. 309.

48. Eliade, *op. cit.*

49. Murdock, *op. cit.*

50. Eliade, *op. cit.*

51. Jilek, *op. cit.*; M. Gelfand, "Psychiatric Disorder as Recognized by the Shona," in Kiev, *op. cit.*; and R. H. Prince and E. D.

Wittkower, "The Care of the Mentally Ill in a Changing Culture (Nigeria)," *American Journal of Psychotherapy*, xviii, No. 4 (1964), 644–648.

52. J. E. Cawte and M. A. Kidson, "Australian Ethnopsychiatry: The Walbiri Doctor," *Medical Journal of Australia*, ii (1964), 977–983. See also C. H. Berndt, "The Role of Native Doctors in Aboriginal Australia," in Kiev, *op. cit.*

53. D. Handelman, "The Development of a Washo Shaman," *Ethnology*, vi (1967), 444–464; and J. H. Tenzel, "Shamanism and Concepts of Disease in a Mayan Indian Community," *Psychiatry*, xxxiii (1970), 372–380.

54. J. L. Maddox, *The Medicine Man: A Sociological Study of the Character and Evolution of Shamanism* (New York: Macmillan, 1923), p. 130.

55. Jilek, *op. cit.*

56. Maddox, *op. cit.*, p. 104.

57. Murphy, *op. cit.*, p. 66.

58. W. LaBarre, "Confession as Cathartic Therapy in American Indian Tribes," in Kiev, *op. cit.*, p. 39.

Chapter 4

1. S. Freud, *Collected Papers, Vol. I*, Second Edition (London: Hogarth Press, 1940), pp. 249–263.

2. J. D. Frank, *Persuasion and Healing* (Baltimore: Johns Hopkins Press, 1961), p. 60.

3. J. D. Frank, "The Role of Hope in Psychotherapy," *International Journal of Psychiatry*, v, No. 5 (May, 1968), 383–412.

4. Some of these are reviewed in A. P. Goldstein, *Therapist-Patient Expectancies in Psychotherapy* (New York: Pergamon Press, 1962).

5. H. H. Kelley, "The Effects of Expectations upon First Impressions of Persons," *American Psychologist*, iv (1949), 252. Cited in Goldstein, *op. cit.*

6. C. D. Egbert, G. E. Battit, C. E. Welch, and M. K. Bartlett, "Reduction of Postoperative Pain by Encouragement and Instruction of Patients," *New England Journal of Medicine*, cclxx, No. 16 (1964), 825–827. See also I. L. Janis, *Psychological Stress* (New York: John Wiley and Sons, 1958).

7. H. J. Friedman, "Patient-Expectancy and Symptom Reduction," *Archives of General Psychiatry*, viii (1963), 61–67.

8. E. H. Uhlenhuth and D. B. Duncan, "Subjective Change with Medical Student Therapists: Some Determinants of Change in

Psychoneurotic Outpatients," *Archives of General Psychiatry*, xviii (May, 1968), 532–540.

9. A. K. Shapiro, "The Placebo Effect in the History of Medical Treatment: Implications for Psychiatry," *American Journal of Psychiatry*, cxvi (1959), 298–304.

10. D. C. Jarvis, *Folk Medicine: A Vermont Doctor's Guide to Good Health* (New York: Henry Holt and Company, 1958).

11. L. H. Gliedman, E. H. Nash, S. D. Imber, A. R. Stone, and J. D. Frank, "Reduction of Symptoms by Pharmacologically Inert Substances and by Short-Term Psychotherapy," *American Medical Association Archives of Neurology and Psychiatry*, lxxix (1958), 345–351.

12. J. D. Frank, E. H. Nash, A. R. Stone, and S. D. Imber, "Immediate and Long-Term Symptomatic Course of Psychiatric Outpatients," *American Journal of Psychiatry*, cxx (1963), 429–439. Other studies of placebos are reviewed by Goldstein, *op. cit.*

13. Frank, *op. cit.*, p. 72.

14. See for example C. P. Kimball, "Psychologic Responses to Open Heart Surgery," *American Journal of Psychiatry*, cxxvi (1969), 348–359.

15. W. B. Cannon, "Voodoo Death," *American Anthropologist*, xliv (1942), 169–181. See also Frank, *op. cit.*

16. H. A. Wilmer, "Transference to a Medical Center," *California Medicine*, xcvi, No. 3 (1962), 173–180. I have borrowed this term from Wilmer's description of it.

17. Frank, Nash, Stone, and Imber, *op. cit.*

18. See, for instance, M. J. Field, *Search for Security: An Ethnopsychiatric Study of Rural Ghana* (Evanston, Illinois: Northwestern University Press, 1960).

19. Goldstein, *op. cit.*

20. M. Eliade, *Shamanism: Archaic Techniques of Ecstasy*, trans. W. R. Trask (New York: Pantheon, 1964). See also A. Kiev, "Primitive Holistic Medicine," *International Journal of Social Psychiatry*, viii, No. 1 (1962), 58–61.

21. J. L. Maddox, *The Medicine Man: A Sociological Study of the Character and Evolution of Shamanism* (New York: Macmillan, 1923).

22. *Ibid.*, p. 91.

23. W. LaBarre, "Confession as Cathartic Therapy in American Indian Tribes," in A. Kiev, ed., *Magic, Faith and Healing* (New York: The Free Press, 1964).

24. A. Zempleni, "Traditional Interpretation and Therapy of Mental Disorder Among the Wolof and the Lebou of Senegal," *Trans-*

cultural Psychiatric Research, vi (1969), 69–74, is an example.

25. See W. G. Jilek, "The Image of the African Medicine-Man," in N. Petrilowitsch, "Contributions to Comparative Psychiatry," *Bibliotheca Psychiatrica et Neurologica*, cxxxiii, No. 6 (1967), 165–178.

26. S. H. Posinsky, "Yoruk Shamanism," *Psychiatric Quarterly*, xxxix (1965), 227–243.

27. R. Prince, "Some Notes on Yoruba Native Doctors and Their Management of Mental Illness," in T. A. Lambo, ed., *First Pan-African Psychiatric Conference* (Ibadan, Nigeria: Government Printer, 1962).

28. For examples of the last see Eliade, *op. cit.*

29. Kiev, *Magic . . . op. cit.*, p. 15.

30. E. Holtved, "Eskimo Shamanism," in C. M. Edsman, ed., *Studies in Shamanism* (Stockholm: Almquist and Weksell, 1967), p. 28.

31. H. Sigerst, *History of Medicine, Vol. 1* (New York: Oxford University Press, 1951), p. 169.

32. M. K. Opler, "Dream Analysis in Ute Indian Therapy," in M. K. Opler, ed., *Culture and Mental Health* (New York: The Macmillan Company, 1959), p. 106.

33. Posinsky, *op. cit.*

34. Maddox, *op. cit.*, p. 104.

35. Prince, *op. cit.*

36. G. P. Murdock, "Tenino Shamanism," *Ethnology*, iv (1965), 165–171.

37. *Ibid.*

38. Maddox, *op. cit.*, p. 58.

39. T. A. Lambo, ed., *First Pan-African Psychiatric Conference* (Ibadan, Nigeria: Government Printer, 1962).

40. J. M. Murphy, "Psychotherapeutic Aspects of Shamanism on St. Lawrence Island, Alaska," in Kiev, *op. cit.*

41. J. F. Rock, "Contributions to the Shamanism of the Tibetan-Chinese Borderland," *Anthropos*, liv (1959), 796–818.

42. Prince, *op. cit.*, and R. Prince, A. Leighton, and R. May, "The Therapeutic Process in Cross-Cultural Perspective: A Symposium," *American Journal of Psychiatry*, cxxiv, No. 9 (March, 1968), 1171–1176.

Chapter 5

1. E. C. Del Pozo, "Empiricism and Magic in Aztec Pharmacology," in D. H. Efron, B. Holmstedt, and N. Kline, eds., *Ethnopharmacologic Search for Psychoactive Drugs* (Washington, D.C.:

Public Health Service Publication No. 1645, 1967). This book, and L. Lewin, *Phantastica: Narcotic and Stimulating Drugs* (New York: E. P. Dutton and Co., 1964), give a good overview of what is known in the field of ethnopharmacology, It is disappointingly little.

2. R. H. Prince, "The Use of Rauwolfia for the Treatment of Psychoses by Nigerian Native Doctors," *American Journal of Psychiatry*, cxviii (1960), 147–149.

3. R. H. Prince and E. D. Wittkower, "The Care of the Mentally Ill in a Changing Culture (Nigeria)," *American Journal of Psychotherapy*, xviii, No. 4 (1964), 644–648.

4. H. D. Lamson, *Social Pathology in China* (Shanghai: Commercial Press, 1928).

5. Efron, Holmstedt, and Kline, *op. cit.*

6. A. C. Pacheco e Silva, "A Lance Broken on Behalf of Transcultural Psychopharmacology," *International Journal of Psychiatry*, viii, No. 5 (1969), 828–830.

7. J. P. Hes, "The Changing Social Role of the Yemenite Mori," in A. Kiev, ed., *Magic, Faith and Healing* (New York: The Free Press, 1964).

8. R. Prince, "Indigenous Yoruba Psychiatry," in Kiev, *Magic . . . . op. cit.*

9. E. M. Schimmel, "The Physician as Pathogen," *Journal of Chronic Disease*, xvi (1963), 1–4; and E. M. Schimmel, "The Hazards of Hospitalization," *Annals of Internal Medicine*, lx, No. 1 (January, 1964), 100–110.

10. A. Kiev, *Curanderismo: Mexican-American Folk Psychiatry* (New York: The Free Press, 1968).

11. P. Kellaway, "The Part Played by Electric Fish in the Early History of Bioelectricity and Electrotherapy," *Bulletin of the History of Medicine*, xx (1946), 112–137.

12. *Ibid.*

13. U. Cerletti, "Old and New Information about Electro-Shock," *American Journal of Psychiatry*, cvii (1950), 87–94.

14. A. L. Hessin, "Treatment of the Mentally Ill by San Blas Indian Healers (Panama)." *Transcultural Psychiatric Research*, xv (October, 1963), 70.

15. A. Leighton and D. Leighton, "Elements of Psychotherapy in Navaho Religion," *Psychiatry*, iv (1941), 515–523.

16. J. Dawson, "Urbanization and Mental Health in a West African Community," in Kiev, *Magic . . . . op. cit.*

17. D. W. James, "Chinese Medicine," *The Lancet*, i (1955), 1068–1069.

18. J. Cernay, "Psychiatry in China," *Czechoslovenska Psychiatrie,* LIX, No. 4 (1963), 273–282; reported in *Transcultural Psychiatric Research* I (April, 1964), 34–36.

19. V. W. Turner, "An Ndembu Doctor in Practice," in Kiev, *Magic* . . . . *op. cit.* See also D. Metzger and G. Williams, "Tenejapa Medicine I: The Curer," *Southwestern Journal of Anthropology,* XIX (1963), 216–234.

20. G. Jahoda, "Traditional Healers and Other Institutions Concerned with Mental Illness in Ghana," *International Journal of Social Psychiatry,* VII, No. 4 (1961), 245–268.

21. J. G. Kennedy, "Nubian Zar Ceremonies as Psychotherapy," *Human Organization,* XXVI (1967), 185–194.

22. Hes, *op cit.;* A. Kiev, "Psychotherapy in Haitian Voodoo," *American Journal of Psychotherapy,* XVI (July, 1962), 469–476; and W. R. Holland and R. G. Tharp, "Highland Maya Psychotherapy," *American Anthropologist,* LXVI (February, 1964), 41–52.

23. T. Kora, "Morita Therapy," *Transcultural Psychiatric Research,* II (October, 1965), 101–103.

24. W. LaBarre, "Confession as Cathartic Therapy in American Indian Tribes," in Kiev, *Magic* . . . . *op. cit.*

25. For this distinction between confession as guilt-sharing, catharsis, and abreaction I am indebted to Dr. Peggy Golde, Department of Anthropology, Stanford University.

26. W. LaBarre, "Primitive Psychotherapy in Native American Cultures: Peyotism and Confession," *Journal of Abnormal and Social Psychology,* XLII (1947), 294–309. See also C. Castaneda, *The Teachings of Don Juan: A Yaqui Way of Knowledge* (New York: Ballantine Books, 1969), p. 152, for a nice illustration of peyote producing an abreaction with the person's father.

27. J. Gillin, "Magical Fright," *Psychiatry,* XI (November, 1948), 387–400.

28. Kiev, *Curanderismo, op. cit.* and A. J. Rubel, "The Epidemiology of a Folk Illness: Susto in Hispanic America," *Ethnology,* III (1964), 268–283.

29. E. F. Torrey, "The Zar Cult in Ethiopia," *International Journal of Social Psychiatry,* XIII (1967), 216–223; Dawson, *op. cit.;* and S. D. Messing, "Group Therapy and Social Status in the Zar Cult in Ethiopia," in M. K. Opler, ed., *Culture and Mental Health* (New York: The Macmillan Company, 1959), pp. 319–332.

30. J. D. Frank, *Persuasion and Healing* (Baltimore: Johns Hopkins Press, 1961).

31. M. G. Whisson, "Some Aspects of Functional Disorders among the Kenya Luo," in Kiev, *Magic . . . . op. cit.*

32. Prince, "Indigenous Yoruba Psychiatry," *op. cit.*

33. W. M. Hudson, ed., *The Healer of Los Olmos* (Dallas: Southern Methodist University Press, 1951) (Texas Folklore Society Publication No. 24).

34. M. E. Opler, "Some Points of Comparison and Contrast Between the Treatment of Functional Disorders by Apache Shamans and Modern Psychiatric Practice," *American Journal of Psychiatry,* xii (1963), 1371–1387.

35. Prince, "Indigenous Yoruba Psychiatry," *op. cit.*

36. T. A. Baasher, "Traditional Psychotherapeutic Practices in the Sudan," *Transcultural Psychiatric Research Review,* iv (October, 1967), 158–160.

37. Prince, "Indigenous Yoruba Psychiatry," *op. cit.*

38. Holland and Tharp, *op. cit.*

39. E. F. Torrey, "A Medical Survey of the Saysay People in the Blue Nile Gorge," *Ethiopian Medical Journal,* iv (July, 1966), 4–11.

40. J. L. McCartney, "Neuropsychiatry in China: A Preliminary Observation," *China Medical Journal,* xl (1926), 617–626.

41. J. Hallaji, "Hypnotherapeutic Techniques in a Central Asian Community," *International Journal of Clinical and Experimental Hypnosis.* Reported in *Transcultural Psychiatric Resarch,* i (October, 1964), 110–111.

42. D. Handelman, "The Development of a Washo Shaman," *Ethnology,* vi, No. 4 (1967), 444–464.

43. F. L. Marcuse, ed., *Hypnosis Throughout the World* (Springfield: Charles C Thomas, 1964).

44. M. Gill and M. Brenman, *Hypnosis and Related States: Psychoanalytic Studies of Regression* (New York: International Universities Press, 1961). See also K. Ravenscroft, "Voodoo Possession and Hypnosis," *International Journal of Clinical and Experimental Hynosis,* xiii, No. 3 (1965), 157–182, for an excellent analysis of Haitian *Voodoo* as a form of mass hypnosis.

45. R. G. D'Andrade, "Anthropological Studies of Dreams," in F. L. K. Hsu, *Psychological Anthropology* (Homewood, Illinois: Dorsey Press, 1961).

46. A. F. C. Wallace, "The Institutionalization of Cathartic and Control Strategies in Iroquois Religious Psychotherapy," in Opler, *Culture . . . . op. cit.*

47. A. F. C. Wallace, "Dreams and the Wishes of the Soul: A Type

of Psychoanalytic Theory Among Seventeenth Century Iroquois," *American Anthropologist,* LX (1958), 234–248.

48. O. Pfister, "Instinctive Psychoanalysis Among the Navahos," *Journal of Nervous and Mental Disease,* LXXVI (1932), 234–254.
49. M. K. Opler, "Dream Analysis in Ute Indian Therapy," in Opler, *Culture . . . . op. cit.*
50. G. Toffelmier and K. Luomala, "Dreams and Dream Interpretation of the Diegueño Indians of Southern California," *Psychoanalytic Quarterly,* II (1936), 195–225.
51. O. M. Ozturk, "Folk Treatment of Mental Illness in Turkey," in Kiev, *Magic . . . . op. cit.*
52. Jahoda, *op. cit.*
53. Dawson, *op. cit.*
54. K. Stewart, *Pygmies and Dream Giants* (London: Victor Gollancz Ltd., 1955).
55. E. Sangmuah, "The Healing (Spiritual) Therapy in Ghana," paper presented at the Second Pan-African Conference on Psychiatry, Dakar, 1968.
56. J. H. Masserman, "The Timeless Therapeutic Trinity," in Masserman, J. H. ed., *Current Psychiatric Therapies,* Vol. 7 (New York: Grune and Stratton, 1967), pp. 231–243.
57. See L. Krasner, "Studies of the Conditioning of Verbal Behavior," *Psychological Bulletin,* LV (1958), 148–170; and J. Greenspoon, "The Reinforcing Effect of Two Spoken Sounds on the Frequency of Two Responses," *American Journal of Psychology,* LXVIII (1955), 409–416.
58. T. A. Lambo, ed., *First Pan-African Psychiatric Conference* (Ibadan, Nigeria: Government Printer, 1962).
59. W. Mischel and F. Mischel, "Psychological Aspects of Spirit Possession," *American Anthropologist,* LX (1958), 249–260; E. Bourguignon, "The Theory of Spirit Possession," in M. Spiro, ed., *Context and Meaning in Cultural Anthropology* (New York: The Free Press, 1965); and especially several excellent chapters in R. Prince, ed., *Trance and Possession States* (Montreal: R. M. Bucke Memorial Society, 1968).
60. Mischel and Mischel, *op. cit.*
61. R. Prince, A. Leighton and R. May, "The Therapeutic Process in Cross-Cultural Perspective: A Symposium," *American Journal of Psychiatry,* CXXIV, No. 9 (March, 1968), 1171–1176.
62. E. Douyon, "Trance in Haitian Voodoo," *Transcultural Psychiatric Research,* II (October, 1965), 155–159. See also L. H. Rogler and A. B. Hollingshead, "The Puerto Rican Spiritualist as Psychiatrist," *American Journal of Sociology,* LXVII (1961), 17–21.

63. J. Belo, *Trance in Bali* (New York: Columbia University Press, 1960).

64. W. Sargant, "Witch Doctoring, Zar and Voodoo: Their Relation to Modern Psychiatric Treatments," *Transcultural Psychiatric Research*, v (October, 1968), 130–132.

65. J. L. Gibbs, "The Kpelle Moot: A Therapeutic Model for the Informal Settlement of Disputes," *Journal of Africa*, xxxiii, No. 1 (1963), 1–11.

66. Whisson, *op. cit.*

67. Dawson, *op. cit.*

68. Prince, "Indigenous Yoruba Psychiatry," *op. cit.*

69. Dawson, *op. cit.*

70. J. R. Fox, "Witchcraft and Clanship in Cochiti Therapy," in Kiev, *Magic* .... *op. cit.*

71. Turner, *op. cit.*

72. Kora, *op. cit.*

73. T. A. Lambo, "Patterns of Psychiatric Care in Developing African Countries," in Kiev, *Magic* .... *op. cit.* For other innovations in hospitalization in developing countries see J. E. Bell, *The Family in the Hospital: Lessons from Developing Countries* (Washington, D.C.: U.S. Government Printing Office, 1969).

74. For a good summary of the literature on modal personality and national character, see A. Inkeles and D. J. Levinson, "National Character: The Study of Modal Personality and Sociocultural Systems," in G. Lindzey, ed., *Handbook of Social Psychology* (Cambridge: Addison-Wesley, 1954), pp. 927–1020.

75. A. Kiev, "Primitive Therapy: A Cross-Cultural Study of the Relationship Between Child Training and Therapeutic Practices Related to Illness," in W. Muensterberger and S. Axelrod, eds., *Psychoanalytic Study of Society*, Vol. 1 (New York: International Universities Press, 1961), pp. 185–217.

76. Even within Western cultures there are different emphases on certain techniques in specific countries which are related to the values of those countries. See V. D. Sauna, "Socio-cultural Aspects of Psychotherapy and Treatment: A Review of the Literature," in *Progress in Clinical Psychology* (New York: Grune and Stratton, 1966); and M. Shepherd, "Comparative Psychiatric Treatment in Different Countries," in D. Richter, J. M. Tanner, Lord Taylor, and O. L. Zangwill, eds., *Aspects of Psychiatric Research* (London: Oxford University Press, 1962), pp. 110–124. See also S. K. Pande, "The Mystique of 'Western' Psychotherapy: An Eastern Interpretation," *Journal of Nervous and Mental Disease*, cxlvi, No. 6 (1968), 425–432, for a cogent analy-

sis of the relationship of Western psychotherapy to deficits in Western cultural values.

77. Prince, "Indigenous Yoruba Psychiatry," *op. cit.*

78. B. Kaplan and D. Johnson, "The Social Meaning of Navaho Psychopathology and Psychotherapy," in Kiev, *Magic* . . . . *op. cit.*, pp. 221–227.

79. S. Nishimaru, "Mental Climate and Eastern Psychotherapy," *Transcultural Psychiatric Research*, II (April, 1965), 24.

80. See Kora, *op. cit.* See also W. Caudill, "Observations on the Cultural Context of Japanese Psychiatry," in Opler, *Culture* . . . , *op. cit.* and Caudill in I. Galdston, ed., *Man's Image in Medicine and Anthropology* (New York: International Universities Press, 1963).

81. Wallace, "The Institutionalization . . ." *op. cit.*

82. Another aspect of this temporal dimension is the problem of acculturation. Ideas about treatment techniques change faster in acculturating societies than concepts about causation. The result is a society left with diseases whose cause is known but the treatment for which has been discredited. The stress can be reduced by adapting new treatment techniques to the existing ideas of causation. See Fox, *op. cit.* and also Chapter 10.

Chapter 6

1. E. F. Torrey, "The Zar Cult in Ethiopia," *International Journal of Social Psychiatry*, XIII, No. 3 (1967), 216–223.

2. H. M. Workineh, "Teaching of the Ethiopian Orthodox Church on Matters Related to Health and Disease," in E. F. Torrey, ed., *Introduction to Health and Health Education in Ethiopia* (Addis Ababa: Berhanena Selam Press, 1966). This priest was Director-General of His Imperial Majesty's private cabinet on Church Affairs.

3. R. Giel, Y. Gezahegn, and J. N. Van Luijk, "Faith-Healing and Spirit-Possession in Ghion, Ethiopia," *Transcultural Psychiatric Research*, V (1968), 64–66.

4. *Ibid.*

5. *Ibid.* The other was Dr. Tigani El Mahi, former Mental Health Advisor to the Eastern Mediterranean Regional Office of the World Health Organization.

6. See S. D. Messing, "Group Therapy and Social Status in the Zar Cult in Ethiopia," in M. K. Opler, ed., *Culture and Mental Health* (New York: The Macmillan Company, 1959), pp. 319–332, for a good description of this.

7. Giel, Gezahegn, and Van Luijk, *op. cit.*
8. D. Freeman, "Shaman and Incubus," *Psychoanalytic Study of Society*, IV (1967), 315–343.
9. K. E. Schmidt, "Folk Psychiatry in Sarawak: A Tentative System of Psychiatry of the Iban," in A. Kiev, ed., *Magic, Faith and Healing* (New York: The Free Press, 1964).
10. J. Perham, "Manangism in Borneo," *Journal of the Straits Branch of the Royal Asiatic Society* (Singapore, 1887), pp. 87–103.
11. W. Howell and D. J. S. Bailey, *A Sea Dyak Dictionary* (Singapore: American Mission Press, 1900).
12. Perham, *op. cit.*, p. 101.
13. *Ibid.* and Howell and Bailey, *op. cit.*
14. M. Eliade, *Shamanism: Archaic Techniques of Ecstasy*, trans. W. R. Trask (New York: Pantheon, 1964).
15. During my visit to Sarawak I unfortunately did not witness a healing ceremony, partly because everybody was busy burning their rice paddies for a new season. The following account is based on a case Digat had recently seen and that he described to me. It corresponds with healing ceremonies described to me by two other *manangs*, with those of Digat that Mr. Beavitt had observed in the past, and with accounts of Iban healing ceremonies in the missionary and anthropological literature dating back 75 years. There is remarkably little variation among these accounts.
16. See Freeman, *op. cit.*
17. For one of the rare ethnographic accounts of these interesting people. see H. Miner, "Body Ritual of the Nacirema," *American Anthropologist*, LVIII (1956), 503–507.

Chapter 7

1. M. K. Opler, "Dream Analysis in Ute Indian Therapy," in M. K. Opler, ed., *Culture and Mental Health* (New York: The Macmillan Company, 1959).
2. M. E. Opler, "Some Points of Comparison and Contrast Between the Treatment of Functional Disorders by Apache Shamans and Modern Psychiatric Practice," *American Journal of Psychiatry*, XCII (1936), 1371–1387.
3. S. H. Posinsky, "Yoruk Shamanism," *Psychiatric Quarterly*, XXXIX (1965), 227–243.
4. A. F. C. Wallace, "Dreams and the Wishes of the Soul: A Type of Psychoanalytic Theory Among Seventeenth Century Iroquois," *American Anthropologist*, LX (1958), 234–248.

5. J. Gillin, "Magical Fright," *Psychiatry*, xi (November, 1948), 387–400.
6. J. H. Tenzel, "Shamanism and Concepts of Disease in a Mayan Indian Community," *Psychiatry*, xxxiii (1970), 372–380.
7. A. Kiev, "Psychotherapy in Haitian Voodoo," *American Journal of Psychotherapy*, xvi (July, 1962), 469–476.
8. P. Singer. E. Araneta, and L. Aarons, "Integration of Indigenous Healing Practices of the Kali Cult with Western Psychiatric Modalities in British Guiana," *Transcultural Psychiatric Research*, iv (April, 1967), 65–67.
9. L. H. Rogler and A. B. Hollingshead, *Trapped: Families and Schizophrenia* (New York: John Wiley and Sons, 1965).
10. L. H. Rogler and A. B. Hollingshead, "The Puerto Rican Spiritualist as Psychiatrist," *American Journal of Sociology*, lxvii (1961), 17–21.
11. R. Prince, "Indigenous Yoruba Psychiatry," in A. Kiev, ed., *Magic, Faith and Healing* (New York: The Free Press, 1964).
12. R. Prince, A. Leighton, and R. May, "The Therapeutic Process in Cross-Cultural Perspective: A Symposium," *American Journal of Psychiatry*, cxxiv, No. 9 (March, 1968), 1171–1176.
13. T. A. Lambo, ed., *First Pan-African Psychiatric Conference* (Ibadan, Nigeria: Government Printer, 1962).
14. T. A. Lambo, "Patterns of Psychiatric Care in Developing African Countries," in Kiev, *op. cit.*, pp. 443–454.
15. "African Sees Gain for Mentally Ill," *New York Times*, March 24, 1968, p. 27.
16. *Ibid.*
17. G. Jahoda, "Traditional Healers and Other Institutions Concerned with Mental Illness in Ghana," *International Journal of Social Psychiatry*, vii, No. 4 (1961), 245–268.
18. S. K. Weinberg, "Mental Healing and Social Change in West Africa," *Social Problems*, ii, No. 3 (1964), 257–269.
19. M. J. Field, *Search for Security: An Ethnopsychiatric Study of Rural Ghana* (Evanston, Illinois: Northwestern University Press, 1960); and M. J. Field, "Witchcraft as a Primitive Interpretation of Mental Disorder," *Journal of Mental Science*, ci (1955), 826–833.
20. Lambo, *First Pan-African . . . op. cit.*
21. J. P. Lehman and H. M. Foté, "The Circle of the Prophet and the Sorcerer: Reflections on a Functional Hysterical Paralysis of a Thirteen-year-old Child," *Transcultural Psychiatric Research*, v (October, 1968), 165–168; and "Healer Offers Unique Brand of

Psychotherapy," *Medical World News*, September 29, 1967, pp. 36–37.

22. R. Wintrob and E. D. Wittkower, "Magic and Witchcraft in Liberia; Their Psychiatric Implications," *Transcultural Psychiatric Research, III* (October, 1966), 149–152.

23. W. G. Jilek, "The Image of the African Medicine-Man," in N. Petrilowitsch, "Contributions to Comparative Psychiatry," *Bibliotheca Psychiatrica et Neurologica*, CXXXIII, No. 6 (1967), 165–178.

24. N. S. Vahia, S. L. Vinekar, and D. R. Doongaji, "Some Ancient Indian Concepts in the Treatment of Psychiatric Disorders," *British Journal of Psychiatry*, CXII, No. 489 (1966), 1089–1096.

25. N. E. Miller, "Learning of Visceral and Glandular Responses," *Science*, CLXIII, No. 3866 (January 31, 1969), 434–445.

26. G. Myrdal, *Asian Drama*, Vol. 3 (New York: Pantheon, 1968), p. 1561.

27. N. C. Surya, K. P. Unnikrishnan, R. Shivathanuvan Thampi, K. Sathyavathi, and N. Sundararaj, "Ayurvedic Treatment in Mental Illness: A Report," *Transactions of All-India Institute of Mental Health*, v (Bangalore, 1965), 28–39.

28. G. Bermann, "China," in A. Kiev, ed., *Psychiatry in the Communist World* (New York: Science House, 1968).

29. D. W. James, "Chinese Medicine," *The Lancet*, I (1958), 1068–1069.

30. Bermann, *op. cit.*

31. S. Liu and S. Chi, "Using Mao Tse-Tung's Thoughts to Open Up a 'Forbidden Zone:' Curing Deaf-Mutes," *Peking Review*, XLVI (November 15, 1968), 14–17. See also C. Pu-yu, "To Be a Revolutionary Health Fighter Boundlessly Loyal to Chairman Mao," *Peking Review*, XXV (June 20, 1969), 7–9.

32. O. Von Riesemann, *Rachmaninoff's Recollections* (New York: The Macmillan Company, 1934), p. 112.

33. H. J. Eysenck, "The Effects of Psychotherapy: An Evaluation," *Journal of Consulting Psychology*, XVI (1952), 319–324.

34. E. E. Leavitt, "The Results of Psychotherapy with Children," *Journal of Consulting Psychology*, XXI (1957), 189–196.

35. For a general review of difficulties inherent in such a task, see A. E. Bergin, "The Effects of Psychotherapy: Negative Results Revisited," *Journal of Counseling Psychology*, X (1963), 244–255.

36. *Community Mental Health Center News*, I (Washington: Morris Associates, November, 1969), 3.

37. See for example H. Modlin and J. B. Taylor, "Professional Role

Development for Mental Health Tasks," *Archives of General Psychiatry*, xx (May, 1969), 524–527. My own experience with health aides is summarized in H. B. Wise, E. F. Torrey, A. McDade, G. Perry, and H. Bograd, "The Family Health Worker," *American Journal of Public Health*, LVIII, No. 10 (1968), 1828–1838.

38. R. Heine, ed., *The Student Physician as Psychotherapist* (Chicago: The University of Chicago Press, 1962).

39. E. H. Uhlenhuth and D. B. Duncan, "Subjective Change with Medical Student Therapists: Course of Relief in Psychoneurotic Outpatients," *Archives of General Psychiatry*, XVIII (April, 1968), 428–438.

40. W. Yeager, W. T. Sowder, and A. V. Hardy, "The Mental Health Worker: A New Public Health Professional," *American Journal of Public Health*, LII, No. 9 (1962), 1625–1630.

41. M. J. Rioch, "Pilot Projects in Training Mental Health Counselors," in E. L. Cowen, E. A. Gardner, and M. Zax, eds., *Emergent Approaches to Mental Health Problems* (New York: Appleton-Century-Crofts, 1967). See also M. J. Rioch, "Changing Concepts in the Training of Therapists," *Journal of Consulting Psychology*, xxx, No. 4 (1966), 290–292.

42. R. Sanders, "New Manpower for Mental Service," in Cowen, Gardner, and Zax, *op. cit.*

43. J. C. Beck, D. Kantor, and V. A. Gelineau, "Follow-up Study of Chronic Psychotic Patients 'Treated' by College Case-Aide Volunteers," *American Journal of Psychiatry*, CXX (1963), 269–271.

44. J. D. Holzberg, R. H. Knapp, and J. C. Turner, "College Students as Companions to the Mentally Ill," in Cowen, Gardner, and Zax, *op. cit.*

45. G. Goodman, "An Experiment with Companionship Therapy: College Students and Troubled Boys—Assumptions, Selection, and Design," *American Journal of Public Health*, LVII, No. 10 (October, 1967), 1772–1777; and J. R. Hilgard and U. S. Moore, "Affiliative Therapy with Young Adolescents," *Journal of the American Academy of Child Psychiatry*, VIII, No. 4 (1969), 577–605.

46. E. G. Poser, "The Effect of Therapists' Training on Group Therapeutic Outcome," *Journal of Consulting Psychology*, xxx, No. 4 (1966), 283–289.

47. F. E. Fiedler, "A Comparison of Therapeutic Relationships in Psychoanalytic, Non-Directive and Adlerian Therapy," *Journal of Consulting Psychology*, XIV (1950), 436–445.

48. P. J. Paulbaum, "Apprenticeship Revisited," *Archives of General Psychiatry*, XIII (1965), 304–309.

49. F. Riessman and E. Hallowitz, "The Neighborhood Service Center: An Innovation in Preventive Psychiatry," *American Journal of Psychiatry*, CXXIII, No. 11 (May, 1967), 1408–1413; M. Roman and M. S. Jacobson, "Progress Report: Training of Mental Health Aides" (Lincoln Hospital Mental Health Services, Bronx, New York, 1965) (Mimeographed.); H. B. Peck, S. R. Kaplan, and M. Roman, "Prevention Treatment, and Social Action: A Strategy of Intervention in a Disadvantaged Urban Area," *American Journal of Orthopsychiatry*, XXXVI (1966), 57–69; and E. Hallowitz and F. Riessman, "The Role of the Indigenous Nonprofessional in a Community Mental Health Neighborhood Service Center Program," Paper read at American Orthopsychiatry Association Meetings, San Francisco, April, 1966.

50. E. A. Gardner, "Indigenous Persons as Clinic Therapists in a Community Mental Health Center: Implications for New Careers," Paper read at meeting of the American Psychiatric Association, Boston, May, 1968.

51. B. G. Berenson and R. R. Carkhuff, eds., *Sources of Gain in Counseling and Psychotherapy* (New York: Holt, Rinehart and Winston, 1967); R. R. Carkhuff and C. B. Truax, "Training in Counseling and Psychotherapy: An Evaluation of an Integrated Didactic and Experimental Approach," *Journal of Consulting Psychology*, XXIX (1965), 333–336; and R. R. Carkhuff and C. B. Truax, "Lay Mental Health Counseling: The Effects of Lay Group Counseling," *Journal of Consulting Psychology*, XXIX (1965), 426.

52. R. B. Ellsworth, *Nonprofessionals in Psychiatric Rehabilitation* (New York: Appleton-Century-Crofts, 1968).

53. L. Appleby, "Evaluation of Treatment Methods for Chronic Schizophrenia," *Archives of General Psychiatry*, VIII (1963), 8–21.

54. W. M. Mendel and S. Rapport, "Outpatient Treatment for Chronic Schizophrenic Patients: Therapeutic Consequences of an Existential View," *Archives of General Psychiatry*, VIII (1963), 190–196.

55. W. F. Needham, H. White, and B. J. Fitzgerald, "A Patient-Therapist Program," *Hospital and Community Psychiatry*, XVII, No. 3 (March, 1966), 84–85. See also E. Pfeiffer, "Patients as Therapists," *American Journal of Psychiatry*, CXXIII, No. 11 (May, 1967), 1413–1418.

Chapter 8

1. W. R. Holland, "Mexican-American Medical Beliefs: Science or Magic?" *Arizona Medicine,* xx (May, 1963), 89–102.
2. These figures are all exclusive of a small satellite in southern Santa Clara County whose funding comes from a different source and whose statistics were not as available. Since it serves an area of only 3 percent of the population, it has not been included.
3. M. Karno and R. B. Edgerton, "Perception of Mental Illness in a Mexican-American Community," *Archives of General Psychiatry,* xx (1969), 233–238.
4. J. Yamamoto, Q. C. James, and N. Palley, "Cultural Problems in Psychiatric Therapy," *Archives of General Psychiatry,* xix (1968), 45–49.
5. E. G. Jaco, "Mental Health of the Spanish-Americans in Texas," in M. K. Opler (ed.), *Culture and Mental Health* (New York: The Macmillan Company, 1958), pp. 467–485.
6. *Ibid.*
7. R. Diaz-Guerrero, "Neurosis and the Mexican Family Structure," *American Journal of Psychiatry,* cxii (1955), 411–417.
8. Santa Clara County, Ad Hoc Comprehensive Mental Health Planning Committee for Santa Clara County, *Joint Venture in Mental Health 1968* (San Jose, California, 1968).
9. See, for example, A. B. Hollingshead and F. C. Redlich, *Social Class and Mental Illness* (New York: John Wiley and Sons, 1958).
10. See, for example, L. Tyhurst, "Displacement and Migration," *American Journal of Psychiatry,* cviii (1951), 561–568. See also T. S. Langner, "Psychophysiological Symptoms and the Status of Women in Two Mexican Communities," in J. M. Murphy and A. H. Leighton (eds.), *Approaches to Cross-Cultural Psychiatry* (Ithaca: Cornell University Press, 1965), pp. 360–392.
11. M. Karno, R. N. Ross, and R. A. Caper, "Mental Health Roles of Physicians in a Mexican-American Community," *Community Mental Health Journal,* v, No. 1 (1969), 62–69.
12. M. Karno, personal communication, 1969.
13. W. Madsen, *Society and Health in the Lower Rio Grande Valley* (Austin, Texas: Hogg Foundation for Mental Health, University of Texas, 1961).
14. D. Senter, "Witches and Psychiatrists," *Psychiatry,* x (1947), 49–56.
15. L. Saunders and J. Samora, "A Medical Care Program in a

Colorado County," in B. Paul, ed., *Health, Culture and Community* (New York: Russell Sage Foundation, 1955).

16. O. Lewis, "Medicine and Politics in a Mexican Village," in Paul, *op. cit.*

17. I. Kelly, *Folk Practices in North Mexico* (Austin, Texas: University of Texas Press, 1965).

18. A. Kiev, *Curanderismo: Mexican-American Folk Psychiatry* (New York: The Free Press, 1968).

19. W. R. Holland and R. G. Tharp, "Highland Maya Psychotherapy," *American Anthropologist*, LXVI (February, 1964), 41–52.

20. W. M. Hudson, ed., *The Healer of Los Olmos* (Dallas: Southern Methodist University Press, 1951), Texas Folklore Society Publication No. 24.

21. W. Madsen, *The Mexican-Americans of South Texas* (New York: Holt, Rinehart and Winston, 1964).

22. Kiev, *op. cit.*

23. Karno and his co-workers claim that *curanderos* are *not* important mental health resources for Mexican-Americans. Definitive resolution of this issue will require more data. See R. B. Edgerton, M. Karno, and I. Fernandez, "Curanderismo in the Metropolis: The Diminished Role of Folk Psychiatry among Los Angeles Mexican-Americans," *American Journal of Psychotherapy*, XXIV (1970), 124–134.

24. C. Martinez and H. W. Martin, "Folk Diseases among Urban Mexican-Americans." *Journal of the American Medical Association*, CXCVI (1966), 161–164.

25. G. Caplan, *Principles of Preventive Psychiatry* (New York: Basic Books, 1964); and E. Lindemann, "The Health Needs of Communities," in J. H. Knowles (ed.), *Hospitals, Doctors and the Public Interest* (Cambridge: Harvard University Press, 1965).

26. See, for example, Diaz-Guerrero, *op. cit.*; S. Ramirez and R. Parres, "Some Dynamic Patterns in the Organization of the Mexican Family," *International Journal of Social Psychiatry*, III (1957), 18–21; and O. Lewis, *Life in a Mexican Village: Tepoztlan Restudied* (Urbana, Illinois: University of Illinois Press, 1951).

27. A. Meadow and D. Stoker, "Symptomatic Behavior of Hospitalized Patients: A Study of Mexican-American and Anglo-American Patients," *Archives of General Psychiatry*, XII (March, 1965), 267–277.

28. Langner, *op. cit.*

29. Ramirez and Parres, *op. cit.*

30. W. Madsen, "Value Conflicts and Folk Psychotherapy in South Texas," in A. Kiev (ed.), *Magic, Faith and Healing* (New York: The Free Press, 1964).
31. Meadow and Stoker, *op. cit.*
32. Lewis, *op. cit.*
33. Jaco, *op. cit.*
34. See M. Clark, *Health in the Mexican-American Culture: A Community Study* (Berkeley: University of California Press, 1959); and Holland, *op. cit.*
35. A. J. Rubel, *Across the Tracks: Mexican Americans in a Texas City* (Austin, Texas: University of Texas Press, 1966).
36. Madsen, *The Mexican-Americans . . . , op. cit.*
37. Kiev, *Curanderismo, op. cit.* See also Lewis, *op. cit.*
38. See F. C. Nall and J. Speilberg, "Social and Cultural Factors in the Responses of Mexican-Americans to Medical Treatment," *Journal of Health and Social Behavior*, viii, No. 4 (December, 1967), 299–308.
39. Martinez and Martin, *op. cit.*
40. A. J. Rubel, "The Epidemiology of a Folk Illness: Susto in Hispanic America," *Ethnology*, iii (1964), 268–283.
41. Madsen, *Society and Health . . . , op. cit.*
42. Rubel, *op. cit.*
43. Holland, *op. cit.*
44. Madsen, *Society and Health . . . , op. cit.*
45. *Ibid.*
46. Rubel, *op. cit.*
47. Kiev, *Curanderismo, op. cit.*
48. Rubel, *op. cit.*
49. See Madsen, *The Mexican-Americans . . . , op. cit.;* Madsen, "Value Conflicts . . . ," *op. cit.;* and Clark, *op. cit.*
50. Kiev, *Curanderismo, op. cit.*
51. Martinez and Martin, *op. cit.*
52. Holland, *op. cit.*
53. Karno and his co-workers in East Los Angeles disagree that cultural factors are as important as I have suggested. As proof they cite their interview data on 444 Mexican-Americans. According to their report "the core content of the interview was formed by small vignettes describing in everyday language imaginary persons who were depicted as suffering *from what psychiatrists generally consider to be psychiatric disorders.*" (italics mine) Thus the very structure of the vignettes is already locked into an Anglo cognitive set, and it is not surprising that their Mexican-American respondents, many brought up in the United

States, could respond appropriately within the desired Anglo framework and label the vignettes as depressed, psychotic, etc. The obverse would be to take a group of Americans raised in Mexico, describe a vignette of *susto,* and they too should be able to correctly label the picture as *susto* even though they didn't necessarily accept it as a disease entity. See Karno and Edgerton, *op. cit.*

54. *San Jose Mercury,* October 1, 1969.
55. For another example of this see Yamamoto, James, and Palley, *op. cit.*
56. See Holland and Tharp, *op. cit.*
57. See Hudson, *op. cit.,* for a good example.
58. Kiev, *Curanderismo, op. cit.*
59. *Ibid.*

Chapter 9

1. For an example of a program which claims to use translators successfully, see H. Bluestone, R. Bisi, and A. J. Katz, "The Establishment of a Mental Health Service in a Predominantly Spanish-Speaking Neighborhood of New York City," *Behavioral Neuropsychiatry,* i, No. 5 (1969), 12–16.
2. B. Betz, "Experiences in Research in Psychotherapy with Schizophrenic Patients," in H. Strupp and L. Luborsky, eds., *Research in Psychotherapy,* (Washington, D.C.: American Psychological Association 1962), pp. 41–60.
3. *Action for Mental Health,* Final Report of the Joint Commission on Mental Illness and Health, 1961 (New York: John Wiley and Sons, 1961), p. 249.
4. H. I. Lief, "Subprofessional Training in Mental Health," *Archives of General Psychiatry,* xv (December, 1966), 660–664. See also W. Schofield, *Psychotherapy: The Purchase of Friendship* (Englewood Cliffs, New Jersey: Prentice-Hall, 1964); and R. R. Holt, "Editorial: New Directions in the Training of Psychotherapists," *Journal of Nervous and Mental Disease,* cxxxvii (1963), 413.
5. W. N. Deane, "The Culture of the Patient: An Underestimated Dimension in Psychotherapy," *International Journal of Social Psychiatry,* vii (1961), 181–186.
6. See M. P. Dumont, "Tavern Culture: The Sustenance of Homeless Men," *American Journal of Orthopsychiatry,* xxxvii, No. 5 (October, 1967), 938–945; J. Shapiro "Dominant Leaders among

Slum Hotel Residents," *American Journal of Orthopsychiatry,* xxxix, No. 4 (July, 1969), 644–650; and J. G. Kelly, "The Mental Health Agent in the Urban Community," in *Urban America and the Planning of Mental Health Services, Symposium No. 10* (New York: Group for the Advancement of Psychiatry, 1964), pp. 474–494.

7. E. F. Torrey, "The Case for the Indigenous Therapist," *Archives of General Psychiatry,* xx (1969), 365–373.

8. See D. C. Tinling, "Voodoo, Root Work, and Medicine," *Psychosomatic Medicine,* xxix (1967), 483–490. See also J. E. Snell, "Hypnosis in the Treatment of the 'Hexed' Patient," *American Journal of Psychiatry,* cxxiv (September, 1967), 3. Information on this was also given to me by C. P. Kimball, M.D., Department of Psychiatry, Yale Medical Center, by personal communication, 1969.

9. H. Wise, R. Brooke, and A. Harwood, "Proposal for an Ethnographic Study of Health Areas 24 and 26, with Particular Reference to Medical and Paramedical Beliefs and Practices" (Neighborhood Medical Care Demonstration, Bronx, New York, 1967) (Mimeographed).

10. S. Fisch, "Herb Pharmacopoeia" (Neighborhood Medical Care Demonstration, Bronx, New York, 1968) (Mimeographed).

11. L. H. Rogler and A. B. Hollingshead, *Trapped: Families and Schizophrenia* (New York: John Wiley and Sons, 1965).

12. A. Harwood, "Annual Report of the Ethnographic Study of Health Areas 24 and 26" (Neighborhood Medical Care Demonstration, Bronx, New York, 1969) (Mimeographed).

13. L. B. Boyer, "Further Remarks Concerning Shamans and Shamanism," *The Israel Annals of Psychiatry and Related Disciplines,* ii, No. 2 (1964), 235–257.

14. Among young adults the Indian suicide rate is four times the U.S. national average. See "Suicide and Homicides among Indians" (Washington, D.C.: Department of Health, Education and Welfare, 1969).

15. "Innovations in Mental Health Training: Summaries of Experimental and Special Training Projects" (Washington, D.C.: Division of Manpower and Training, National Institute of Mental Health, 1969) (Mimeographed).

16. A. Leighton and D. Leighton, "Elements of Psychotherapy in Navaho Religion," *Psychiatry,* iv (1941), 515–523.

17. "Innovations in Mental Health Training," *op. cit.*

18. M. J. Field, *Search for Security: An Ethnopsychiatric Study of*

Rural Ghana (Evanston, Illinois: Northwestern University Press, 1960).

19. G. Myrdal, *Asian Drama*, Vol. 3 (New York: Pantheon, 1968), p. 1599.
20. See M. G. Jayasundera, "Mental Health Surveys in Ceylon," in W. Caudill and T. Lin, eds., *Mental Health Research in Asia and the Pacific* (Honolulu: East-West Center Press, 1969); and Myrdal, *op. cit.*, p. 1599.
21. Y. Sasaki, "Psychiatric Study of the Shaman in Japan," in Caudill and Lin, *op. cit.*
22. C. M. U. MacLean, "Hospitals or Healers? An Attitude Survey in Ibadan," *Human Organization*, xxv, No. 2 (Summer, 1966), 131–139.
23. T. A. Lambo, "Patterns of Psychiatric Care in Developing African Countries," in A. Kiev, ed., *Magic, Faith and Healing* (New York: The Free Press, 1964), pp. 443–454.
24. *Ibid.*
25. G. Jahoda, "Traditional Healers and Other Institutions Concerned with Mental Illness in Ghana," *International Journal of Social Psychiatry*, vii. No. 4 (1961), 245–268.
26. Field, *op. cit.*
27. J. E. Cawte and M. A. Kidson, "Australian Ethnopsychiatry: The Walbiri Doctor," *Medical Journal of Australia*, ii (1964), 977–983. See also Jahoda, *op. cit.*
28. D. Akstein, "Terpsichore Trance Therapy: A Form of Group Psychotherapy Based on Ritual Possession," *Transcultural Psychiatric Research*, v (April, 1968), 74–75.
29. Myrdal, *op. cit.*, p. 1576.
30. *Hospital Tribune*, May 6, 1968.
31. Jayasundera, *op. cit.*

Chapter 10

1. These facilities are for the entire native population.
2. J. M. Murphy, "Psychotherapeutic Aspects of Shamanism on St. Lawrence Island, Alaska," in A. Kiev, ed., *Magic, Faith and Healing* (New York: The Free Press, 1964).
3. N. A. Chance, *The Eskimo of North Alaska* (New York: Holt, Rinehart and Winston, 1966).
4. Murphy, *op. cit.*
5. R. F. Spencer, *The North Alaskan Eskimo: A Study in Ecology*

and Society (Washington, D.C.: U.S. Government Printing Office. 1959).

6. J. M. Murphy and A. H. Leighton, "Native Conceptions of Psychiatric Disorders," in J. M. Murphy and A. H. Leighton, eds., *Approaches to Cross Cultural Psychiatry* (Ithaca: Cornell University Press, 1965), pp. 64–107.

7. See G. Caplan, *Principles of Preventive Psychiatry* (New York: Basic Books, 1964); and G. Caplan and H. Grunebaum, "Perspectives on Primary Prevention," *Archives of General Psychiatry*, XVII, No. 3 (1967), 331–346.

8. Chance, *op. cit.*

9. C. S. Hughes, "Under Four Flags: Recent Culture Change among the Eskimos," *Current Anthropology*, VI (1965), 3–69.

10. O. Lewis, *Life in a Mexican Village: Tepoztlan Restudied* (Urbana, Illinois: University of Illinois Press, 1951), p. 107.

11. See L. Y. Kline, "Some Factors in the Psychiatric Treatment of Spanish-Americans," *American Journal of Psychiatry*, CXXV, No. 12 (June, 1969), 1674–1681; and W. Madsen, *Society and Health in the Lower Rio Grande Valley* (Austin, Texas: Hogg Foundation for Mental Health, University of Texas, 1961), for a similar opinion.

12. See M. Clark, *Health in the Mexican-American Culture: A Community Study* (Berkeley: University of California Press, 1959), p. 205.

13. Madsen, *op. cit.*

14. L. Saunders and J. Samora, "A Medical Care Program in a Colorado County," in B. Paul, ed., *Health, Culture and Community* (New York: Russell Sage Foundation, 1955).

15. I. Kelly, *Folk Practices in North Mexico* (Austin, Texas: University of Texas Press, 1965).

16. W. Madsen, *The Mexican-Americans of South Texas* (New York: Holt, Rinehart and Winston, 1964).

17. Clark, *op. cit.*

18. R. Reiff and S. Scribner, "Issues in the New National Mental Health Program Relating to Labor and Low Income Groups," in F. Reissman, J. Cohen, and A. Pearl, eds., *Mental Health of the Poor* (New York: The Free Press, 1964).

19. Kelly, *op. cit.*

20. C. Martinez and H. W. Martin, "Folk Diseases among Urban Mexican-Americans," *Journal of the American Medical Association*, CXCVI (1966), 161–164. See also A. J. Rubel, *Across the Tracks: Mexican Americans in a Texas City* (Austin, Texas: University of Texas Press, 1966).

21. Rubel, *op. cit.*
22. See Saunders and Samora, *op. cit.*, and O. Lewis, "Medicine and Politics in a Mexican Village," in Paul, *op. cit.*, for examples.

Chapter 11

1. T. A. Lambo, ed., *First Pan-African Psychiatric Conference* (Ibadan, Nigeria: Government Printer, 1962).
2. See M. J. Field, *Search for Security: An Ethnopsychiatric Study of Rural Ghana* (Evanston, Illinois: Northwestern University Press, 1960). See also R. Prince, "Indigenous Yoruba Psychiatry," in A. Kiev, ed., *Magic, Faith and Healing* (New York: The Free Press, 1964).
3. A. M. Wellner, "A State-Wide Survey of Community Needs for Mental Health Technicians," *Mental Hygiene*, LII (1968), 204–206.
4. *Community Mental Health Center News*, I (Washington, D.C.: Morris Associates, November, 1969), 3.
5. "Protest Against Licensing of Cultists," *Journal of the American Medical Association*, CCIX, No. 6 (August 11, 1969), 950.
6. See Field, *op. cit.*, for examples of such referrals.
7. One of the few articles to deal with this issue, usually left unstated, is I. N. Berlin, "Resistance to Change in Mental Health Professionals," *American Journal of Orthopsychiatry*, XXXIX, No. 1 (January, 1969), 109–115.

Chapter 12

1. A. Leighton, Discussion, in A. V. S. De Rueck and R. Porter, eds. *Transcultural Psychiatry* (Boston: Little, Brown, 1965).

Bibliography

Abel, T. "Cultural Patterns as They Affect Psychotherapeutic Procedures," *American Journal of Psychotherapy*, x (1956), 728–740.

Ackerknecht, E. H. "Natural Diseases and Rational Treatment in Primitive Medicine," *Bulletin of the History of Medicine*, xix (1946), 467–497.

————. "Psychopathology, Primitive Medicine, and Primitive Culture," *Bulletin of the History of Medicine*, xiv (1943), 30–67.

————. "Problems of Primitive Medicine," *Bulletin of the History of Medicine*, xi (1942), 503–521.

Action for Mental Health. Final Report of the Joint Commission on Mental Illness and Health, 1961. New York: John Wiley and Sons, 1961.

"African Sees Gain for Mentally Ill," *New York Times*. March 24, 1968, p. 27.

Akstein, D. "Terpsichore Trance Therapy: A Form of Group Psychotherapy Based on Ritual Possession," *Transcultural Psychiatric Research*, v (April, 1968), 74–75.

Albee, G. W. "Myths, Models and Manpower," *Mental Hygiene*, lii, No. 2 (1968), 168–180.

Allport, G. W., and T. F. Pettigrew. "Cultural Influences on the Perception of Movement: The Trapezoidal Illusion Among the Zulus," *Journal of Abnormal Psychology*, LV, No. 1 (1957), 104–113.

Appleby, L. "Evaluation of Treatment Methods for Chronic Schizophrenia," *Archives of General Psychiatry*, VIII (1963), 8–21.

Aspy, D. N. "A Study of Three Facilitative Conditions and Their Relationships to the Achievement of Third Grade Students." Unpublished Doctoral dissertation, University of Kentucky, 1965. Summarized in Truax, C. B. and R. R. Carkhuff. *Toward Effective Counseling and Psychotherapy: Training and Practice.* Chicago: Aldine Publishing Company, 1967.

Baasher, T. A. "Traditional Psychotherapeutic Practices in the Sudan," *Transcultural Psychiatric Review*, IV (October, 1967), 158–160.

Beck, J. C., D. Kantor, and V. A. Gelineau. "Follow-up Study of Chronic Psychotic Patients 'Treated' by College Case-Aide Volunteers," *American Journal of Psychiatry*, CXX (1963), 269–271.

Becker, E. "The Relevance to Psychiatry of Recent Research in Anthropology," *American Journal of Psychotherapy*, XVI, No. 4 (1962), 600–617.

Bell, J. E. *The Family in the Hospital: Lessons from Developing Countries.* Washington, D.C.: U.S. Government Printing Office, 1969.

Belo, J. *Trance in Bali.* New York: Columbia University Press, 1960.

Benoist, A., et al. "Depression Among French Canadians in Montreal," *Transcultural Psychiatric Research*, II (April, 1965), 52–54.

Berenson, B. G., and R. R. Caukhuff (eds.). *Sources of Gain in Counseling and Psychotherapy.* New York: Holt, Rinehart and Winston, 1967.

Bergin, A. E. "The Effects of Psychotherapy: Negative Results Revisited," *Journal of Counseling Psychology*, X (1963), 244–255.

————. "Some Implications of Psychotherapy Research for Therapeutic Practice," *Journal of Abnormal Psychology*, LXXI, No. 1 (1966), 235–246.

Bergman, A. B., S. W. Dassel, and R. J. Wedgewood. "Time-Motion Study of Practicing Pediatricians," *Pediatrics*, XXXVIII, No. 2 (1966), 254–263.

————, J. L. Probstfield, and R. J. Wedgwood. "Task Identification in Pediatric Practice," *American Journal of the Diseases of Children*, CXVIII (1969), 459–468.

Berlin, I. N. "Resistance to Change in Mental Health Professionals," *American Journal of Orthopsychiatry*, XXXIX, No. 1 (January, 1969), 109–115.

Bermann, G. "China," in A. Kiev (ed.), *Psychiatry in the Communist World.* New York: Science House, 1968.

Berndt, C. H. "The Role of Native Doctors in Aboriginal Australia," in A. Kiev (ed.), *Magic, Faith and Healing*. New York: The Free Press, 1964.

Berne, E. "The Cultural Problem: Psychopathology in Tahiti," *American Journal of Psychiatry*, cxvi (1960), 1076–1081.

Betz, B. J. "Experiences in Research in Psychotherapy with Schizophrenic Patients," in H. Strupp, and L. Luborsky (eds.), *Research in Psychotherapy*. Washington, D.C.: American Psychological Association, 1962, pp. 41–60.

Bishop, M. M., and G. Winokur. "Cross-Cultural Psychotherapy," *Journal of Nervous and Mental Disease*, cxxiii (1956), 369–375.

Blachly, P. H., II. J. Osterud, and R. Josslin. "Suicide in Professional Groups," *New England Journal of Medicine*, cclxviii, No. 23 (1963), 1278–1282.

Bloom, L. "The Izinyanga of Durban, South Africa," *Transcultural Psychiatric Research*, xiv (April, 1963), 43–45.

Bluestone, H., R. Bisi, and A. J. Katz. "The Establishment of a Mental Health Service in a Predominantly Spanish-Speaking Neighborhood of New York City," *Behavioral Neuropsychiatry*, i, No. 5 (1969), 12–16.

Boas, F. "On Grammatical Categories," in D. Hymes. *Language in Culture and Society*. New York: Harper and Row, 1964.

Boghen, D., and M. Boghen. "Medical Attitudes, Beliefs and Practices in Martinique," *Transcultural Psychiatric Research*, iii (April, 1966), 47–49.

Bogoras, W. *The Chukchee*. New York: American Museum of Natural History, 1907.

Bolman, W. "Cross-Cultural Psychotherapy," *American Journal of Psychiatry* cxxiv, No. 9 (1968), 1237–1244.

Bourguignon, E. "The Theory of Spirit Possession," in M. Spiro (ed.), *Context and Meaning in Cultural Anthropology*. New York: The Free Press, 1965.

Boyer, L. B. "Folk Psychiatry of the Apaches of the Mescalero Indian Reservation," in A. Kiev (ed.), *Magic, Faith and Healing*. New York: The Free Press, 1964.

————. "Further Remarks Concerning Shamans and Shamanism," *The Israel Annals of Psychiatry and Related Disciplines*, ii, No. 2 (1964), 235–257.

————. "Notes on the Personality Structure of a North American Indian Shaman," *Journal of Hillside Hospital*, x (January, 1961), 14–33.

————. "Remarks on the Personality of Shamans," *Psychoanalytic Study of Society*, ii (1961), 233–254.

————, *et al.* "Comparison of the Shamans and Pseudoshamans of the Apaches of the Mescalero Indian Reservation: A Rorschach Study," *Journal of Projective Techniques and Personality Assessment,* XXVIII, No. 2 (1964), 173–180.

Braceland, F. J. (ed.). *Faith, Reason and Modern Psychiatry.* New York: P. J. Kennedy and Sons, 1955.

Bram, J. "Spirits, Mediums and Believers in Contemporary Puerto Rico," *Transactions of the New York Academy of Sciences* (1957), pp. 340–347.

Bromberg, W. *The Mind of Man: A History of Psychotherapy and Psychoanalysis.* New York: Harper and Row, 1959.

Brown, B. M. "Cognitive Aspects of Wolpe's Behavior Therapy," *American Journal of Psychiatry,* CXXIV (December, 1967), 6.

Brown, R. W., and E. Lenneberg. "A Study in Language and Cognition," *Journal of Abnormal and Social Psychology,* XLIX (1954), 454–462.

Burton-Bradley, B. G., and C. Julius. "Folk Psychiatry of Certain Villages in the Central District of Papua," *Transcultural Psychiatric Research,* III (April, 1966), 22–24.

Bustamente, J. A. "Importance of Cultural Patterns in Psychotherapy," *American Journal of Psychotherapy,* XI (1957), 803–812.

Cannon, W. B. "Voodoo Death," *American Anthropologist,* XLVI (1942), 169–181.

Caplan, G. *Principles of Preventive Psychiatry.* New York: Basic Books, 1964.

————, and H. Grunebaum. "Perspectives on Primary Prevention," *Archives of General Psychiatry,* XVII, No. 3 (1967), 331–346.

Carkhuff, R. R., and C. B. Truax. "Lay Mental Health Counseling: The Effects of Lay Group Counseling," *Journal of Consulting Psychology,* XXIX (1965), 426.

————, and C. B. Truax. "Training in Counseling and Psychotherapy: An Evaluation of an Integrated Didactic and Experimental Approach," *Journal of Consulting Psychology,* XXIX (1965), 333–336.

Carstairs, G. M. "Medicine and Faith in Rural Rajasthan," in B. D. Paul (ed.), *Health, Culture and Community.* New York: Russell Sage Foundation, 1955.

Castaneda, C. *The Teachings of Don Juan: A Yaqui Way of Knowledge.* New York: Ballantine Books, 1969.

Caudill, W. "Around the Clock Patient Care in Japanese Psychiatric Hospitals: The Role of the Tsukisoi," *American Sociological Review,* XXVI, No. 2 (April, 1961), 204–214.

————. "Observations on the Cultural Context of Japanese Psychiatry," in M. Opler (ed.), *Culture and Mental Health*. New York: The Macmillan Company, 1959, pp. 213–242.

————, and C. Schooler. "Symptom Patterns and Background Characteristics of Japanese Psychiatric Patients," *Transcultural Psychiatric Research*, v (October, 1968), 133–137.

Cawte, J. E. "Australian Ethnopsychiatry in the Field: A Sampling in North Kimberley," *Medical Journal of Australia*, i (1964), 467–472.

————, and M. A. Kidson. "Australian Ethnopsychiatry: The Walbiri Doctor," *Medical Journal of Australia*, ii (1964), 977–983.

Cerletti, U. "Old and New Information about Electroshock," *American Journal of Psychiatry*, cvii (1950), 87–94.

Cernay, J. "Psychiatry in China," *Ceskoslovenska Psychiatrie*, lix, No. 4 (1963), 273–282. Reported in *Transcultural Psychiatric Research*, i (April, 1964), 34–36.

Chance, N. A. "Culture Change and Integration: An Eskimo Example," *American Anthropologist*, lxii, No. 6 (1960), 1028–1044.

————. *The Eskimo of North Alaska*. New York: Holt, Rinehart and Winston, 1966.

Charatan, F. B., and I. Rosenblatt. "Psychotherapy: The Views of Psychiatrists from Scotland and Nassau County, New York," *American Journal of Psychiatry*, cxxv, No. 8 (1969), 1120–1122.

Clark, M. *Health in the Mexican-American Culture: A Community Study*. Berkeley: University of California Press, 1959.

Colby, K. M. "Computer Simulation of Change in Personal Belief Systems," *Behavioral Science*, xii, No. 3 (1967), 248–253.

————. "Computer Simulation of Neurotic Processes," in R. W. Stacey and B. Waxman (eds.), *Computers in Biomedical Research*. New York: Academic Press, 1965.

————, J. B. Watt and J. P. Gilbert. "A Computer Method of Psychotherapy: Preliminary Communication," *Journal of Nervous and Mental Disease*, cxlii, No. 2 (1966), 148–152.

Community Mental Health Center News (Washington, D.C.: Morris Associates), i (November, 1969), 3.

Conklin, H. "Hanunoo Color Categories," *Southwest Journal of Anthropology* xi (Winter, 1955), 339–344.

Cowen, E. L., E. A. Gardner, and M. Zax. *Emergent Approaches to Mental Health Problems*. New York: Appleton-Century-Crofts, 1967.

Currier, R. L. "The Hot-Cold Syndrome and Symbolic Balance in Mexican and Spanish-American Folk Medicine," *Ethnology*, v, No. 3 (1966), 251–263.

D'Andrade, R. G. "Anthropological Studies of Dreams," in F. L. K.

Hsu *Psychological Anthropology*. Momewood, Illinois: Dorsey Press, 1961.

Davis, K. "Mental Hygiene and the Class Structure," *Psychiatry*, I (1938), 55–65.

Dawson, J. "Urbanization and Mental Health in a West African Community," in A. Kiev (ed.) *Magic, Faith and Healing*. New York: The Free Press, 1964.

Deane, W. N. "The Culture of the Patient: An Underestimated Dimension in Psychotherapy," *International Journal of Social Psychiatry*, VII (1961), 181–186.

Del Pozo, E. C. "Empiricism and Magic in Aztec Pharmacology," in D. H. Efron, B. Holmstedt, and N. Kline (eds.), *Ethnopharmacologic Search for Psychoactive Drugs*. (Public Health Service Publication No. 1645.) Washington, D.C.: U.S. Government Printing Office, 1967.

Denko, J. D. "How Preliterate Peoples Explain Disturbed Behavior," *Archives of General Psychiatry*, XV (1966), 398–409.

DeReuck, A. V. S., and R. Porter (eds.). *Transcultural Psychiatry*. Boston: Little, Brown and Company, 1965.

Devereux, G. "Dream Learning and Individual Ritual Differences in Mohave Shamanism," *American Anthropologist*, LIX (1957), 1036–1045.

———. *Mohave Ethnopsychiatry and Suicide: The Psychiatric Knowledge and the Psychic Disturbances of an Indian Tribe*. (Bureau of American Ethnology Bulletin No. 175.) Washington, D.C.: Smithsonian Institution, 1961.

———. *Reality and Dream: Psychotherapy of a Plains Indian*. New York: International Universities Press, 1950.

———. "Shamans as Neurotics," *American Anthropologist*, LXIII (1961), 1088–1090.

———. "Three Technical Problems in Psychotherapy of Plains Indian Patients," *American Journal of Psychotherapy*, V (1951), 411–423.

Diaz-Guerrero, R. "Neurosis and the Mexican Family Structure," *American Journal of Psychiatry*, CXII (1955), 411–417.

Douyon, E. "Trance in Haitian Voodoo," *Transcultural Psychiatric Research*, II (October, 1965), 155–159.

Dubos, R. *Man Adapting*. New Haven: Yale University Press, 1965.

Dumont, M. P. "Tavern Culture: The Sustenance of Homeless Men," *American Journal of Orthopsychiatry*, XXXVII, No. 5 (October, 1967), 938–945.

Edgerton, R. B., M. Karno, and I. Fernandez. "Curanderismo in the Metropolis: The Diminished Role of Folk Psychiatry among Los

Angeles Mexican-Americans," *American Journal of Psychotherapy*, xxiv (1970), 124–134.

Edsman, C. M. (ed.) *Studies in Shamanism*. Stockholm: Almquist and Weksell, 1967.

Efron, D. H., B. Holmstedt, and N. Kline (eds.) *Ethnopharmacologic Search for Psychoactive Drugs*. (Public Health Service Publication No. 1645.) Washington, D.C.: U.S. Government Printing Office, 1967.

Egbert, C. D., G. E. Battit, C. E. Welch, and M. K. Bartlett. "Reduction of Postoperative Pain by Encouragement and Instruction of Patients," *New England Journal of Medicine*, clxx, No. 16 (1964), 825–827.

Eliade, M. *Shamanism: Archaic Techniques of Ecstasy*. Translated by W. R. Trask. New York: Pantheon, 1964.

Ellsworth, R. B. *Nonprofessionals in Psychiatric Rehabilitation*. New York: Appleton-Century-Crofts, 1968.

Erasmus, C. J. "Changing Folk Beliefs and the Relativity of Empirical Knowledge," *Southwest Journal of Anthropology*, viii (1952), 411–428.

Erikson, E. H. *Observations on the Yoruk: Childhood and World Image*. (University of California Publications in American Archaeology and Ethnology.) Berkeley: University of California Press, 1943, p. 262. Quoted in S. H. Posinsky, "Yoruk Shamanism," *Psychiatric Quarterly*, xxxix (1965), 227–243.

Eysenck, H. J. "The Effects of Psychotherapy: An Evaluation." *Journal of Consulting Psychology*, xvi (1952), 319–324.

Ezriel, H "Experimentation within the Psychoanalytic Session," *British Journal of Philosophy and Science*, vii (1956), 25. Quoted in W. M. Mendel, "The Non-Specifics of Psychotherapy," *International Journal of Psychiatry*, v, No. 5 (1968), 400–402.

Fejos, P. "Magic, Witchcraft and Medical Theory in Primitive Cultures," in I. Galdston (ed.), *Man's Image in Medicine and Anthropology*. New York: International Universities Press, 1963.

Fiedler, F. E. "A Comparison of Therapeutic Relationships in Psychoanalytic, Non-Directive and Adlerian Therapy," *Journal of Consulting Psychology*, xiv (1950), 436–445.

Field, M. J. *Search for Security: An Ethnopsychiatric Study of Rural Ghana*. Evanston, Illinois: Northwestern University Press, 1960.

———. "Witchcraft as a Primitive Interpretation of Mental Disorder," *Journal of Mental Science*, ci (1955), 826–833.

Fisch, S. "Herb Pharmacopoeia." Bronx: Neighborhood Medical Care Demonstration, 1968. (Mimeographed.)

Ford, C. S., and F. A. Beach. *Patterns of Sexual Behavior.* New York: Harper, 1951.

Foster, G. M. "Nagualism in Mexico and Guatemala," *Acta Americana*, II (1944), 85–105.

————. "Relationships between Spanish and Spanish-American Folk Medicine," *Journal of American Folklore*, LXVI (1953), 201–217.

Fox, J. R. "Pueblo Baseball: A New Use for Old Witchcraft," *Journal of American Folklore*, LXXIV (1961), 291.

————. "Witchcraft and Clanship in Cochiti Therapy," in A. Kiev (ed.) *Magic, Faith and Healing.* New York: The Free Press, 1964.

Frake, C. O. "The Diagnosis of Disease Among the Subanun of Mindanao," *American Anthropologist*, LXIII (1961), 113–132.

Frank, J. D. *Persuasion and Healing.* Baltimore: Johns Hopkins Press, 1961.

————. "The Role of Hope in Psychotherapy." *International Journal of Psychiatry*, V, No. 5 (May, 1968), 383–412.

————, E. H. Nash, A. R. Stone, and S. D. Imber. "Immediate and Long-Term Symptomatic Course of Psychiatric Outpatients," *American Journal of Psychiatry*, CXX (1963), 429–439.

Freud, S. *Collected Papers.* Vol. I. 2d ed. London: Hogarth Press, 1940, pp. 249–263.

Freeman, D. "Shaman and Incubus," *Psychoanalytic Study of Society*, IV (1967), 315–343.

Freeman, W. "Psychiatrists Who Kill Themselves: A Study in Suicide," *American Journal of Psychiatry*, CXXIV, No. 6 (1967), 846–847.

Friedman, H. J. "Patient-Expectancy and Symptom Reduction," *Archives of General Psychiatry*, VIII (1963), 61–67.

Fuchs, S. "Magic Healing Techniques Among the Balahis in Central India," in Kiev, A. (ed.) *Magic, Faith and Healing.* New York: The Free Press, 1964.

Galdston, I. (ed.). *Man's Image in Medicine and Anthropology.* New York: International Universities Press, 1963.

Gardner, E. A. "Indigenous Persons as Clinic Therapists in a Community Mental Health Center: Implications for New Careers." Paper presented at meeting of the American Psychiatric Association, Boston, May, 1968.

Gardner, G. G. "The Psychotherapeutic Relationship," *Psychological Bulletin*, LXI (1964), 426–437.

Gavin, J., and A. Ludwig. "A Case of Witchcraft," *Journal of Nervous and Mental Disease*, CXXXIII (1961), 161–168.

Gelfand, M. "Psychiatric Disorder as Recognized by the Shona," in

A. Kiev (ed.), *Magic, Faith and Healing*. New York: The Free Press, 1964.

Gibbs, J. L. "The Kpelle Moot: A Therapeutic Model for the Informal Settlement of Disputes," *Journal of Africa*, xxxiii, No. 1 (1963), 1–11.

Giel, R., Y. Gezahegn, and J. N. van Luijk. "Faith Healing and Spirit Possession in Ghion, Ethiopia," *Transcultural Psychiatric Research*, v (April, 1968), 64–67.

Gill, M., and M. Brenman. *Hypnosis and Related States: Psychoanalytic Studies of Regression*. New York: International Universities Press, 1961.

Gillin, J. "Magical Fright," *Psychiatry*, xi (November, 1948), 387–400.

Gliedman, L. H., E. H. Nash, S. D. Imber, A. R. Stone, and J. D. Frank. "Reduction of Symptoms by Pharmacologically Inert Substances and by Short-Term Psychotherapy," *American Medical Association Archives of Neurology and Psychiatry*, lxxix (1958), 345–351.

Goldstein, A. P. "Domains and Dilemmas," *International Journal of Psychiatry*, vii, No. 3 (1969), 128–134.

————. *Therapist-Patient Expectancies in Psychotherapy*. New York: Pergamon Press, 1962.

Goodman, G. "An Experiment with Companionship Therapy: College Students and Troubled Boys—Assumptions, Selection, and Design," *American Journal of Public Health*, lvii, No. 10 (October, 1967), 1772–1777.

Greenblatt, M., and D. Kantor. "Student Volunteer Movement and the Manpower Shortage," *American Journal of Psychiatry*, cxviii (1962), 809–814.

Greenspoon, J. "The Reinforcing Effect of Two Spoken Sounds on the Frequency of Two Responses," *American Journal of Psychology*, lxviii (1955), 409–416.

Gursslin, O. R., R. G. Hunt, and J. L. Roach. "Social Class and the Mental Health Movement," in F. Riessman, J. Cohen, and A. Pearl, *Mental Health of the Poor*. New York: The Free Press, 1964.

Haley, J. *Strategies of Psychotherapy*. New York: Grune and Stratton, 1963.

Hallaji, J. "Hypnotherapeutic Techniques in a Central Asian Community," *International Journal of Clinical and Experimental Hypnosis*. Reported in *Transcultural Psychiatric Research*, i (October, 1964), 110–111.

Hallowell, A. I. "Ojibwa Ontology, Behavior and World View," in

S. Diamond (ed.), *Culture in History*. New York: Columbia University Press, 1960.

―――――. "Some Empirical Aspects of Northern Salteaux Religion," *American Anthropologist*, xxxvi (1934), 389–405.

Hallowitz, E., and F. Riessman. "The Role of the Indigenous Nonprofessional in a Community Mental Health Neighborhood Service Center Program." Presented at American Orthopsychiatry Association meetings, San Francisco, April, 1966.

Handelman, D. "The Development of a Washo Shaman," *Ethnology*, vi, No. 4 (1967), 444–464.

Hansell, N., M. Wodarczyk, and H. M. Visotsky. "The Mental Health Expediter: A Review after Two Years of the Project and One Year of the Expediter in Action," *Archives of General Psychiatry*, xviii (April, 1968), 392–399.

Harlow, H. F. "The Nature of Love," *American Psychologist*, xiii (1958), 673–685.

―――――. "Primary Affectional Patterns in Primates," *American Journal of Orthopsychiatry*, xxx (1960), 676–684.

Harrison, T. J. "Training for Village Health Aides in the Kotzebue Area of Alaska," *Public Health Reports*, lxxx, No. 7 (1965), 565–572.

Harwood, A. "Annual Report of the Ethnographic Study of Health Areas 24 and 26." New York: Neighborhood Medical Care Demonstration, 1969. (Mimeographed.)

"Healer Offers Unique Brand of Psychotherapy," *Medical World News*, September 29, 1967, pp. 36–37.

Heine, R. (ed.). *The Student Physician as Psychotherapist*. Chicago: The University of Chicago Press, 1962.

Henry, J. "The Inner Experience of Culture," *Psychiatry*, xiv (1951), 87–103.

Hertz, D. "Problems of Urbanization in Liberia as Reflected in the Mental Health Services," *Transcultural Psychiatric Research*, i (April, 1964), 58–60.

Hes, J. P. "The Changing Social Role of the Yemenite Mori," in A. Kiev (ed.) *Magic, Faith and Healing*. New York: The Free Press, 1964.

Hessin, A. L. "Treatment of the Mentally Ill by San Blas Indian Healers (Panama)," *Transcultural Psychiatric Research*, xv (October, 1963), 70.

Hilgard, J. R., D. C. Staight, and U. S. Moore. "Better-Adjusted Peers as Resources in Group Therapy with Adolescents," *Journal of Psychology*, lxxiii (1969), 75–100.

―――――, and U. S. Moore. "Affiliative Therapy with Young Adolescents," *Journal of the American Academy of Child Psychiatry*, VIII, No. 4 (1969), 577–605.

Hill, D. *Magic and Superstition*. New York: Hamlyn Publishing, 1968.

Holland, W. R. "Mexican-American Medical Beliefs: Science or Magic?" *Arizona Medicine*, xx (May, 1963), 89–102.

————, and R. G. Tharp. "Highland Maya Psychotherapy," *American Anthropologist*, LXVI (February, 1964), 41–52.

Hollingshead, A. B., and F. C. Redlich. *Social Class and Mental Illness*. New York: John Wiley and Sons, 1958.

Holt, R. R. "Editorial: New Directions in the Training of Psychotherapists," *Journal of Nervous and Mental Disease*, CXXXVII (1963), 413.

————, and L. Luborsky. *Personality Patterns of Psychiatrists*. New York: Basic Books, 1958.

Holtved, E. "Eskimo Shamanism," in C. M. Edsman (ed.), *Studies in Shamanism*. Stockholm: Almquist and Weksell, 1967.

Holzberg, J. D., R. H. Knapp, and J. C. Turner. "College Students as Companions to the Mentally Ill," in E. L., Cowen, E. A. Gardner, and M. Zax, *Emergent Approaches to Mental Health Problems*. New York: Appleton-Century-Crofts, 1967.

Howell, W., and D. J. S. Bailey. *A Sea Dyak Dictionary*. Singapore: American Mission Press, 1900.

Hudson, W. M. (ed.). *The Healer of Los Olmos*. Dallas: Southern Methodist University Press, 1951. (Texas Folklore Society Publication No. 24.)

Hughes, C. S. "Under Four Flags: Recent Culture Change Among the Eskimos," *Current Anthropology*, VI (1965), 3–69.

Hunt, R. G. "Social Class and Mental Illness: Some Implications for Clinical Theory and Practice," *American Journal of Psychiatry*, CXVI (June, 1960), 1065–1069.

Indian Health Highlights. Washington, D.C.: Department of Health, Education and Welfare, 1966.

Inkeles, A., and D. J. Levinson. "National Character: The Study of Modal Personality and Socio-Cultural Systems," in G. Lindzey (ed.), *Handbook of Social Psychology*. Cambridge, Massachusetts: Addison-Wesley, 1954, pp. 927–1020.

"Innovations in Mental Health Training: Summaries of Experimental and Special Traning Projects," Washington, D.C.: National Institute of Mental Health Division of Manpower and Training, 1969. (Mimeographed.)

Jaco, E. G. "Mental Health of the Spanish-American in Texas," in M. K. Opler (ed.), *Culture and Mental Health*. New York: The Macmillan Company, 1959, pp. 467–485.

Jahoda, G. "Traditional Healers and Other Institutions Concerned with Mental Illness in Ghana," *International Journal of Social Psychiatry*, VII, No. 4 (1961), 245–268.

James, D. W. "Chinese Medicine," *The Lancet*, I (1958), 1068–1069.

Janis, I. L. *Psychological Stress.* New York: John Wiley and Sons, 1958.

Jarvis, D. C. *Folk Medicine: A Vermont Doctor's Guide to Good Health.* New York: Henry Holt and Company, 1958.

Jayasundera, M. G. "Mental Health Surveys in Ceylon," in W. Caudill and T. Lin (eds.), *Mental Health Research in Asia and the Pacific.* Honolulu: East-West Center Press, 1969.

Jilek, W. G. "The Image of the African Medicine-Man," in N. Petrilowitsch, "Contributions to Comparative Psychiatry," *Bibliotheca Psychiatrica et Neurologica*, CXXXIII, No. 6 (1967), 165–178.

Johnson, D. L., and C. A. Johnson. "Totally Discouraged: A Depressive Syndrome of the Dakota Sioux," *Transcultural Psychiatric Research*, II (October, 1965), 141–143.

"Joint Venture in Mental Health, 1968." Report of the Ad Hoc Comprehensive Mental Health Planning Committee for Santa Clara County. San Jose, California, 1968.

Jones, R. "Ethnic Family Patterns: The Mexican Family in the United States," *American Journal of Sociology*, LIII (1948), 450–452.

Kaplan, B. (ed.). *Studying Personality Cross-Culturally.* New York: Row, Peterson and Company, 1961.

————, and D. Johnson. "The Social Meaning of Navaho Psychopathology and Psychotherapy," in A. Kiev (ed.) *Magic, Faith and Healing.* New York: The Free Press, 1964.

Karno, M. "The Enigma of Ethnicity in a Psychiatric Clinic," *Archives of General Psychiatry*, XIV, No. 5 (1966), 516–520.

————, and R. B. Edgerton. "Perception of Mental Illness in a Mexican-American Community," *Archives of General Psychiatry*, XX (1969), 233–238.

————, R. N. Ross, and R. A. Caper. "Mental Health Roles of Physicians in a Mexican-American Community," *Community Mental Health Journal*, V, No. 1 (1969), 62–69.

Kellaway, P. "The Part Played by Electric Fish in the Early History of Bioelectricity and Electrotherapy," *Bulletin of the History of Medicine*, XX (1946), 112–137.

Kelley, H. H. "The Effects of Expectations upon First Impressions of Persons," *American Psychologist*, IV (1949), 252.

Kelly, Isabel. *Folk Practices in North Mexico.* Austin: University of Texas Press, 1965.

Kelly, J. G. "The Mental Health Agent in the Urban Community," in *Urban America and the Planning of Mental Health Services.* (Symposium No. 10.) New York: Group for the Advancement of Psychiatry, 1964, pp. 474–494.

Kennedy, J. G. "Nubian Zar Ceremonies as Psychotherapy," *Human Organization,* xxvi (1967), 185–194.

Kiev, A. *Curanderismo: Mexican-American Folk Psychiatry.* New York: The Free Press, 1968.

————. "Prescientific Psychiatry," in S. Arieti (ed.) *American Handbook of Psychiatry.* Vol. iii. New York: Basic Books, 1966.

————. "Primitive Holistic Medicine," *International Journal of Social Psychiatry,* viii, No. 1 (1962), 58–61.

————. "Primitive Therapy: A Cross-Cultural Study of the Relationship Between Child Training and Therapeutic Practices Related to Illness," in W. Muensterberger and S. Axelrod (eds.), *Psychoanalytic Study of Society,* Vol. i (New York: International Universities Press, 1961), 185–217.

————. "The Psychotherapeutic Aspects of Primitive Medicine," *Human Organization,* xxi (1962), 25–29.

————. "Psychotherapy in Haitian Voodoo," *American Journal of Psychotherapy,* xvi (July, 1962), 469–476.

————. "Spirit Possession in Haiti," *American Journal of Psychiatry,* cxviii (1961), 133–138.

———— (ed.). *Magic, Faith and Healing.* New York: The Free Press, 1964.

Kimball, C. P. "Psychologic Responses to Open Heart Surgery," *American Journal of Psychiatry,* cxxvi (1969), 348–359.

Kline, L. Y. "Some Factors in the Psychiatric Treatment of Spanish-Americans," *American Journal of Psychiatry,* cxxv, No. 12 (June, 1969), 1674–1681.

Kluckhohn, C., and D. Leighton. *The Navaho.* Garden City, New York: Anchor Books, 1962.

Knupfer, G., D. D. Jackson, and G. Krieger. "Personality Differences Between More and Less Competent Psychotherapists as a Function of Criteria of Competence," *Journal of Nervous and Mental Disease,* cxxix (1959), 375–384.

Kora, T. "Morita Therapy," *Transcultural Psychiatric Research,* ii (October, 1965), 101–103.

Krasner, L. "Studies of the Conditioning of Verbal Behavior," *Psychological Bulletin,* lv (1958), 148–170.

Kroeber, A. L. "Psychosis or Social Sanction," in *The Nature of Culture.* Chicago: University of Chicago Press, 1952, pp. 310–319.

Kubie, L. S. "The Need for a New Subdiscipline in the Medical Profession," *Archives of Neurology and Psychiatry,* LXXVIII (September, 1957), 283–293.

LaBarre, W. "Confession as Cathartic Therapy in American Indian Tribes," in A. Kiev (ed.), *Magic, Faith and Healing.* New York: The Free Press, 1964.

————. "Primitive Psychotherapy in Native American Cultures: Peyotism and Confession," *Journal of Abnormal and Social Psychology,* XLII (1947), 294–309.

Lambo, T. A. "Patterns of Psychiatric Care in Developing African Countries," in A. Kiev (ed.), *Magic, Faith and Healing.* New York: The Free Press, 1964, pp. 443–454.

———— (ed.). *First Pan-African Psychiatric Conference.* Ibadan, Nigeria: Government Printer, 1962.

Lamson, H. D. *Social Pathology in China.* Shanghai: Commercial Press, 1928.

Langner, T. S. "Psychophysiological Symptoms and the Status of Women in Two Mexican Communities," in J. M. Murphy and A. H. Leighton (eds.), *Approaches to Cross-Cultural Psychiatry.* Ithaca, New York: Cornell University Press, 1965, pp. 360–392.

Leavitt, E. E. "The Results of Psychotherapy with Children," *Journal of Consulting Psychology,* XXI (1957), 189–196.

Lebra, W. P. "The Okinawan Shaman," in A. H. Smith (ed.) *Ryukyuan Culture and Society.* Honolulu: University of Hawaii Press, 1964.

————. "Shaman and Client in Okinawa," in W. Caudill and T. Lin (eds.), *Mental Health Research in Asia and the Pacific.* Honolulu: East-West Center Press, 1969.

Lehman, J. P., and H. M. Foté. "The Circle of the Prophet and the Sorcerer: Reflections on a Functional Hysterical Paralysis of a Thirteen-year-old Child," *Transcultural Psychiatric Research,* V (October, 1968), 165–168.

Leighton, A., and D. Leighton. "Elements of Psychotherapy in Navaho Religion," *Psychiatry,* IV (1941), 515–523.

Levenson, A. I., *et al.* "Manpower and Training in Federally-Funded Community Mental Health Centers," *Hospital and Community Psychiatry,* March, 1969.

Levinson, P., and J. Schiller. "Role Analysis of the Indigenous Nonprofessional," *Social Work,* XI, No. 3 (1966), 95–101.

Lévi-Strauss, C. *Structural Anthropology.* New York: Basic Books, 1963.

Levy, R. I. "Tahitian Folk Psychotherapy," *International Public Health Research Newsletter*, IX, No. 4 (1967), 12–15. Abstracted in *Transcultural Psychiatric Research*, VI (April, 1969), 51–55.

Lewin, L. *Phantastica: Narcotic and Stimulating Drugs*. New York: E. P. Dutton and Company, 1964. (First published in 1924.)

Lewis, L. S. "Rational Behavior and the Treatment of Illness," *Journal of Health and Human Behavior*, IV, No. 4 (Winter, 1963), 235–239.

Lewis, O. "The Culture of Poverty," *Scientific American*, CCXV, No. 1 (1966), 19–25.

————. *Life in a Mexican Village: Tepoztlan Restudied*. Urbana: University of Illinois Press, 1951.

————. "Medicine and Politics in a Mexican Village," in B. Paul (ed.), *Health, Culture and Community*. New York: Russell Sage Foundation, 1955.

Lief, H. I. "Subprofessional Training in Mental Health," *Archives of General Psychiatry*, XV (December, 1966), 660–664.

Lindemann, E. "The Health Needs of Communities," in J. H. Knowles (ed.), *Hospitals, Doctors and the Public Interest*. Cambridge, Massachusetts: Harvard University Press, 1965.

Linton, R. *Culture and Mental Disorders*. Springfield, Illinois: Charles C. Thomas, 1956.

Liu, S., and S. Chi. "Using Mao Tse-Tung's Thoughts to Open Up a 'Forbidden Zone:' Curing Deaf-Mutes," *Peking Review*, XLVI (November 15, 1968), 14–17.

Loeb, E. "Shaman and Seer," *American Anthropologist*, XXXI (1929), 61–84.

Maclean, C. M. U. "Hospitals or Healers? An Attitude Survey in Ibadan," *Human Organization*, XXV, No. 2 (Summer, 1966), 131–139.

Maddox, J. L. *The Medicine Man: A Sociological Study of the Character and Evolution of Shamanism*. New York: Macmillan, 1923.

Madsen, W. *The Mexican-Americans of South Texas*. New York: Holt, Rinehart and Winston, 1964.

————. *Society and Health in the Lower Rio Grande Valley*. Austin: Hogg Foundation for Mental Health, University of Texas, 1961.

————. "Value Conflicts and Folk Psychotherapy in South Texas," in A. Kiev (ed.), *Magic, Faith and Healing*. New York: The Free Press, 1964, pp. 420–440.

Marcuse, F. L. (ed.). *Hypnosis Throughout the World*. Springfield, Illinois: Charles C. Thomas, 1964.

Margetts, E. L. "The Future of Psychiatry in East Africa," *East African Medical Journal*, xxxvii (1960), 448–456.

Margolin, S. G. "On Some Principles of Therapy," *American Journal of Psychiatry*, cxiv (1958), 1087–1094.

Martinez, C., and H. W. Martin. "Folk Diseases Among Urban Mexican-Americans," *Journal of the American Medical Association*, cxcvi (1966), 161–164.

Masserman, J. H. "The Timeless Therapeutic Trinity," in J. H. Masserman (ed.), *Current Psychiatric Therapies*. Vol. vii. New York: Grune and Stratton, 1967, 231–243.

McCartney, J. L. "Neuropsychiatry in China: A Preliminary Observation," *China Medical Journal*, xl (1926), 617–626.

Meadow, A., and D. Stoker. "Symptomatic Behavior of Hospitalized Patients: A Study of Mexican-American and Anglo-American Patients," *Archives of General Psychiatry*, xii (March, 1965), 267–277.

Mendel, W. M. "The Non-Specifics of Psychotherapy," *International Journal of Psychiatry*, v, No. 5 (1968), 400–402.

————, and S. Rapport. "Outpatient Treatment for Chronic Schizophrenic Patients: Therapeutic Consequences of an Existential View," *Archives of General Psychiatry*, viii (1963), 190–196.

"Mental Health Activities in the Indian Health Program." Washington, D.C.: Department of Health, Education and Welfare, 1967.

Messing, S. D. "Group Therapy and Social Status in the Zar Cult in Ethiopia," in M. K. Opler (ed.), *Culture and Mental Health*. New York: The Macmillan Company, 1959, pp. 319–332.

Metzger, D., and G. Williams. "Tenejapa Medicine I: The Curer," *Southwestern Journal of Anthropology*, xix (1963), 216–234.

Miller, N. E. "Learning of Visceral and Glandular Responses," *Science*, clxiii, No. 3866 (January 31, 1969), 434–445.

Miner, H. "Body Ritual of the Nacirema," *American Anthropologist*, lviii (1956), 503–507.

Mischel, W., and F. Mischel. "Psychological Aspects of Spirit Possession," *American Anthropologist*, lx (1958), 249–260.

Modlin, H., and J. B. Taylor. "Professional Role Development for Mental Health Tasks," *Archives of General Psychiatry*, xx (May, 1969), 524–527.

Murdock, G. P. "Tenino Shamanism," *Ethnology*, iv (1965), 165–171.

Murphy, J. M. "Psychotherapeutic Aspects of Shamanism on St. Lawrence Island, Alaska," in A. Kiev (ed.), *Magic, Faith and Healing*. New York: The Free Press, 1964, pp. 53–83.

————, and A. H. Leighton. "Native Conceptions of Psychiatric Disorders," in J. M. Murphy and A. H. Leighton (eds.), *Ap-*

proaches to Cross Cultural Psychiatry. Ithaca, New York: Cornell University Press, 1965, pp. 64–107.

Myrdal, G. *Asian Drama.* Vol. III. New York: Pantheon, 1968.

Nall, F. C., and J. Speilberg. "Social and Cultural Factors in the Responses of Mexican-Americans to Medical Treatment," *Journal of Health and Social Behavior,* VIII, No. 4 (December, 1967), 299–308.

Needham, W. E., H. White, and B. J. Fitzgerald. "A Patient-Therapist Program," *Hospital and Community Psychiatry,* XVII, No. 3 (March, 1966), 84–85.

Nishimaru, S. "Mental Climate and Eastern Psychotherapy," *Transcultural Psychiatric Research,* II (April, 1965), 24.

Nisson, M. P., and K. E. Schmidt. "Land-Dayak Concepts of Mental Illness," *Medical Journal of Malaya,* XXI, No. 4 (June, 1967), 352–357.

———, and K. E. Schmidt. "Land-Dayak Concepts of Mental Illness," *Transcultural Psychiatric Research,* III (April, 1966), 21–22.

Opler, M. E. "Some Points of Comparison and Contrast Between the Treatment of Functional Disorders by Apache Shamans and Modern Psychiatric Practice," *American Journal of Psychiatry,* XCII (1936), 1371–1387.

Opler, M. K. *Culture, Psychiatry and Human Values.* Springfield, Illinois: Charles C. Thomas, 1956.

———. "Dream Analysis in Ute Indian Therapy," in M. K. Opler (ed.), *Culture and Mental Health.* New York: The Macmillan Company, 1959.

Orne, M. T. "On the Nature of Effective Hope," *International Journal of Psychiatry,* V, No. 5 (1968), 403–410.

Ozturk, O. M. "Folk Treatment of Mental Illness in Turkey," in A. Kiev (ed.), *Magic, Faith and Healing.* New York: The Free Press, 1965.

Pacheco e Silva, A. C. "A Lance Broken on Behalf of Transcultural Psychopharmacology," *International Journal of Psychiatry,* VIII, No. 5 (1969), 828–830.

Pande, S. K. "The Mystique of 'Western' Psychotherapy: An Eastern Interpretation," *Journal of Nervous and Mental Disease,* CXLVI, No. 6 (1968), 425–432.

Parks, W. Z. "Paviotso Shamanism," *American Anthropologist,* XXXVI (1934), 98–113.

———. *Shamanism in Western North America.* Chicago: Northwestern University Press, 1938.

Paulbaum, P. J. "Apprenticeship Revisited," *Archives of General Psychiatry*, XIII (1965), 304–309.

Peck, H. B., S. R. Kaplan, and M. Roman. "Prevention, Treatment, and Social Action: A Strategy of Intervention in a Disadvantaged Urban Area," *American Journal of Orthopsychiatry*, XXXVI (1966), 57–69.

————, T. Levin, and M. Roman. "The Health Careers Institute: A Mental Health Strategy for an Urban Community," *American Journal of Psychiatry*, CXXIX, No. 9 (March, 1969), 1180–1186.

Pelto, P. J. "Psychological Anthropology," in B. J. Siegel, and A. R. Beals (eds.), *Biennial Review of Anthropology*. Stanford: Stanford University Press, 1967, pp. 140–208.

Perham, J. "Manangism in Borneo," *Journal of the Straits Branch of the Royal Asiatic Society* (Singapore, 1887), pp. 87–103.

Pfeiffer, E. "Patients as Therapists," *American Journal of Psychiatry*, CXXIII, No. 11 (May, 1967), 1413–1418.

Pfeiffer, W. M. "Meditation and Trance States in Indonesian Tribes," *Transcultural Psychiatric Research*, II (October, 1965), 106–110.

Pfister, O. "Instinctive Psychoanalysis Among the Navahos," *Journal of Nervous and Mental Disease*, LXXVI (1932), 234–254.

Pollack, I. W., F. M. Ochberg, and E. Meyer, "Social Class and the Subjective Sense of Time," *Archives of General Psychiatry*, XXI (July, 1969), 1–14.

Poser, E. G. "The Effect of Therapists' Training on Group Therapeutic Outcome," *Journal of Consulting Psychology*, XXX, No. 4 (1966), 283–289.

Posinsky, S. H. "Yoruk Shamanism," *Psychiatric Quarterly*, XXXIX (1965), 227–243.

Prince, R. "Indigenous Yoruba Psychiatry," in A. Kiev (ed.), *Magic, Faith and Healing*. New York: The Free Press, 1964.

————. "Psychotherapy and the Chronically Poor: What Can We Learn from Primitive Psychotherapy?" in J. Finney (ed.), *Social Change, Poverty, and Mental Health*. Lexington: University of Kentucky Press, 1968.

————. "Some Notes on Yoruba Native Doctors and Their Management of Mental Illness," in T. A. Lambo (ed.), *First Pan-African Psychiatric Conference*. Ibadan, Nigeria: Government Printer, 1962.

————. "The Use of Rauwolfia for the Treatment of Psychoses by Nigerian Native Doctors," *American Journal of Psychiatry*, CXVIII (1960), 147–149.

———— (ed.). *Trance and Possession States*. Montreal: R. M. Bucke Memorial Society, 1968.

————, A. Leighton, and R. May. "The Therapeutic Process in Cross-Cultural Perspective: A Symposium," *American Journal of Psychiatry*, cxxiv, No. 9 (March, 1968), 1171–1176.

————, and E. D. Wittkower. "The Care of the Mentally Ill in a Changing Culture (Nigeria)," *American Journal of Psychotherapy*, xviii, No. 4 (1964), 644–648.

"Protest Against Licensing of Cultists," *Journal of the American Medical Association*, ccix, No. 6 (August 11, 1969), 950.

Pu-Yu, C. "To Be a Revolutionary Health Fighter Boundlessly Loyal to Chairman Mao," *Peking Review*, xxv (June 20, 1969), 7–9.

Quinn, R. D. Mental Health Centers Staffing Branch, National Institute of Mental Health. Personal communication.

Radin, P. *Primitive Religion: Its Nature and Origin.* New York: Dover Publications, 1937.

Ramirez, S., and R. Parres. "Some Dynamic Patterns in the Organization of the Mexican Family," *International Journal of Social Psychiatry*, iii (1957), 18–21.

Ravenscroft, K. "Voodoo Possession and Hypnosis," *International Journal of Clinical and Experimental Hypnosis*, xiii, No. 3 (1965), 157–182.

Redlich, F. C., and D. X. Freedman. *The Theory and Practice of Psychiatry.* New York: Basic Books, 1966.

Rieff, R., and F. Riessman. "The Indigenous Non-Professional." New York: National Institute of Labor Education, 1964.

————, and S. Scribner. "Issues in the New National Mental Health Program Relating to Labor and Low Income Groups," in F. Riessman, J. Cohen, and A. Pearl (eds.), *Mental Health of the Poor.* New York: The Free Press, 1964.

Riessman, F. "The 'Helper' Therapy Principle," *Social Work*, x (April, 1965), 27–32.

————, and E. Hallowitz. "The Neighborhood Service Center: An Innovation in Preventive Psychiatry," *American Journal of Psychiatry*, cxxiii, No. 11 (May, 1967), 1408–1413.

————, E. F. Lynton, M. Ginsberg, S. Barr, and M. Battle. "The New Nonprofessional," *American Child*, xlix, No. 1 (Winter, 1967), 1–32.

————, J. Cohen, and A. Pearl (eds.). *Mental Health of the Poor.* New York: The Free Press, 1964.

Rin, H. "A Study of the Aetiology of Koro in Respect to the Chinese Concept of Illness," *International Journal of Social Psychiatry*, xi, No. 1 (1965), 7–13.

Rioch, M. J. "Changing Concepts in the Training of Therapists," *Journal of Consulting Psychology*, xxx, No. 4 (1966), 290–292.

————. "Pilot Projects in Training Mental Health Counselors," in E. L. Cowen, E. A., Gardner, and M. Zax (eds.). *Emergent Approaches to Mental Health Problems*. New York: Appleton-Century-Crofts, 1967.

Rioch, M. J., C. Elkes, A. A. Flint, B. S. Usdansky, R. G. Newman, and E. Silber. "National Institute of Mental Health Pilot Study in Training Mental Health Counselors," *American Journal of Orthopsychiatry*, XXXIII (1963), 678–689.

Robinson, H. A., F. C., Redlich, and J. K. Myers. "Social Structure and Psychiatric Treatment," *American Journal of Orthopsychiatry*, XXIV, No. 2 (1954), 307–316.

Rock, J. F. "Contributions to the Shamanism of the Tibetan-Chinese Borderland," *Anthropos*, LIV (1959), 796–818.

Rogers, C. R. "The Necessary and Sufficient Conditions of Therapeutic Personality Change," *Journal of Consulting Psychology*, XXI (1957), 95–103.

————, and R. F. Dymond (eds.). *Psychotherapy and Personality Change*. Chicago: University of Chicago Press, 1954.

Rogler, L. H., and A. B. Hollingshead. "The Puerto Rican Spiritualist as Psychiatrist," *American Journal of Sociology*, LXVII (1961), 17–21.

————, and A. B. Hollingshead. *Trapped: Families and Schizophrenia*. New York: John Wiley and Sons, 1965.

Roman, M., and M. S. Jacobson. "Progress Report: Training of Mental Health Aides. Lincoln Hospital Mental Health Series (Bronx, New York), 1965. (Mimeographed.)

Romney, A. K., and R. G. D'Andrade (eds.). "Transcultural Studies in Cognition," *American Anthropologist*, LXVI, No. 3 (Special Edition, 1964).

Rosenbaum, M. "Some Comments on the Use of Untrained Therapists," *Journal of Consulting Psychology*, XXX, No. 4 (1966), 292–294.

Rothenberg, A. "Puerto Rico and Aggression," *American Journal of Psychiatry*, CXX (1964), 962–970.

Rubel, A. J. *Across the Tracks: Mexican Americans in a Texas City*. Austin: University of Texas Press, 1966.

————. "Concepts of Disease in Mexican-American Culture," *American Anthropologist*, LXII (1960), 793–814.

————. "The Epidemiology of a Folk Illness: Susto in Hispanic America," *Ethnology*, III (1964), 268–283.

Sachs, W. *Black Hamlet*. Boston: Little, Brown and Company, 1947.

Sanders, R. "New Manpower for Mental Hospital Service," in E. L. Cowen, E. A. Gardner, and M. Zax. *Emergent Approaches to*

Mental Health Problems. New York: Appleton-Century-Crofts, 1967.

Sangmuah, E. "The Healing (Spiritual) Therapy in Ghana," Paper presented at the 2nd Pan-African Conference on Psychiatry, Dakar, 1968.

Sargant, W. "Witch Doctoring, Zar and Voodoo: Their Relation to Modern Psychiatric Treatments," *Transcultural Psychiatric Research*, v (October, 1968), 130–132.

Sasaki, Y. "Psychiatric Study of the Shaman in Japan," in W. Caudill, and T. Lin (eds.). *Mental Health Research in Asia and the Pacific*. Honolulu: East-West Center Press, 1969.

Sauna, V. D. "Socio-Cultural Aspects of Psychotherapy and Treatment: A Review of the Literature," in *Progress in Clinical Psychology*. New York: Grune and Stratton, 1966.

Saunders, L. *Cultural Differences and Medical Care: The Case of the Spanish-Speaking People of the Southwest*. New York: Russell Sage Foundation, 1954.

—————. "Healing Ways in the Spanish Southwest," in E. G. Jaco (ed.), *Patients, Physicians, and Illnesses*. New York: The Free Press, 1958, pp. 189–206.

—————, and J. Samora. "A Medical Care Program in a Colorado County," in B. Paul (ed.), *Health, Culture and Community*. New York: Russell Sage Foundation, 1955.

Scheibe, K. E. "College Students Spend Eight Weeks in a Mental Hospital," *Psychotherapy*, II (1965), 117–120.

Schimmel, E. M. "The Hazards of Hospitalization," *Annals of Internal Medicine*, LX, No. 1 (January, 1964), 100–110.

—————. "The Physician as Pathogen," *Journal of Chronic Disease*, XVI (1963), 1–4.

Schmidt, K. E. "Folk Psychiatry in Sarawak: A Tentative System of Psychiatry of the Iban," in A. Kiev (ed.), *Magic, Faith and Healing*. New York: The Free Press, 1964.

Schofield, W. *Psychotherapy: The Purchase of Friendship*. Englewood Cliffs, New Jersey: Prentice-Hall, 1964.

Schulman, S., and A. M. Smith. "The Concept of 'Health' Among Spanish-Speaking Villages in New Mexico and Colorado." *Journal of Health and Human Behovior*, IV, No. 4 (Winter, 1963), 226–234.

Segall, M. H., D. T. Campbell, and M. J. Herskovits. *The Influence of Culture on Visual Perception*. Indianapolis: The Bobbs-Merrill Company, 1966.

Seguin, C. A. "Language and Psychotherapy," *Journal of Nervous and Mental Disease*, CXXI (1955), 564–567.

Senter, D. "Witches and Psychiatrists," *Psychiatry,* x (1947), 49–56.

Sereno, R. "Obeah, Magic and Social Structure in the Lesser Antilles, *Psychiatry,* xi (1948), 15–31.

Seward, G. *Psychotherapy and Culture Conflict.* New York: The Ronald Press, 1956.

Shapiro, A. K. "The Placebo Effect in the History of Medical Treatment: Implications for Psychiatry," *American Journal of Psychiatry,* cxvi (1959), 298–304.

Shapiro, J. "Dominant Leaders Among Slum Hotel Residents," *American Journal of Orthopsychiatry,* xxxix, No. 4 (July, 1969), 644–650.

Shepherd, M. "Comparative Psychiatric Treatment in Different Countries," in D. Richter, J. M. Tanner, L. Taylor and O. L. Zangwill (eds.), *Aspects of Psychiatric Research.* London: Oxford University Press, 1962, pp. 110–124.

Sigerist, H. *History of Medicine.* Vol. I. New York: Oxford University Press, 1951, p. 175.

Silver, H. K., L. C. Ford, and L. R. Day. "The Pediatric Nurse-Practitioner Program," *Journal of the American Medical Association,* cciv, No. 4 (1968), 298–302.

Silverman, J. "Shamans and Acute Schizophrenia," *American Anthropologist,* lxix, No. 1 (1967), 21–31.

Simmons, O. G. "The Mutual Images and Expectations of Anglo-Americans and Mexican-Americans," *Daedalus,* xc (Spring, 1961), 286–299.

Singer, P., E. Araneta, and L. Aarons. "Integration of Indigenous Healing Practices of the Kali Cult with Western Psychiatric Modalities in British Guiana," *Transcultural Psychiatric Research,* iv (April, 1967), 65–67.

Snell, J. E. "Hypnosis in the Treatment of the 'Hexed' Patient," *American Journal of Psychiatry,* cxxiv (September, 1967), 3.

Soddy, K. (ed.). *Identity: Mental Health and Value Systems.* London: Tavistock Publications, 1961.

Spencer, R. F. *The North Alaskan Eskimo: A Study in Ecology and Society.* Washington, D.C.: U.S. Government Printing Office, 1959.

Stead, E. A. "Training and Use of Paramedical Personnel," *New England Journal of Medicine,* cclxxvii, No. 15 (1967), 800–801.

Stewart, K. *Pygmies and Dream Giants.* London: Victor Gollancz, 1955.

Strupp, H. H., and A. E. Bergin. "Some Empirical and Conceptual Bases for Coordinated Research in Psychotherapy," *International Journal of Psychiatry,* vii, No. 2 (1969), 18–90.

Stunkard, A. "Some Interpersonal Aspects of an Oriental Religion," *Psychiatry*, xiv (1951), 419–431.

Suicide and Homicides Among Indians. Washington: Department of Health, Education and Welfare, 1969.

Surya, N. C., K. P. Unnikrishnan, R. Shivathanuvan Thampi, K. Sathyavathi, and N. Sundararaj. "Ayurvedic Treatment in Mental Illness: A Report," *Transactions of the All-India Institute of Mental Health*, v (Bangalore, 1965), 28–39.

Szasz, T. S. *The Ethics of Psychoanalysis*. New York: Basic Books, 1965.

Tenzel, J. H. "Shamanism and Concepts of Disease in a Mayan Indian Community," *Psychiatry*, xxxiii (1970), 372–380.

Tinling, D. C. "Voodoo, Root Work and Medicine," *Psychosomatic Medicine*, xxix (1967), 483–490.

Toffelmier, G., and K. Luomala. "Dreams and Dream Interpretation of the Diegueño Indians of Southern California," *Psychoanalytic Quarterly*, ii (1936), 195–225.

Torrey, E. F. "The Case for the Indigenous Therapist," *Archives of General Psychiatry*, xx (1969), 365–373.

————. "A Medical Survey of the Saysay People in the Blue Nile Gorge," *Ethiopian Medical Journal*, iv (July, 1966), 4–11.

————. "Mental Health Services for American Indians and Eskimos," *Community Mental Health Journal*, vi, No. 6 (1970), 455–463.

————. "The Zar Cult in Ethiopia," *International Journal of Social Psychiatry*, xiii, No. 3 (1967), 216–223.

———— (ed.). *An Introduction to Health and Health Education in Ethiopia*. Addis Ababa: Berhanena Selam Press, 1966.

————, F. J. Van Rheenan, and H. A. Katchadourian. "Problems of Foreign Students: An Overview," *Journal of the American College Health Association*, ixx, No. 2 (1970), 83–86.

Truax, C. B., and R. R. Carkhuff. *Toward Effective Counseling and Psychotherapy: Training and Practice*. Chicago: Aldine Publishing Company, 1967.

————, and D. Wargo. "Human Encounters that Change Behavior for Better or Worse," *American Journal of Psychotherapy*, xx (1966), 499–520.

————, D. Wargo, J. Frank, S. Imber, C. Battle, R. Hoehn-Saric, E. Nash, and A. Stone. "Therapeutic Empathy, Genuineness, and Warmth and Patient Therapeutic Outcome," *Journal of Consulting Psychology*, xxx (1966), 395–401.

Turner, V. W. "An Ndembu Doctor in Practice," in A. Kiev (ed.) *Magic, Faith and Healing*. New York: The Free Press, 1964.

Tyhurst, L. "Displacement and Migration," *American Journal of Psychiatry*, CVIII (1951), 561–568.

Uhlenhuth, E. H., and D. B. Duncan. "Subjective Change with Medical Student Therapists: Course of Relief in Psychoneurotic Outpatients," *Archives of General Psychiatry*, XVIII (April, 1968), 428–438.

————, and D. B. Duncan. "Subjective Change with Medical Student Therapists: Some Determinants of Change in Psychoneurotic Outpatients," *Archives of General Psychiatry*, XVIII (May, 1968), 532–540.

Umbarger, C. C., J. S. Dalsimer, A. P. Morrison, and P. R. Breggin. *College Students in a Mental Hospital.* New York: Grune and Stratton, 1962.

Van Rheenen, F. J., E. F. Torrey, and H. A. Katchadourian. "Preventive Psychiatry: Group Work with Foreign Students," to be published.

Vahia, N. S., S. L. Vinekar, and D. R. Doongaji. "Some Ancient Indian Concepts in the Treatment of Psychiatric Disorders," *British Journal of Psychiatry*, CXII, No. 489 (1966), 1089–1096.

Vidaver, R. M. "The Mental Health Technician: Maryland's Design for a New Health Career," *American Journal of Psychiatry*, CXXV, No. 8 (February, 1969), 1013–1023.

Von Riesemann, O. *Rachmaninoff's Recollections.* New York: The Macmillan Company, 1934, p. 112.

Wakefield, D. *Island in the City.* Boston: Houghton Mifflin Company, 1959.

Wallace, A. F. C. "Cultural Determinants of Response to Hallucinatory Experience," *Archives of General Psychiatry*, I, No. 1 (July, 1959), 58–69.

————. *Culture and Personality.* New York: Random House, 1961.

————. "Dreams and the Wishes of the Soul: A Type of Psychoanalytic Theory Among Seventeenth Century Iroquois," *American Anthropologist*, LX (1958), 234–248.

————. "The Institutionalization of Cathartic and Control Strategies in Iroquois Religious Psychotherapy," in M. K. Opler. *Culture and Mental Health.* New York: Macmillan, 1959.

Weed, V., and W. H. Denham. "Toward More Effective Use of the Nonprofessional Worker," *Social Work*, VI (October, 1963), 29.

Weinberg, S. K. "Mental Healing and Social Change in West Africa," *Social Problems*, II, No. 3 (1964), 257–269.

Weinstein, E. A. *Cultural Aspects of Delusion: A Psychiatric Study of the Virgin Islands.* New York: The Free Press, 1962.

Wellner, A. M. "A State-Wide Survey of Community Needs for

Mental Health Technicians," *Mental Hygiene,* LII (1968), 204–206.

Whisson, M. G. "Some Aspects of Functional Disorders Among the Kenya Luo," in A. Kiev (ed.), *Magic, Faith and Healing.* New York: The Free Press, 1964.

Whiting, J. W., and I. L. Child. *Child Training and Personality: A Cross-Cultural Study.* New Haven: Yale University Press, 1953.

Whorf, B. L. "Science and Linguistics," in J. B. Carroll (ed.), *Language, Thought and Reality.* Cambridge, Massachusetts: The Technology Press of Massachusetts Institute of Technology, 1957.

Wilmer, H. A. "Transference to a Medical Center," *California Medicine,* XCVI, No. 3 (1962), 173–180.

Wintrob, R., and E. D. Wittkower. "Magic and Witchcraft in Liberia: Their Psychiatric Implications," *Transcultural Psychiatric Research,* III (October, 1966), 149–152.

Wise, H., R. Brooke, and A. Harwood. "Proposal for an Ethnographic Study of Health Areas 24 and 26, with Particular Reference to Medical and Paramedical Beliefs and Practices." Neighborhood Medical Care Demonstration, Bronx, New York, 1967. (Mimeographed.)

Wise, H. B., E. F. Torrey, A. McDade, and H. Bograd. "The Family Health Worker," *American Journal of Public Health,* LVIII, No. 10 (1968), 1828–1838.

Wittkower, E. D., H. B. Murphy, J. Fried, and H. Ellenberger. "Cross-Cultural Inquiry into the Symptomatology of Schizophrenia," *Annals of the New York Academy of Sciences,* LXXXIV (1960), 854–863.

Workineh, H. M. "Teaching of the Ethiopian Orthodox Church on Matters Related to Health and Disease," in E. F. Torrey (ed.), *An Introduction to Health and Health Education in Ethiopia.* Addis Ababa: Berhanena Selam Press, 1966.

Yamamoto, J., Q. C. James, and N. Palley. "Cultural Problems in Psychiatric Therapy," *Archives of General Psychiatry,* XIX (1968), 45–49.

Yap, P. M. "Mental Diseases Peculiar to Certain Cultures: A Survey of Comparative Psychiatry," *Journal of Mental Science,* XCVII (1951), 313–327.

Yeager, W., W. T. Sowder, and A. V. Hardy. "The Mental Health Worker: A New Public Health Professional," *American Journal of Public Health,* LII, No. 9 (1962), 1625–1630.

Zempleni, A. "Traditional Interpretation and Therapy of Mental Disorder Among the Wolof and the Lebou of Senegal," *Transcultural Psychiatric Research,* VI (1969), 69–74.

Index